King David

King David

A Biography

Steven L. McKenzie

OXFORD
UNIVERSITY PRESS

2000

OXFORD

UNIVERSITY PRESS

Oxford New York
Athens Auckland Bangkok Bogotá
Buenos Aires Calcutta Cape Town Chennai Dar es Salaam
Delhi Florence Hong Kong Istanbul Karachi
Kuala Lumpur Madrid Melbourne
Mexico City Mumbai Nairobi Paris São Paolo Singapore
Taipei Tokyo Toronto Warsaw

and associated companies in
Berlin Ibadan

Published by Oxford University Press, Inc.
198 Madison Avenue, New York, New York 10016

Oxford is a registered trademark of Oxford University Press, Inc.

Library of Congress Cataloging-in-Publication Data
McKenzie, Steven L., 1953–
King David : a biography / by Steven L. McKenzie.
p. cm. Includes bibliographical references
ISBN 0-19-513273-4
1. David, King of Israel.
2. Bible. O.T.—Biography. I. Title.
BS580.D3 M 1999 222.4'092—dc21
[B]   99–044315

9 8 7 6 5 4 3 2 1

Printed in the United States of America
on acid-free paper

Contents

Acknowledgments

There are many people who have contributed, sometimes un-
awares, to my work with David and to whom I owe an expression of gratitude. First and foremost, I want to thank my students at Rhodes College,
especially those in the "Historical Literature of the Bible" course, for their
stimulation over the years. It was they who first made the off-handed suggestion that I should write David's biography.

I am indebted also to my colleagues at Rhodes for their support on this
project: to the Faculty Development Committee for a summer grant to
work on David; to Susan Kus in anthropology for her advice on ethnoar-
chaeology; to Richard Batey of my own department of religious studies for
his encouragement; and special thanks to my colleagues in Hebrew Bible,
John Kaltner and Carey Walsh, for their shared expertise on specific parts
of the manuscript. Karen Winterton, whose title of secretary belies her
skill as an editor and literary critic, made helpful comments on an earlier
incarnation of this manuscript. My friend Shaul Bar of the University of
Memphis helped me with materials in modern Hebrew.

I am grateful to Oxford University Press for agreeing to publish this book.
The manuscript benefited enormously from the editorial pen of Cynthia
Read of OUP. Nina Sherwin helped prepare the illustrations and maps incor-
porated into this volume, and Helen Mules guided the book through produc-
tion. Thanks are due to Hebrew Union College, Jerusalem, and to the Israel
Exploration Society, respectively, for permission to reproduce the photograph
of the Tel Dan inscription and the drawings of lyres from N. Avigad's article,
"The King's Daughter and the Lyre," in the 1978 *Israel Exploration Journal.*

Finally, I have been privileged over the years to sit at the feet of the lead-ing scholars in various areas of study relating to ancient Israel. This book owes a debt to three of them in particular. Bill Dever's 1995 summer semi-nar on "Imagining the Past," sponsored by the National Endowment for the Humanities at the University of Arizona, helped me to set my image of David into the background provided by the archaeology of ancient Israel, in which Bill is the world's leading expert. Kyle McCarter was my first teacher at Harvard—in a course on textual criticism in the books of Samuel! His two-volume commentary on these books is a classic of biblical scholarship, and my dependence on it will be obvious throughout this biography. John Van Seters revolutionized my view of the Bible when I met him a decade ago in his NEH seminar on historiography at the University of North Carolina, and his combination of critical insight and sober judg-ment on both the historical and literary levels continues as the standard I strive to achieve. My interest in this volume in providing biographical information for David has led me to take a more positive view than John does of the potential historical value of the biblical material. He should not, therefore, be held responsible for any of my shortcomings or excesses. The same is true for Bill Dever and Kyle McCarter with regard to my state-ments about archaeology and the narrative of 1–2 Samuel. But this biogra-phy, whatever its failings or contributions, would never have existed without the work of these three scholars.

King David

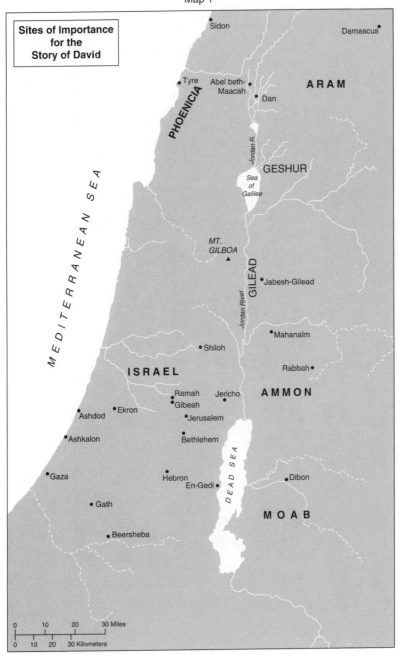

Map 1

**Sites of Importance
for the
Story of David**

Sidon

Damascus

ARAM

Tyre

PHOENICIA

Abel beth-
Maacah

Dan

Jordan R.

GESHUR

Sea
of
Galilee

MEDITERRANEAN SEA

MT.
GILBOA

GILEAD

Jordan River

Jabesh-Gilead

Mahanaim

Shiloh

ISRAEL

Rabbah

Ramah

Jericho

Gibeah

AMMON

Ashdod

Ekron

Jerusalem

Ashkalon

Bethlehem

DEAD SEA

Gaza

Hebron

En-Gedi

Dibon

Gath

MOAB

Beersheba

0   10   20   30 Miles

0   10   20   30 Kilometers

Map 2

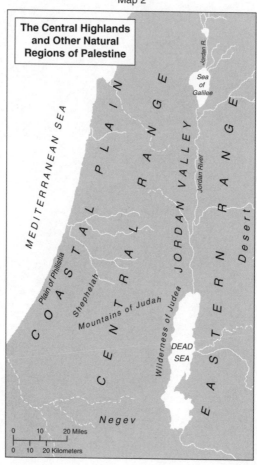

The Central Highlands and Other Natural Regions of Palestine

MEDITERRANEAN SEA

Jordan R.

Sea of Galilee

COASTAL PLAIN

CENTRAL RANGE

JORDAN VALLEY

Jordan River

EASTERN RANGE

Desert

Plain of Philistia

Shephelah

Mountains of Judah

Wilderness of Judea

DEAD SEA

Negev

0   10   20 Miles

0   10   20 Kilometers

Map 3

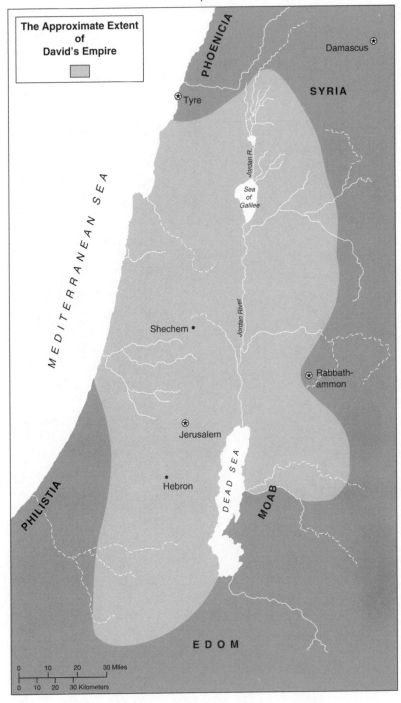

The Approximate Extent
of
David's Empire

PHOENICIA

Damascus

SYRIA

Tyre

Jordan R.

Sea
of
Galilee

M E D I T E R R A N E A N   S E A

Jordan River

Shechem

Rabbath-
ammon

Jerusalem

Hebron

DEAD SEA

MOAB

PHILISTIA

E D O M

0   10   20   30 Miles

0   10   20   30 Kilometers

Map 4

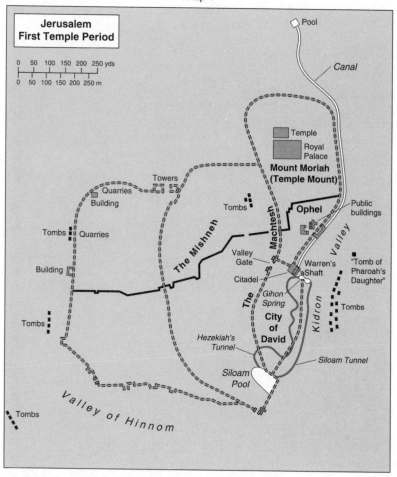

**Jerusalem
First Temple Period**

0   50 100 150 200 250 yds
0   50 100 150 200 250 m

Pool

Canal

Temple

Royal
Palace

**Mount Moriah
(Temple Mount)**

Towers

Quarries

Building

Tombs

The Mishneh

Machtesh

Ophel

Public
buildings

Tombs   Quarries

Valley
Gate

Warren's
Shaft

Kidron Valley

"Tomb of
Pharoah's
Daughter"

Building

Citadel

*Gihon
Spring*

The

**City
of
David**

Tombs

*Hezekiah's
Tunnel*

Siloam Tunnel

Tombs

*Siloam
Pool*

Tombs

Valley of Hinnom

Introduction

Images

The Need for a Biography of David

Sing the Man who Judah's Scepter bore,
  In that right Hand which held the Crook before;
  Who from best Poet, best of Kings did grow;
  The two chief Gifts Heav'n could on Man bestow.

—Abraham Cowley, *Davideis*

Images of David in Literature

It is arguably the best known single work of art in the world, certainly the most famous sculpture. Michelangelo's *David* shows the power of an image (*Fig. 1*). No one knows what David looked like, though he is one of the most popular subjects in Western art.[1] Of the hundreds, perhaps thousands, of depictions of him, none has had the influence of Michelangelo's statue. Its size (over 15 feet high) is, ironically, Goliath-like. David's pose is graceful. His youthful, athletic body constitutes perfection. About to battle Goliath, his expression is humble but confident. This image has shaped people's ideas about David for generations and has come to represent the essence of the man.

Whereas artists use physical images to communicate ideas and inner qualities, writers use words and ideas to describe characters and create images of them in the mind. The literary images of David in Western civilization are as diverse and powerful as the artistic ones. To begin with, there is the Bible, which devotes more space to David than to any other character. Moses and Jesus rival him for sheer number of pages until you add the Psalms. Then David wins hands down. But even without the Psalms, there is more about David's life than about the lives of the other biblical characters. Most of the "Books of Moses" is *torah*, "law" or "instruction." Similarly, most of the Gospels is teachings. David is no lawgiver or teacher but a man of deeds and actions. The David of the Bible is also a complex character. He is pious and faithful at times but is also capable of heinous crimes. He is a powerful and decisive man, except around his children, whom he cannot control.

The complexity of the biblical character helps to account for his popularity and diversity of portrayal in subsequent literature, especially during the Renaissance.[2] Shakespeare himself may have borrowed from the plot of the Bible's story of David, as the following comparison suggests.

> A young man, with a right to the throne, is set in conflict with a king who alternately flatters him and tries to kill him. The young man feigns madness. He comes upon his enemy, helpless and oblivious of his presence, but forgoes the perfect opportunity for revenge. This partial outline of the plot of Hamlet is also that of the biblical story of David, which likewise includes a ghost, fratricide, incest, and a dissembling avenger who invites his enemy to a feast so that he might be killed, unsuspecting and unprepared.[3]

Even today writers remain fascinated with David. Half a dozen new novels about him have appeared in just the last few years—some by world-class authors. We will look at these in the course of this book.

Writers have viewed David in different ways. For poets, he was the psalmist, inspired by God and inspiring them to the highest form of praise. Abraham Cowley's *Davideis* (1656), quoted at the beginning of this Introduction, was subtitled "A Sacred Poem."[4] Christopher Smart's "A Song to David" (1753) praised him as the ideal man:[5]

> Great, valiant, pious, good, and clean,
> Sublime, contemplative, serene,
>   Strong, constant, pleasant, wise!
> Bright effluence of exceeding grace;

Best man!—the swiftness and the race,
The peril, and the prize! (lines 19–24)

Smart's "Song" was actually a defense of David. It was aimed at a group of people in the England of Smart's day who had attacked David's moral character even to the point of suggesting that his name be removed from Scripture. Smart upheld David's reputation and scolded his detractors:

O DAVID, highest in the list
Of worthies, on God's ways insist,
The genuine word repeat:
Vain are the documents of men,
And vain the flourish of the pen
That keeps the fool's conceit. (lines 289–294)

Robert Browning's "Saul" (1845) portrayed David as a psalmist in a more intimate way.[6] Writing in the first person, Browning described David's feelings of awe and devotion for Saul when he played the lyre for him the first time. David's humility and innocence stand out.

he spoke not, but slow
Lifted up the hand slack at his side, till he laid it with care
Soft and grave, but in mild settled will, on my brow: thro' my hair
The large fingers were pushed, and he bent back my head, with kind power—
All my face back, intent to peruse it, as men do a flower.
Thus held he me there with his great eyes that scrutinized mine—
And oh, all my heart how it loved him! but where was the sign?
I yearned—"Could I help thee, my father, inventing a bliss,
I would add, to that life of the past, both the future and this;
I would give thee new life altogether, as good, ages hence,
As this moment—had love but the warrant, love's heart to dispense!"
(lines 226–236)

For some, poets and prose writers alike, David was primarily a champion. His victory over Goliath was the triumph of truth, beauty, and virtue over hideous evil. According to Michael Drayton's "David and Goliath" (1630), David was God's "most deare delight" (line 31), "this holy Youth so humble," "so wonderously faire" (lines 192, 723).[7] And the slave poet Phillis Wheatley in "Goliath of Gath" (1772) called him "the wond'rous hero" with "warlike courage far beyond his years" (lines 73, 44).[8] Ann Fairbairn's novel *Five Smooth Stones* (1966) defined Goliath, the evil enemy, as racism. Her hero was David Champlin, a warrior for civil rights.[9]

But for other writers, David was less heroic. Some depicted him as a man of unbridled and insatiable sexual appetite. When John Dryden in "Absalom and Achitophel" (1681) satirized King Charles II as promiscuous, he chose David for the caricature:[10]

In pious times, ere priestcraft did begin,
Before polygamy was made a sin;
When man on many multiplied his kind,
Ere one to one was cursedly confin'd;
When nature prompted, and no law denied
Promiscuous use of concubine and bride;
Then Israel's monarch after Heaven's own heart,
His vigorous warmth did variously impart
To wives and slaves; and, wide as his command,
Scatter'd his Maker's image thro' the land
Michal, of royal blood, the crown did wear;
A soil ungrateful to the tiller's care:
Not so the rest; for several mothers bore
To godlike David several sons before. (lines 1–14)

In this century, D. H. Lawrence's *David: A Play* (1926) used David as a way of exploring his own ideas about different kinds of love.[11] Casting David in his own image (same first name, red hair, and all), Lawrence described his relationships with Saul, Jonathan, and Michal. One of the most recent novels about David, Allan Massie's *King David* (1995) similarly paints David as a very active sexual being with lovers of both genders.[12]

Other modern novelists have described David in a much more negative way, as someone who lusted not just for sexual fulfillment but for power and control. More than that, they see his personality as thoroughly malig-nant—cruel and manipulative. William Faulkner's *Absalom, Absalom!* (1936) may have begun this trend in the present century.[13] He built the character of Thomas Sutpen on the model of David as cold and ruthless. More recently, the German writer Grete Weil empathized with Michal's loneliness and isolation and blamed it on David's callousness. In her *The Bride Price* (1991) she has Michal say, "[David] became a hero and a hero is what I got for a husband in the end, though I had wished for a singer."[14] For Torgny Lindgren, the leading novelist of Sweden, David was worse than indifferent; he was devious and mean. In his *Bathsheba* (1989) he writes, "Holiness has made King David very cunning and shrewd."[15] Lindgren's Bathsheba learns from David and then surpasses him in shrewdness, manipulating all the major events of his reign.

There are many more literary works about David. We will survey some of them in future chapters. But these samples indicate the great interest generated by the biblical story of David as well as the diversity of characterization it has inspired.

The Quest for the Historical David

Given this literary preoccupation with David and the wide disagreement about his character, one would expect to find many biographies of David. But that is not the case. There are, to be sure, works about David that describe themselves as biographies. But their perspective is almost always inspirational rather than historical. What their authors really want to know is what made David "a man after God's own heart." In David they hope to isolate those personal qualities that are especially pleasing to God so that they and their readers can cultivate them in their lives.[16] Of those works that are not inspirational, some are in need of updating and the others focus more on the setting of the times than on David per se.[17]

The quest of this book is strictly historical. We will read the Bible not for its model of David as a religious hero nor for the artistry of its story about him, but for the historical information about him that it may provide. The Bible is, of necessity, the primary source about David's life. But we will analyze it critically using the best methods of biblical scholarship for discerning history. We will look to sources outside of the Bible, such as those uncovered by archaeology, to fill in the historical and social background, from the details of daily living to the actions typically undertaken by Middle Eastern kings. My purpose is not simply to retell the biblical story but to recount the events and details of David's life to the extent that they can be surmised from the available sources. This includes matters such as his real character and personality, physical appearance, deeds and accomplishments, and true motives and ambitions.

The Challenges of a Biography of David

Trying to reconstruct any event from the past is a lot harder than it first appears. Take the JFK assassination. It was only thirty-five years ago, had plenty of eyewitnesses, and was captured on film. Yet, the controversy surrounding it appears to be endless. It may be impossible now to know exactly what happened, much less the motives and intentions of the people involved.

Historians have long realized that every account of the past involves interpretation. The greater the distance from the past to the present, the greater the role played by interpretation will be. This is particularly significant for a biography of David, because the distance between his time and the present is considerable, some three thousand years. One scholar has referred to the historical image of David as a hologram—a likeness that is fleeting, indistinct, and varies according to the spectator's point of view.[18] Others are more skeptical; they conclude that there is no substance to any image of David because he never existed historically. This is an issue I will discuss in the first chapter. But it is important to admit at the outset that our biography of David is actually an interpretation of the historical character—a hologram or a portrait, if you will.

A further challenge for a biography of David is presented by the abundance of material about him. There is more detailed information available about David than about any other person who lived so long ago. The challenge comes in trying to separate historical fact from its literary presentation. How much of the David material is history and how much story? To what extent is the historical David influenced by theology? To what extent is his story fictional?

Biblical scholarship has made it clear that the Bible cannot be taken at face value as history. This is not to say anything against the Bible. Its human authors were simply more concerned with theology than with history. But modern scholars have developed critical methods of analysis that can be used to delve beneath the literary and theological presentations of David in search of historical information. It is the use of these critical methods that distinguishes this biography from most other works about David. I take the Bible seriously—but also critically—as a source of historical information.

While some of the conclusions about David's actions and character may seem shocking to lay readers, they are "old hat" to scholars. Part of my purpose in writing this book is to make available to a broad audience views that most scholars have long held. Thus, a significant part of this biography consists of conclusions reached by other scholars using methods of biblical criticism. I have assembled them into a comprehensive history of David's life. I have tried to put them together in a form that is easy to read. I have limited technical discussions to the footnotes and kept those to a minimum. But I also want to give credit where it is due. That is the reason for the extensive bibliography at the end. Of course, I have a few new ideas of my own to add. But the portrait of David that is painted here, at least in its broad strokes, is one that is widely endorsed among scholars.

Prospectus

The plan of this book is simple. Chapter One discusses the nature of sources outside of the Bible for David's life. They are basically two: inscriptions and the results of archaeology. Is there evidence from these sources to indicate that David was a real person and not just the invention of the biblical writers? If so, what can they tell us about his life, and how do they relate to the biblical material? Chapter Two focuses on the Bible. It describes the different parts of the Bible that deal with David and their historical value. It also lays out the approach that will be used in the rest of the book to mine the biographical information about David. Chapters Three through Nine are the biography proper. David's life is divided into periods, and the information about him from the Bible and other sources is integrated to reconstruct his activities in each period. The final chapter brings the results of the individual chapters together into a single biographical synthesis of the life of King David.

One final note. Since the Bible is our primary source for David's life, you may find it helpful to look over the section of the Bible about him in 1 Samuel 16—1 Kings 2 before beginning this biography. An outline of this section may be found in Chapter Two. It may also be helpful to have a copy of the Bible handy for reference while you read.

I

Was There a King David?

Extrabiblical Sources

"Do we, the late-born, really know anything at all about someone who lived in the past?"

—Grete Weil, *The Bride Price*

The November 21, 1997, issue of the *Chronicle of Higher Education* contained an unusual article. The *Chronicle* monitors trends in higher education, typically reporting on matters like tuition costs, tenure, and the impact of technology. The lead for this article on the cover read, "Did King David Exist? Bitter Divisions Among Biblical Scholars." Even more provocative was the one-line synopsis: "Biblical scholars get nasty in a transatlantic debate over whether King David existed." The article lived up to its billing, with quotations from biblical scholars and archaeologists characterizing one another as "fundamentalist," "minimalist," and "anti-Zionist," and each others' views as "scandalous," "absurd," and "insanity."[1]

The heat of this debate reflects the emotion that many people feel—one way or the other—about the Bible and its main characters. But beyond the emotion and personal conflicts, the article also makes clear the two major questions that must be answered before a biography of David can begin: (1) Do sources outside of the Bible indicate that David really existed or give additional information about him? and (2) How may the Bible be used to reconstruct David's life? These two questions are the topics of this chapter and the next.

More than a decade before the firestorm of controversy erupted on the pages of the *Chronicle of Higher Education*, a scholar penned these words in an article titled "The Historical David":

> The Bible is our only source of information about David. No ancient inscription mentions him. No archaeological discovery can be securely linked to him. The quest for the historical David, therefore, is primarily exegetical.[2]

This statement may seem surprising. You would think that a person as famous and active as David is in the Bible would have left plenty of indications of his historical existence for archaeologists to dig up. You would also expect to find him mentioned frequently in the records of the ancient countries he conquered or had dealings with.

The scholar who wrote those words, P. Kyle McCarter, is not one of the so-called minimalists who deny David's historical existence. Yet he must concede that there is little concrete information about David outside of the Bible. It is easy to see how one might suspect that there never was such a person and that the story about him in the Bible is fictional. But McCarter and others like him also have good reasons for believing in a historical David. McCarter's statement, therefore, provides a useful structure for surveying the evidence outside of the Bible that bears, pro and con, on the question of the David of history.

"No ancient inscription mentions him"

During the past two centuries, thousands of ancient documents from hundreds of sites throughout the Middle East have been excavated. They provide information about history, politics, religion, laws, customs, and almost every other aspect of life in the ancient world. However, the vast majority of these documents have come from Egypt and Iraq (ancient Mesopotamia), both of which were in stages of rebuilding in 1000 B.C.E., the approximate time of David's reign according to the Bible's chronology. This means that their contact with other countries was limited during this period. In Mesopotamia this era has been called a "dark age," and we have fewer records than for other periods.

The relative paucity of documents from this period may help to explain why no mention of David was found for such a long time. But in the summer of 1993 he finally showed up. The occurrence of David's name in a newly discovered inscription led to the publication of new readings for two previously known inscriptions. Thus, McCarter's statement that "no ancient inscription mentions [David]" is no longer true.

The Tel Dan Stele

The new discovery was a piece of an inscribed monument or "stele." It was found by accident, as such things usually are, at an archaeological dig in the ruin ("tel") of the ancient city of Dan in northern Israel. It had been reused as building material for a later wall and was near the wall's base. You can imagine the excitement of the person who found it. She was walking along looking at the ground when something about that one stone caught her eye. She knelt to take a closer look and noticed the lines of markings cut into the rock. She recognized it as writing of some kind and immediately called the project director.

The fragment measured 32 by 22 cm. at its widest point. It was broken on all sides except the right margin, so the size of the original monument could not be determined. It was made of basalt, which was a very expensive stone in antiquity. Since it would have been costly to produce, the monument could not have been erected by just anybody. It was most likely the work of a king (*Fig. 2*).

There were thirteen lines of writing preserved on the fragment in an early form of the alphabet. The letters were clear and elegantly inscribed. The language was instantly recognized as Aramaic, the mother tongue of ancient Syria. As with Hebrew, the writing went from right to left. It was the ninth line that caught the collective eye of the first readers. There were the consonants that spelled out the name of David: DWD.

But the name did not stand alone. It was part of a larger word rendered "house of David." This was one source of the controversy generated by the inscription in the first year after its discovery. The occurrence of David's name was not as obvious as it had appeared at first. The same letters used to write his name could have other meanings as well, especially since Aramaic, like ancient Hebrew, was written without vowels. One common pro-

posal was that the phrase actually meant "temple of (a god named) Dod."³
The broken piece did not preserve enough of the original context to decide
between these two (and other) possible readings.

Much of the controversy, however, ended a year later, almost to the day,
when the same person who had found the initial fragment spotted two more
pieces.⁴ Together, they filled in parts of eight of the thirteen lines found the
previous year. The original translators read all three pieces together as follows (the portions within brackets are reconstructed and are not actually
on the inscription):

1. [...   ...] and cut [...]
2. [...] my father went up [against him when] he fought at [...]
3. And my father lay down, he went to his [ancestors] (viz. became sick
    and died). And the king of I[s-]
4. rael entered previously in my father's land. [And] Hadad made me king.
5. And Hadad went in front of me, [and] I departed from [the] seven [...-]
6. s of my kingdom, and I slew [seve]nty kin[gs], who harnessed thou[sands
    of cha-]
7. riots and thousands of horsemen (or: horses). [I killed Jeho]ram son of
    [Ahab]
8. king of Israel, and [I] killed [Ahaz]iahu son of [Jehoram kin-]
9. g of the House of David. And I set [their towns into ruins and turned]
10. their land into [desolation ...]
11. other [...   and Jehu ru-]
12. led over Is[rael ...   and I laid]
13. siege upon [...   ]⁵

It is obvious that the inscription is badly broken. Still, the two new fragments have provided additional context and helped to clarify the date and
setting of the inscription. The monument was erected by one of the kings of
Aram (ancient Syria) a little before 800 B.C.E. Dan was the northernmost city
of ancient Israel and bordered on the territory of Aram (*Map 1*). The Bible
uses the expression "from Dan to Beersheba" several times to refer to the full
extent of Israel (Judg. 20:1; 1 Sam. 3:20; 2 Sam. 3:10; 17:11; 24:2, 15). The two
new fragments mention the names of Jehoram, king of Israel, and Ahaziah,
king of Judah, both of whom the author of the inscription claims to have
killed. This claim contradicts the Bible, which credits the Israelite general

Jehu with the two assassinations (2 Kings 9–10). The contradiction is further reason for considering the inscription genuine. A modern forger would almost certainly parrot the Bible rather than inventing a blatant contradiction to it. The context of the references to these two kings makes it relatively certain that the phrase in line nine means "the house of David."

However, "the house of David" was a title for the nation of Judah or its ruling dynasty. It tells us nothing about David the person or his life. Its occurrence in the Tel Dan stele does seem to support the Bible's claim that David was the founder of the country of Judah and its ruling family. The inscription was written within one hundred fifty years of David's lifetime. It is much closer than anything we had before and shows that David was not a late fiction. But a century and a half is still enough time for legends to develop, especially in a culture without photographs or newspapers. So we must be cautious. The Tel Dan inscription does not prove that David was a historical figure, though it does seem to tip the scales in that direction. Unfortunately, the other two inscriptions are just as ambiguous if not more so and add further complications.

The Mesha Stele

The Tel Dan stele prompted the announcement of the discovery of the same expression, "the house of David," in another, previously known inscription. The Mesha stele or Moabite stone is the greatest tragedy in the history of archaeology in Palestine[6] (*Fig. 3*). It was found intact in 1868 among the ruins of Dibon, the ancient capital of Moab, the country on the other side of the Dead Sea from Israel (*Map 1*). It was the most spectacular artifact ever found in Palestine, and the European powers were quickly embroiled in a bitter competition to acquire it. The Bedouin tribe that controlled it felt threatened by its presence and decided to get rid of it. They hoisted the stone in the air and dipped it alternately in fire and water until it broke in pieces. Most of the inscription of more than thirty lines was later reconstructed from recovered fragments and a "squeeze" (an impression left on plaster-soaked paper). The squeeze was also fragmentary, having been torn away in the middle of a gunfight before the stone was destroyed. Both the reconstruction and the squeeze have been in the Louvre Museum in Paris ever since.

The monument was commissioned by Mesha, king of Moab, sometime in the latter half of the ninth century (850–800 B.C.E.), so it is contemporary with the Tel Dan stele. In its inscription Mesha tells how he broke free from Israel after many years of subjugation. There is a story about Mesha in the Bible (2 Kings 3) that sounds similar. But it is not clear that it describes the same battle as the Mesha stele.

The basic content of the inscription has been known since the last century. However, for the past few years, the French scholar André Lemaire has been studying both the monument fragments and the squeeze. Living in Paris, he has a unique opportunity to examine it closely and repeatedly. He hopes, therefore, to solve some of the problems of the reconstruction and produce a definitive edition of the inscription.

Lemaire has now found what he believes to be an additional occurrence of the expression "the house of David." The phrase occurs near the end of the inscription in line 31 (out of 34 at least partially preserved lines). The inscription is too long to reproduce in its entirety, but the relevant lines are as follows:

> And the house [of Da]vid dwelt in Horonen[32] [. . . . .] and Kamosh said to me, "Go down! Fight against Horonen." And I went down, and[33] [I fought against the town, and I took it; and] Kamosh [resto]red it in my days.[7]

Since the monument is broken at that point, only about half of the phrase is visible, and it remained undeciphered until recently. Lemaire says he has confirmed the presence of the entire phrase on the original inscription. According to his reading, the statement, "And the house of David dwelt in Horonen" is followed by an order from the Moabite god Kamosh to fight against it. Horonen (also called Horonaim in the Bible, Isa. 15:5; Jer. 48:3, 5, 34) was a city southeast of the Dead Sea in what the Moabites considered their country. In other words, having broken free from Israel, King Mesha is being ordered to war by his god to take back the territory around Horonen, which Judah had annexed. There are a few words in line 33, but the inscription is basically missing from that point on. Presumably, Mesha reported successful completion of Kamosh's order. As in the Tel Dan inscription, therefore, "the house of David" on the Mesha stele would refer to the nation of Judah or its royal family.

The presence of David's name on the Mesha stele is obviously less certain than in the Tel Dan inscription. One of the letters of his name is missing, and the immediate context is less clear because the inscription breaks off shortly thereafter. But even if we assume that Lemaire's reading is correct, the same reservations hold for the Mesha stele as for the Tel Dan inscription. Neither contains any direct information about David's life or person. They do seem to accord with the Bible's depiction of David as the founder of the nation and dynasty of Judah—"the house of David." Based on their testimony, combined with the Bible's, the assumption that David was a historical figure seems reasonable. The third inscription introduces a complication.

The Shoshenq Relief

The Tel Dan inscription inspired another sighting of David's name on a long-known text. That text is the relief of Pharaoh Shoshenq (called Shishak in the Bible, 1 Kings 14:25–27) carved on the temple of Amun in the ancient Egyptian city of Thebes. The relief hails Shoshenq's raid into Palestine in the year 925 B.C.E. It contains a long list of names of places that Shoshenq claims to have captured.

The British Egyptologist Kenneth Kitchen has very recently suggested that David's name is in that list.[8] The name occurs in an expression that Kitchen translates "highland/heights of David" (*Fig. 4*). The immediate context, he says, is a set of places in southern Judah and the Negev (the southern part of Palestine) where, the Bible reports, David was active when he was fleeing Saul (1 Samuel 21–30). The area, Kitchen concludes, must have been known by David's name.

This occurrence of David's name is even less certain than the one on the Mesha stele. Much of the relief is damaged and illegible. Of the names that can be read, many cannot be identified for certain with any known sites in Palestine. Not all scholars agree with Kitchen that the names on the relief reflect any consistent geographical order. In addition, the Egyptian word translated "highland/heights" is rare, and its exact meaning is uncertain. In an earlier publication Kitchen himself calls the reading of these words "obscure."[9]

Kitchen's reasoning is curious. It is highly unlikely that the highlands of southern Judah and the Negev bore David's name simply because he spent time there. The term "the highland of David" for this region does not occur in the Bible or anywhere else. If this interpretation were correct, it would indicate the opposite of what Kitchen intends. The "highland of David" would most naturally refer to an area within the territory of a clan or tribe. "David" in this expression would then be a clan or its land—like Benjamin, Ephraim, or Judah—not an individual at all. If "David" could refer to a clan or region, as Kitchen's reading suggests, then he may never have existed as a historical figure. The character of David in the stories about him might be an abstraction of the clan treated as its ancestor—what biblical scholars call an "eponymous" ancestor or tradition.

Eponymous traditions are common in the Bible. In Genesis 10, for instance, the nations and peoples of the known world are treated as individuals in a genealogy that goes back to Noah and his sons (note Egypt and Canaan in v. 6 NRSV). In Gen. 25:19–26 the nations of Edom and Israel are treated as individuals, Esau and Jacob. In Genesis 29–30 the twelve tribes of Israel are described as the twelve sons of Jacob/Israel. But outside of Kitchen's interpretation of the Shoshenq relief, "David" was never the designation for a clan or region. The biblical stories about David differ from those about eponymous figures such as Jacob and his sons. There is no hint that David ever represented the dynasty or the nation of Judah. Rather, all the stories are about him as an individual. They deal with the drives, motives, and deeds of an individual man rather than the representative of a group. Kitchen's reading unintentionally highlights an important distinction between the name David and the expression "house of David." The latter is a political designation and refers to the dynasty or kingdom of Judah. But the name David in the Hebrew Bible always refers to the individual.[10] David is the founder of the dynasty known as the "house" or "seed" of David.

The occurrence of David's name on the Shoshenq relief, then, is uncertain. Kitchen's explanation of it is highly speculative and causes more problems than it solves. On the other hand, "the house of David" on the Tel Dan and Mesha steles most naturally refers to the nation or dynasty established by the individual named David. Neither of these inscriptions tells us anything about David or proves that he actually lived. But the fact that they mention him by name as an important figure within such a relatively short period after the years considered to be his lifetime makes it unlikely that he was a complete fiction.

"No archaeological discovery can be securely linked to him"

This part of McCarter's statement remains true today. There have been no new archaeological discoveries in the last ten years that can be securely linked to David. A recent textbook on the archaeology of Palestine by the Israeli archaeologist Amihai Mazar illustrates McCarter's point.[11] Mazar mentions the following archaeological sites as possibly connected to David:

1. The "City of David" is an area about 100 yards south of the walled "Old City" of Jerusalem (*Map 4* and *Fig. 5*). Its name was given to it by archaeologists who identified this area as the site of part of David's Jerusalem; nothing found there names David, though. The site's most prominent feature is an enormous "stepped stone structure," preserved to a height of 16.5 meters, which likely served to support a large building on the crest of the hill (*Fig. 6*). Its excavator dated the structure to the early tenth century B.C.E., the presumed time of David, and suggested that it supported David's citadel, which the Bible calls the "Ophel."[12] There are also the ruins of a few other buildings at this site that archaeologists generally agree date to the tenth century. But none of these—including the stepped stone structure—have any demonstrable connection to David.

2. A deep tunnel on the same hillside as the "City of David," called "Warren's Shaft" after its discoverer, has often been related to the story of David's conquest of Jerusalem. "David had said on that day, 'Whoever would strike down the Jebusites, let him get up the water shaft to attack'" (2 Sam. 5:8, NRSV). But the meaning of this passage is uncertain. Another recent translation renders it very differently: "Whoever smites a Jebusite, let him strike at the windpipe."[13] Is David telling his men how they can enter the city to attack it (how would he know this?) or is he saying that they should fight to kill the Jebusites rather than to wound them? In other words, the passage might not be referring to a water tunnel at all. Furthermore, that water tunnel may not have existed in David's day. It began as a natural fissure, but the date of its enlargement by human hands to serve as part of Jerusalem's water supply system cannot be determined.[14] Comparable systems from other cities are all from later periods.

3. The destruction of a number of sites in different parts of Palestine at around 1000 B.C.E. has been attributed to David. These include Megiddo

in the Jezreel Valley, Tel Masos in southern Judah, and the Philistine cities of Ashdod and Tel Qasile on the Mediterranean coast. The Bible makes reference to David's conquest of the Philistines (2 Sam. 8:1 = 1 Chron. 18:1) but does not mention these places specifically, and David's personal involvement at these sites cannot be shown.

4. Mazar mentions a series of fortified enclosures scattered throughout the central region of southern Palestine (the Negev) as probably tied with David.[15] Some archaeologists think they were Amalekite "fortresses" destroyed by Saul and David. Others say they were built by Saul or David to control the region. The precise date these enclosures were built and their purpose are uncertain, and their connection with David is only supposition.

5. Mazar suggests that five inscribed arrowheads found near Bethlehem belonged to a class of mercenary bowmen who could have been affiliated with David.[16] This proposal is very speculative. There is no real evidence of the existence of this guild of bowmen or of David's involvement with them.

This brief survey well illustrates and confirms McCarter's statement. The links drawn between David and archaeological discoveries made to date are far from secure. Certainly none of them could be used to prove that David existed. At the same time, the lack of certainty about their connections with David does not disprove his historical existence either. This point can be illustrated by surveying the evidence regarding the city of Jerusalem and the kingdom of David and Solomon where the controversy about archaeological evidence for David has concentrated.

David's Jerusalem

The lack of remains from the site known as the "City of David" that can be confidently connected with the time of David (ca. 1000 B.C.E.) should not be seen as decisive evidence that he didn't exist, for several reasons. First, Jerusalem is occupied today, making it impossible to dig anywhere and everywhere in the city. So we still do not have a complete picture of the city's occupational history. Furthermore, Jerusalem has been constantly occupied since the time of David and before. It has been destroyed and rebuilt numerous times, and each time the building materials from previous occupations were reused. It is not surprising, therefore, that few substantial architectural remains from as far back as David's reign have been found.

Also, we know of Jerusalem's existence long before David from a set of documents known as the "Amarna letters," found at the site of el-Amarna in Egypt.[17] They are letters written during the fourteenth century B.C.E. between the rulers of Canaanite city-states and the Egyptian pharaoh. Jerusalem was one of those city-states. It is mentioned several times in the letters, and its king was one of those who corresponded with the pharaoh. Jerusalem with its environs, therefore, was already a site of some importance at that time. So there is no reason to doubt that Jerusalem was in existence some three hundred years later for David to conquer and inhabit. The size and nature of the site, however, are uncertain. What kind of place did David conquer, and what sort of capital did he make of it? Was it a thriving city or only an administrative center over a small region or state? In trying to answer these questions, we will have to examine critically what the Bible really says (and does not say). The Bible may exaggerate or reflect circumstances that actually pertained at a later period. But we must also be careful not to define cities in the ancient Middle East by modern, Western standards.

The Kingdom of David and Solomon

Though the Bible credits David with building activity only in Jerusalem, it ascribes a great deal of building both in and outside of Jerusalem to Solomon. So, the reigns of David and Solomon are usually treated together when it comes to archaeological evidence, particularly from architecture. Archaeologists have sometimes said that the evidence would force them to invent the figures of David and Solomon if the Bible did not give their names. The evidence they have in mind consists of architectural remains from the tenth-century cities of Hazor, Megiddo, and Gezer. These remains indicate the existence of a central government that planned and executed such projects. Most would identify this government as the united monarchy of David and Solomon. The buildings are Solomonic. But David conquered the territory and established the central authority that made it possible for Solomon to carry out his construction.[18] The majority of archaeologists continue to endorse this perspective despite recent attempts to date the "royal cities" a century after Solomon.[19]

However, archaeologists and biblical scholars alike have raised questions about the real extent of David's kingdom. As Mazar puts it, "It thus has to be emphasized that even the traditional chronology hardly justifies the description of the United Monarchy as an 'empire' or even a developed state."[20] As with the city of Jerusalem, in considering the size and nature of David's kingdom (as well as the length of his reign) we will have to read the Bible carefully, keeping in mind the possibility that it contains exaggeration and anachronisms. But again, kingdoms and empires of the ancient Middle East are not modern ones. The notion of a Davidic empire spanning the Middle East, for example, may come more from interpretation of the Bible than from the Bible itself. A close reading of the Bible in its context, balanced with the evidence from archaeology, can give us a more accurate picture of what David and his reign were really like.

Other Contributions of Archaeology

McCarter's statement that no archaeological discovery can be securely linked to David is correct. But to leave it at that would be to misunderstand the nature of archaeology and the contribution it can make to a study of David's life. You might even call this short-sighted view of archaeology the Indiana Jones perspective.

Indiana Jones is a mixed blessing to archaeologists. On the one hand, he excites public interest and attracts young people to the field. On the other hand, he perpetuates a major misconception about what archaeology tries to do. Indiana Jones is always after the big-ticket artifact that will prove the truthfulness of a religious legend. Near the beginning of *Raiders of the Lost Ark*, he tells his colleague, Marcus Jones, that the search for the ark "represents the reason you and I got into archaeology to begin with."

In its early days, archaeology was a lot like an Indiana Jones movie. "Excavations" were really treasure-hunting expeditions to Middle Eastern or Mediterranean countries. They were often sponsored by European governments seeking to enhance their international prestige. The great museums of today are filled with treasures that were plundered by such expeditions in the last century. The discovery of characters and events mentioned in the Bible was a driving force behind such expeditions. And it is still a primary motivation for today's excavations.

Over the past few decades, however, the field of archaeology has experienced great change.[21] This change is the result of archaeologists starting to work in the "New World" of North, Central, and South America. Archaeology was formerly a discipline practiced in the "Old World" of Europe, Asia, and Africa. But when archaeologists began to excavate in the Americas they found that they had to adapt their theories and techniques to a different set of circumstances.

Unlike the classic Old World civilizations, native American sites had no texts—at least none that anyone was able to decipher at the time. In order to learn all they could from the material artifacts alone, archaeologists had to rely on sophisticated scientific analysis for clues. The tiniest mollusk, pollen sample, and rodent bone became subjects of intense study for the information they might yield about ancient climate, geology, horticulture, and domestication of animals. These things, in turn, could tell much about the human occupants—what they ate, how they dressed, why they moved around. The archaeologists also looked to the fields of anthropology and sociology for help. In order to determine the function of artifacts they dug up, they made comparisons with other cultures. They also searched for patterns shared by all human societies as a way of explaining developments among a particular group of people.

Old World archaeologists soon realized that the new methods could be very useful to them as well. The new methods opened up entirely new areas for research. Archaeology had previously focused almost exclusively on the upper classes and on political history. The new methods allowed archaeologists for the first time to concentrate on the everyday existence of the common people. They could also focus on segments of the population whose place in society had been previously neglected. It became possible, for example, to study the role of women in ancient cultures in a more complete and detailed way than ever before.

King David, of course, was a member of the upper class. But according to the Bible he rose to that status from humble or at least common roots. Even without specific artifacts definitely tied to David, archaeology still contributes to our biographical portrait of him in at least three ways. First, it supplies an *everyday context* for the Bible's stories about David. Information from archaeology brings the period to life and allows us a glimpse of what daily life in Palestine at David's time was like. It helps us to understand such things as what people wore and how they made their clothes, how they traveled, what they ate and how they grew and produced food, and what tools and weapons they used and how wars were fought.

Second, archaeology tells us about the even broader *environmental and economic context* of David's life. One archaeologist has shown how environmental and economic factors may have played an important role in David's ascent to kingship.[22] An increase in the population at the beginning of Israel's Iron Age put a strain on natural resources and on the agricultural economy. As the youngest son, there would not have been much inheritance left for David when he came of age. He would have been forced, therefore, to leave home in search of a means of livelihood. He found it in military activity—at first in the service of Saul and then as leader of his own outlaw band of mercenaries eluding Saul.

This leads to the third kind of information that archaeology can furnish for David—*cultural parallels*. In this case, it is actually anthropology or sociology rather than archaeology that is the source.[23] Anthropologists have looked to other cultures, especially in the Middle East, for light on how and why monarchy developed. They have determined that societies follow patterns of leadership as they grow in size and complexity. One such pattern runs: tribal leaders to chiefs to a king.[24] Saul and David were both chosen by tribal leaders. Both ruled over a confined area that could be called a chiefdom. David is described as going further and building a kingdom in Israel and then an empire in Palestine. This matter will be discussed in detail in Chapter Seven.

Anthropologists have also noticed that the steps by which David gained power according to the Bible were similar to the careers of other Middle Eastern despots. One scholar has compared David's ascent to power with that of Ibn Saud, the founding king of Saudi Arabia.[25] He could also be compared to other, more recent and more infamous Middle Eastern dictators, like Saddam Hussein. Both were clever politicians and military commanders. Both led outlaw bands that rivaled the ruling family. Both eventually replaced their rivals, leaving a trail of dead bodies behind. Both gained and retained power through military force.

This comparison may seem offensive at first. But it must be remembered that David and Saddam are culturally much closer to each other than either is to Westerners. They share outlooks about politics, society, and perhaps even religion that are quite different from those that prevail in the West. The concepts of elective democracy and frequent, peaceful transition of power were unheard of in David's day and are still foreign to much of the Middle East today. Rulers have always been installed for life. Comparisons between David and modern Middle Eastern rulers help to isolate the motives for his actions and suggest some of the personality traits that led him to achieve what he did.

Archaeology is sometimes thought to produce "hard," objective evidence in contrast to the Bible, which must be interpreted. But this is a misconception. The foregoing discussion shows that archaeological evidence is subject to interpretation just as the Bible is.[26] Archaeology has not yet proved David's historical existence. But it has not disproved it either. The evidence is interpreted differently by different people. The assumption that David was a real person remains a viable and defensible one. The references to his name in inscriptions add some weight to this assumption, as do the "Solomonic" cities. Parallels with other cultures may help us to understand the process behind David's rise to power and the motives for some of his actions. Archaeology provides background and context for the David stories and thus for our biography and can be interpreted as lending credence to David's historical existence.

"The quest for the historical David, therefore, is primarily exegetical"

Despite archaeology's contributions, on the whole we must affirm McCarter's statement: "The Bible is our only source of information about David"— at least our only direct source. Without the Bible we would barely know David's name, have only a vague idea of who he was, and know almost nothing of what he did. The Bible alone details his actions, reports his conversations, and explains his motives. David's biography, therefore, relies primarily on the Bible.

Biblical scholars use various guidelines for interpreting the Bible, just as archaeologists do for understanding artifacts. The biblical literature about David cannot be taken at face value as biographical, because it has a very complicated history of development. Also, the writer(s) who put together the final product were primarily interested in David not as a historical figure but as a religious model. The historical information contained in the Bible has to be exegeted or "drawn out" from its stories. This would remain a useful enterprise even if we were to determine that David was not a historical person. We are simply asking what conception of David lies behind the stories about him in the Bible. As a next step in the biography of David, therefore, we must consider the nature of the biblical material about him. We must also detail the methods and principles to be used for extracting biographical information from it. That is the task of the next chapter.

2

Royal Propaganda

The Bible's Account of David's Life

David's kingliness caused everything in his vicinity to grow, even stories; his power does not allow anything to remain as it was.

—Torgny Lindgren, *Bathsheba*

Stefan Heym is a well-known writer from the former East Ger-
many. Before the fall of the Berlin Wall, he published a book called *The King
David Report.*[1] It was a clever satire on the repressive censorship and propaganda of the East German government. In the book, King Solomon com-
missions a fictional character named Ethan to write the official report on
King David. The purpose of the report is

to establish for this and all time to come One Truth, thus ending *All Contradiction and Controversy,* eliminating *All Disbelief of the Choice by our Lord Yahveh of
David ben Jesse,* and allaying *All Doubt* of the *Glorious Promises* made to him by
our Lord Yahveh in regard to *his Seed and Progeny.*[2]

Ethan soon realizes that what Solomon and his commission want is not
a factual account of David's life but a way of controlling what people
believe about him. The report cannot be made up; it must contain docu-
mented facts about his life. "But as knowledge of the facts may lead a person to dangerous thoughts, the facts must be presented so as to direct the
mind into the proper channels."[3] In the commission's view, some facts
about David are embarrassing and must be left out. Others, such as his vic-

tory over Goliath, are factually dubious but should be included because they bolster David's image.

Ethan's report fails to satisfy the commission. They ultimately issue an "improved" version of it. But Ethan gets no credit because he has been banished to obscurity. The implication is that the story of David in 1–2 Samuel represents the commission's final, approved report, which was found more suitable as royal propaganda.

The Bible is unique among all the writings and artifacts from the ancient Middle East. Its uniqueness lies in its enormous impact on society and religion over thousands of years and continuing today. "The Bible as we have it is clearly both what it was in its original context and usage, plus what it has become over the centuries as Scripture, constantly reinterpreted by Synagogue and Church."[4] The Bible's stories about David are our best artifact of his life. Heym's depiction of the David story as propaganda is a useful vision of how it originated. But the story of David in the Bible has become something very different from what it was.

The Bible is not a book but a whole library from ancient Israel. David's importance in the Bible is evident from the sheer volume of material devoted to him—more than for any other character, as we have seen. It contains several books devoted to David. They fall into three sections:

1. 1 Samuel 16–2 Samuel 24 + 1 Kings 1–2
2. 1 Chronicles
3. Psalms

The story in Samuel–Kings is by far the most important of the three for our purposes. It contains the longest and most detailed account of David's life. It is also the source for most of the information about him in Chronicles and Psalms.

1 Samuel 16–1 Kings 2 in the Deuteronomistic History

The books of 1–2 Samuel and 1–2 Kings are part of the Deuteronomistic History. This is the name biblical scholars use for the books of Deuteronomy plus Joshua, Judges, 1–2 Samuel, and 1–2 Kings. (The book of Ruth, found in English Bibles between Judges and 1 Samuel, is in a different location in the Hebrew Bible and was not part of the Deuteronomistic History). These books together are identified as an original, unified work because they have many traits in common, especially their structure, writing style, and theological outlook.[5] Together they recount the entire history of Israel from the time of Moses to the destruction of the kingdom of Judah in 586 B.C.E.

The Deuteronomistic History evaluates Israel's history according to the law set forth in Deuteronomy, hence its name. It explains national successes and failures as the consequences of faithfulness or disobedience to the law. So it is not "pure" history but rather a theological history or even a historical theology. Its goal was less to recount what had happened in the past than to use the past to instruct a later audience.

The Structure of the Deuteronomistic History

Deuteronomy—Moses reviews the law for the people of Israel just before his death

Joshua—Israel under Joshua conquers and takes possession of the land of Canaan

Judges—Military leaders deliver the people from different foreign oppressors

1 Samuel 1–15—Samuel becomes Israel's last judge and anoints Saul as its first king

1 Samuel 16–2 Samuel 24—The rise and reign of David

1 Kings 1–11—David's death and the reign of Solomon

1 Kings 12–2 Kings 17—The history of Israel and Judah to the fall of Israel (721 B.C.E.)

2 Kings 18–25—The history of Judah to its fall in 586 B.C.E.

David stands squarely at the center of the Deuteronomistic History. He follows the epochs of Moses, Joshua, and the judges and ushers in the reigns of Solomon and the divided monarchy. Half of the book of 1 Samuel, all of 2 Samuel, and the first two chapters of 1 Kings are devoted to the story of David. With a total of forty-two chapters (Moses and the law get only thirty-four chapters in Deuteronomy), the David story is the centerpiece of the Deuteronomistic History both in placement and in size.

David is the main character of the Deuteronomistic History in other ways as well. He is the standard by which the later kings are judged and mostly found wanting. It was because of him that Judah and Jerusalem lasted as long as they did. For example, even though Abijam's "heart was not true to Yahweh his God as the heart of David his father, yet for David's sake Yahweh his God gave him a fiefdom (or "light") in Jerusalem" (1 Kings 15:3). Eventually, though, Yahweh's patience expired. The fall of Jerusalem and exile of the people of Judah to Babylon in 586 B.C.E. were explained as punishment for the shortcomings of these later kings. But David was also the model for restoring Israel to its former greatness.

Key Dates in Israel's History

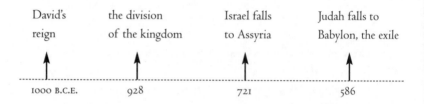

David's reign	the division of the kingdom	Israel falls to Assyria	Judah falls to Babylon, the exile
1000 B.C.E.	928	721	586

The identity of the Deuteronomistic Historian is unknown. He (this author was almost certainly male) is simply called the "Deuteronomist" or "Dtr" for short. He was both an editor (also called a "redactor") and an author. He often included older documents as the basic content of his history. This is especially true for his account of David, as we will see. Dtr did not hesitate to make changes he deemed necessary in these source documents. But his creativity as an author shows primarily in the way that he linked his sources together and in the theological explanations that he added. The Deuteronomistic History was composed sometime during the exile (after 586 B.C.E.), when the work ends. Several passages were later added to the completed history by other writers.

Dtr's Composition of 1 Samuel 8–14

Dtr's account of Saul's reign well illustrates his compositional techniques. It also supplies important background to the David story that is essential for his biography. First Samuel 9–11 contains three different stories about how Saul became king. In 9:1–10:16, Saul is searching for some lost donkeys of his father's and encounters Samuel, who anoints him king; in 10:17–27 he is chosen by lot in a national assembly; and in chapter 11 he leads the people in battle, after which they proclaim him king.[6] The three stories came from three different sources that were available to Dtr. Rather than choosing among them, he combined all three by means of a series of editorial additions.

The first of Dtr's additions comes at the end of the first story (10:14–16). It relates a conversation between Saul and his uncle.

> [14] Saul's uncle said to him and his servant, "Where did you go?" [Saul] said, "To look for the donkeys. But when we saw that they were not to be found we went to Samuel." [15] Saul's uncle said, "Tell me what Samuel said to you." [16] Saul said to his uncle, "He told us that the donkeys had been found." But about the matter of the kingdom [Saul] did not tell [his uncle] what Samuel had said.

This conversation makes clear that Saul's anointing by Samuel was a private matter and that he did not tell anyone else about it. This creates the need for the public proclamation of Saul as king in the second story in 10:17–27. The end of this second story also has an editorial addition from Dtr in 10:27. It tells of some "scoundrels" in the army who question Saul's military capability. They ask, "How can this fellow save us?" This opens the door for Saul to prove himself in the third story, at the end of which the scoundrels are referred to again (11:12–13):

> [12] The people said to Samuel, "Who is it who said Saul would not reign over us? Bring the men so we can execute them." [13] But Samuel said, "No one will be executed today because today Yahweh has effected deliverance in Israel." [14] Samuel said to the people, "Come, let us go to Gilgal and renew the kingship there."

The two references to those who questioned Saul link the second and third stories together. Dtr also added the call to "renew" the kingship in 11:14 as a part of the same link. The original story behind chapter 11 did not presuppose that Saul was king. It told of the people making him king for the first time (11:15): "All the people went to Gilgal and made Saul king there before Yahweh." By means of these additions Dtr united three separate stories into a single one in which Saul becomes king in stages: privately, publicly, and then by proving his prowess as a military leader. He then encased these stories within the framework of the speeches in chapters 8 and 12, which have long been recognized as his composition.

For his account of Saul's reign in chapters 13–14 Dtr used some stories about Saul's and Jonathan's battles against the Philistines. These stories came from much later in Saul's life, since his son, Jonathan, appears in them for the first time as a grown man. Dtr used them to set the stage for David. The stories depict Saul very negatively. Jonathan, rather than Saul, is the hero of the battles. In one story (14:24–45) Saul makes a foolish vow that almost costs Jonathan his life. Dtr made Saul look even worse by inserting the story of his rejection as king in 13:8–15a (Dtr's own composition). It ends with the notice that Yahweh has found "a man after his own heart" to replace Saul. This is an obvious allusion to David. As he customarily did for all kings, Dtr closed his account of Saul's reign with a set of summary notices (14:47–52). Saul would not die for some time, but the focus of the narrative would hereafter shift to David. Saul's recruitment of soldiers in 14:52 paves the way for David's arrival at court in 16:14–23.[7]

In sum, 1 Samuel 7–15 is a good illustration of how the Deuteronomistic History was written. Dtr collected traditions from Israel's history— like those about how Saul became king—and skillfully edited them into a single, flowing narrative. While he generally transmitted them as they were, he was not shy about making changes that he considered necessary. He also provided a framework for the stories he passed on. In this case, the framework included chapters 8, 12, and 14:47–52. Dtr's own history became an important part of Israel's tradition. As a result, later scribes occasionally enlarged upon it by adding their own stories and sources. We will see the same process at work on a larger scale in Dtr's account of David.

The Nature of the David Story

The story of David in Samuel–Kings has two large parts. The first, in 1 Samuel 16–2 Samuel 5, tells of David's conflicts with Saul and eventual ascension to the throne of Israel. The second, beginning with David's coronation in 2 Samuel 5, recounts major events in David's reign, especially the revolt of his son Absalom.

Outline of 1 Samuel 16 — 1 Kings 2

David's Rise

1 Sam. 16—17	David is anointed and comes to Saul's court
1 Sam. 18—20	Tensions mount between David and Saul
1 Sam. 21—27	David flees to the wilderness of Judah with Saul in pursuit
1 Sam. 28—2 Sam. 1	Saul is killed in battle with the Philistines while David is away
2 Sam. 2:1—5:3	David becomes king of Judah and then king of Israel

David's Reign

2 Sam. 5:4—10:19	David consolidates his reign in Jerusalem
2 Sam. 11—12	David's adultery with Bathsheba
2 Sam. 13—20	Amnon's death and the revolts of Absalom and Sheba
2 Sam. 21—24	Miscellaneous stories, poems, and lists from David's reign
1 Kings 1—2	David's death and Solomon's succession

Scholars commonly theorize that these two parts were based on two older narrative sources. The first source is called the "History of David's Rise." The second is known as the "Court History" or "Succession Narrative," so called because it was understood as dealing with who David's successor as king would be.[8] The History of David's Rise is preserved in basic outline in 1 Samuel 16–2 Samuel 5. It presumably began with David's coming to Saul's court as his musician (16:14–23). It then told how Saul became jealous of David and tried to kill him, how David evaded Saul's pursuit in the wilderness, how Saul was killed in battle, and how David was crowned king first over Judah and then over Israel.[9]

The Court History is more controversial. Originally, it probably dealt only with David's reign and did not include the story of the transition to Solomon in 1 Kings 1–2.[10] Its focus was Absalom's revolt in 2 Samuel 13–20. It also included a few other passages from 2 Samuel that I will discuss in more detail in the course of this chapter. These are: the stories of the deaths of Asahel, Abner, and Ishbaal (2 Sam. 2:12–4:12); the introduction of Jonathan's son "Mephibosheth" (2 Samuel 9); and the account of the deaths of Saul's other heirs (2 Sam. 21:1–14). As was his typical practice, Dtr incorporated these two sources more or less wholesale into his history. But he also adapted them to fit his purposes. He joined them together in dovetail fashion so that the ending of the History of David's Rise in 2 Samuel 5 overlaps with the beginning of the Court History in 2 Sam. 2:12–4:12.[11]

More important for our biography of David than the dimensions of these sources is their nature. Scholars have long observed the apologetic tone of the History of David's Rise. "Apology" in this sense is a term for a type of literature that defends someone against accusations. Kings in the ancient Middle East, especially usurpers, used apology to justify their reigns and claim their right to rule.[12] The episodes in the story of David's rise function to legitimate David as Saul's successor by answering charges against him such as the following:[13]

(1) David sought to advance himself as king at Saul's expense.
defense—David came to Saul at the latter's behest (1 Sam. 16:19–22), was completely loyal while there, and did much to help Saul's cause (19:4–5). Marriage to Michal was Saul's idea (as a plot against David, 18:20–21a), and David protested his unworthiness (18:23).

(2) David was a deserter.
defense—David was driven away by Saul (1 Sam. 19:9–17; 26:19), and Saul's own children sided with David and helped him (19:11–17; 20:1–21:1).

(3) David was an outlaw.
defense—David was a fugitive from Saul's injustice and sought reconciliation (1 Sam. 26:18–20), all of which Saul admitted (v. 21).

(4) David was a Philistine mercenary.
defense—David was forced by Saul into Philistine service as a last resort (1 Sam. 27:1); he deceived the Philistines by claiming that he attacked Israel and Judah when he in fact raided their enemies (27:8–12) and enriched Judah (chap. 30).

(5) David murdered Nabal and seized his wife, Abigail, and his property.
defense—Nabal was a mean-spirited fool who deserved to die (1 Sam. 25:3, 17, 25). David was prevented from killing him by God through Abigail (25:18–34). It was Yahweh who struck Nabal, and Abigail married David of her own will (25:38, 41–42).

(6) David was implicated in Saul's death.
defense—David did not kill Saul on two previous occasions when he had the chance (1 Samuel 24 and 26), so he must not have been ultimately responsible for Saul's death. He was not on Mt. Gilboa where Saul died (chap. 29), and his words to Achish (29:8) make it clear that in battle with Israel he would have turned against the Philistines, "the enemies of my lord the king." He executed the man who claimed to have killed Saul (2 Sam. 1:14–16) and profoundly lamented Saul's death (1:18–27).

To grasp the apologetic nature of this material, contrast the fifth entry above about Nabal and Abigail with the story about Bathsheba and Uriah (2 Samuel 11–12). In both cases David was accused of having a man killed and stealing his wife. But the story of Bathsheba and Uriah is not apologetic. (I will explain why this is so momentarily.) It recounts David's adultery and murder openly, and in the end he is denounced and punished for these crimes. With Abigail and Nabal, however, the writer goes to great lengths to explain how David was innocent of any wrongdoing.

The same apologetic tone continues in the story of David's reign,[14] so that we may add to the list of accusations:

(7) David was implicated in Abner's death.
defense—Abner had left Ishbaal, come to an agreement with David, and begun to lobby for him in the North (2 Sam. 3:7–18). He and David had parted peacefully (3:21–23) when Joab, acting alone, killed him as part of a private vendetta (3:22–30). David cursed Joab (v. 29) and led the mourning for Abner (vv. 31–35) to the point that all the observers were convinced of his innocence (v. 37).

(8) David was implicated in Ishbaal's death.
defense—Ishbaal was murdered without David's knowledge by opportunists hoping to gain David's favor (2 Sam. 4:2–8). Instead, he condemned them to death and desecrated their bodies. But he buried Ishbaal honorably.

(9) David annihilated Saul's heirs when he took the throne.

defense—David was forced to allow the execution of Saul's seven sons and grandsons in order to save Israel from Yahweh's punishment of bloodguilt which Saul himself had incurred (2 Sam. 21:1–14). He then "showed kindness for Jonathan's sake" to the one remaining heir, "Mephibosheth," restoring his property and hosting him in the palace (chap. 9). Michal's childlessness (6:23) was the just deserts for her contemptuous treatment of her husband and king.

(10) David had his own sons murdered to preserve his place on the throne.

defense—David's firstborn, Amnon, was murdered by Absalom in revenge for the rape of Tamar (2 Samuel 13). David was so angry that he did not allow Absalom back into Jerusalem for three years, and would not see Absalom even then (chap. 14). Absalom's rebellion (chaps. 15–18) forced David to fight him, and even then David ordered leniency toward him. It was Joab, in direct disobedience of this order, who killed Absalom and broke David's heart (18:1–19:9).

The story of Solomon's appointment as David's successor (1 Kings 1–2) was not in the Court History but was added by Dtr. His language and ideology occur in the concern for the establishment of David's dynasty (1 Kings 1:48; 2:4, 24, 45) and in David's charge to Solomon to "be strong and courageous" and "walk in his ways, keeping his statutes and commandments" (2:1–3). The formula marking the close of David's reign (2:10–12) and the notice about the fulfillment of the prophecy against Eli (2:27b) also come from Dtr. He thus changed the focus of the narrative from Absalom's revolt to the question of who David's successor would be. In other words, he turned the Court History into the Succession Narrative. His motive for this change was theological. Saul's line had been wiped out. The fates of Amnon and Absalom in 2 Samuel 13–20 seemed to threaten the same thing for David. God had promised David that his son would succeed him as king and establish a dynasty (2 Samuel 7). Dtr wanted to make it plain that Solomon was the fulfillment of that promise.[15]

The greatest change to the Court History, however, was not Dtr's doing. Dtr could hardly have known the story of David's sin with Bathsheba and still held him up as a model king who always "did what was right in Yahweh's eyes."[16] This story (2 Samuel 11–12) must have been added after Dtr had finished his history. The addition of the Bathsheba episode placed the story of Absalom's revolt in an entirely new light. That story was originally apologetic. It had depicted David as too gentle to harm his sons. He loved them so much that he could not bring himself to discipline them despite their willfulness and rebellion. The blame for any bloodshed was consistently placed on Joab, the army commander. David's emotional display of mourning over Absalom, like his mourning over Abner, was a sign of his non-involvement in their deaths. With the addition of the Bathsheba affair, though, David's family troubles and the deaths of his sons were understood in a new way. They were punishments for or consequences of his sins against Uriah and Bathsheba. His gentleness and love were seen as weakness and failure as a father. Even his mourning for Absalom took on a new poignancy as David's own sin was to blame for his son's death.

Recognition of the apologetic nature of the History of David's Rise and the Court History is extremely important for our biography of David. These sources may bring us close to David chronologically. This is a controversial matter. Some scholars suggest that these source documents were written during or shortly after David's reign.[17] They point out that accusations listed earlier were against David personally, not his dynasty. These would have been controversial only during David's lifetime or shortly afterward, and an apologetic response would have been unnecessary after he had been dead for several generations and his dynasty firmly established. But other scholars object that the high literary quality of these two sources presupposes widespread literacy and interest in the past, which would not have been the case with Israel before the eighth century B.C.E. at the earliest.[18]

More important, these sources bring us close to David historically. That is, whatever their date of writing, they seem to contain genuine historical information about David. It is hard to believe that they are pure fiction. Who would invent such allegations against David just to try to explain them away? Moreover, the events they relate have the "ring" of authenticity: Saul, Nabal, Abner, and Ishbaal all died at times that were convenient for David's political career; Saul's line was obliterated at David's order; David lived as an outlaw and served the Philistines. The authors could not simply deny these events or ignore the suspicions they raised about David. The best they could do was take on the role of "spin doctors," explaining that David's motives were virtuous and his actions justified.

In short, the story in the Deuteronomistic History (1 Samuel 16–1 Kings 2) is as close to the historical David as we can get. It appears to contain genuine historical information about him. But that information is not immediately accessible. It is clothed in literary and apologetic garb. So we have to read critically in order to make use of it. We must remain aware that Dtr shaped it for his own purposes and that later writers sometimes added to it. We must also keep in mind the apologetic nature of both Dtr's work and that of his sources and be especially cautious about their explanations of the reasons for David's actions. Nevertheless, the Deuteronomistic History provides the paints and canvas for our biographical portrait of David. I will say more about how to use it after surveying the other biblical materials about David.

1 Chronicles

If David is the main hero of the Deuteronomistic History, he is even more so for the books of Chronicles. First and Second Chronicles were written around 350 B.C.E. At that time, the people of Judah and Jerusalem were trying to rebuild the political and religious institutions that had been destroyed since the exile. The author of Chronicles (called the "Chronicler") was strongly interested in the temple and the institutions connected with it. So he (the Chronicler was also male and likely a priest) emphasized the roles of David and Solomon in building the temple and organizing the worship activities there. He put David and Solomon forward as the models after which the restored monarchy should be patterned. The main difference was that the Chronicler's David and Solomon were particularly models of a king's proper ritual activity.[19]

If Chronicles were independent of Samuel–Kings it would be a very valuable resource for the history of the monarchy. The two works could then be compared with one another to help determine what was history and what was added by each writer. But the Deuteronomistic History was the Chronicler's primary source. This means that Chronicles is largely a rehearsal of what is in Samuel and Kings. Often, in fact, Chronicles repeats Samuel–Kings word for word.

The first nine chapters of 1 Chronicles are genealogies. The narrative portion begins in chapter 10 with the account of Saul's death in battle against the Philistines. The chapter is parallel to 1 Samuel 31. Thereafter, the story of David's reign in 1 Chronicles 11–21 is drawn from 2 Samuel, as the following chart illustrates.

Parallels in Chronicles and Samuel Versions of the David Story

Topic	Chronicles	Samuel
Saul's death on Mt. Gilboa	1 Chron. 10:1–12	1 Sam. 31
David anointed king over Israel at Hebron	1 Chron. 11:1–3	2 Sam. 5:1–3
David's conquest of Jerusalem	1 Chron. 11:4–9	2 Sam. 5:6–10
List of David's mighty men	1 Chron. 11:10–47	2 Sam. 23:8–39
First attempt to bring the ark to Jerusalem	1 Chron. 13	2 Sam. 6:1–11
Treaty with Hiram of Tyre and defeat of Philistines	1 Chron. 14	2 Sam. 5:11–25
Ark successfully installed in Jerusalem	1 Chron. 15:25–16:3	2 Sam. 6:12–19
Promise of a dynasty	1 Chron. 17	2 Sam. 7
David's wars	1 Chron. 18	2 Sam. 8
Wars with Ammonites and Aramaeans	1 Chron. 19	2 Sam. 10
Siege of Rabbah	1 Chron. 20:1–3	2 Sam. 11:1; 12:26–31
Victories over Philistine heroes	1 Chron. 20:4–8	2 Sam. 21:18–22
David's census	1 Chron. 21:1–27	2 Sam. 24

The chart shows that the Chronicler changed the order of some passages in Samuel. He also made minor changes in wording in order to accommodate his religious views. Occasionally he even added his own compositions:

Saul died for his rebellion by which he rebelled against Yahweh by not keeping his word and by inquiring of a medium, divining, instead of divining of Yahweh. So Yahweh killed him and turned the kingdom over to David, son of Jesse. (1 Chron. 10:13–14)

Even these two verses, however, attest the Chronicler's familiarity with the book of Samuel, since the events they mention are recounted in full in 1 Samuel 13, 15, and 28.

The Chronicler also drew from other portions of the Bible. First Chronicles 16:3–36, for instance, borrows from Psalms 96, 105, and 106. It is not certain whether the Chronicler had any sources aside from those in the Bible. He refers to such sources as "the records" of Samuel, Nathan, and Gad (1 Chron. 29:29). But these may be the Chronicler's way of alluding to the stories about these prophets in the books of Samuel. Still, Chronicles does occasionally provide details not found elsewhere in the Bible, such as the full list of David's siblings in 1 Chron. 2:13–16.

All in all, 1 Chronicles is not a very reliable source for David's biography. Most of the time it simply repeats what is in 2 Samuel. Where the two diverge, it is usually because of changes introduced by the Chronicler to promote his interests. However, Chronicles cannot be completely or automatically discounted as a historical source. Occasionally, it offers independent information that may be useful for filling in details of David's life.

The Book of Psalms

In Chronicles, David is given credit for organizing the music used in the temple worship. The tradition that David was an expert composer and musician also pervades the book of Psalms. This book is a collection of one hundred fifty songs and hymns from different periods in Israel's history. Nearly half of them, seventy-three psalms, contain headings referring to David. Typically, these references are quite brief—"of David," "a psalm of David," or the like—without any reference to his life. These psalms would be a useful source for David's biography, at least for glimpses of the inner man, if they really were written by him.

However, there are two major difficulties with connecting the psalms to David. First, the headings that refer to him are not necessarily meant as claims of authorship. The Hebrew preposition (l^e) that precedes David's name can be understood in a wide variety of ways: "to David," "for David," "by David," "of David," "belonging to David," "pertaining to David," and so on. The headings may mean that the psalms were dedicated to David or were part of group of psalms known as the "David collection" or were written in the style of David.

Second, the headings were added long after the psalms themselves were written. This means that the connection of the psalms with David is secondary. They reflect a common tendency in the Bible to associate originally anonymous writings with famous biblical characters. Many psalms were attributed to David at a late date because of the tradition that he was the "sweet psalmist of Israel." This same tendency also led to the insertion of psalms into the story of David (e.g., Psalm 18 = 2 Samuel 22).

The Greek translation of the Hebrew Bible, known as the Septuagint (abbreviated LXX), illustrates both of these points. It associates fourteen additional psalms with David. This is because the tendency to connect religious writings to known biblical figures grew over time. The LXX book of Psalms even adds a psalm, number 151, which explicitly claims Davidic authorship. It recaps the story of his early life and triumph over Goliath (1 Samuel 16–17).

Some of the other additional headings in the LXX show the ambiguity of the expression "of David." The LXX heading to Psalm 71,[20] for example, reads, "Of David, by the sons of Jonadab and the first of those who were taken captive." Even though it is a psalm "of David" it was written by someone else at the time of the exile. So whatever "of David" meant, it did not signal Davidic authorship in this instance. Psalm 96 is also called "a song of David" in the LXX. But its heading dates it to the end of the exile, "when the temple was built after the captivity." This was nearly five hundred years after David. Psalm 137, though also "of David," was written "by Jeremiah," according to the LXX.

Psalm Headings with Information about David's Life

Psalm 3	A psalm of David when he fled from Absalom his son
Psalm 7	A *Shiggaion*[21] of David, which he sang to Yahweh about the words of Cush, a Benjaminite
Psalm 18	Of the servant of Yahweh, David, who spoke to Yahweh the words of this song when Yahweh saved him from all his enemies and from Saul
Psalm 30	A psalm. A song at the dedication of the temple. Of David
Psalm 34	Of David, when he feigned madness before Abimelech, so that he drove him out, and he went away
Psalm 51	A psalm of David, when Nathan the prophet came to him because he had had sexual relations with Bathsheba
Psalm 52	A *maskil* of David, when Doeg the Edomite came to Saul and said to him, "David has come to the house of Ahimelech"

Psalm 54	A *maskil* of David, when the Ziphites came and said to Saul, "Is not David hiding with us?"
Psalm 56	Of David. A *maskil* when the Philistines seized him in Gath
Psalm 57	Of David. A *miktam* when he fled from Saul in the cave
Psalm 59	Of David. A *miktam* when Saul had his house watched in order to kill him
Psalm 60	A *miktam* of David, for instruction, when he struggled with Aram Naharaim and Aram Zobah and when Joab returned and killed twelve thousand in the Valley of Salt
Psalm 63	A psalm of David when he was in the wilderness of Judah
Psalm 142	A *maskil* of David, when he was in the cave. A prayer

These fourteen psalms contain headings referring to events in David's life. But these are not very useful for historical reconstruction because they lack details. The heading of Psalm 3, for instance, says it was written when David fled from Absalom. But the psalm itself refers only generally to enemies without ever mentioning Absalom or any part of his revolt. Similarly, Psalm 18 was written when Yahweh had saved David from Saul according to its heading. But it lacks any mention of Saul. In addition, its parallel in 2 Samuel 22 comes long after Saul's death in the narrative. The heading of Psalm 51 assigns it to the occasion of David's repentance after his adultery with Bathsheba. But again, it does not name Bathsheba or the nature of the sin that the author regrets. It was the general content of these psalms that led a later editor to associate them with David.

Others of these fourteen headings do not match the information in Samuel. Psalm 7 mentions an enemy of David named Cush, the Benjaminite, about whom there is no information elsewhere in the Bible. Psalm 34 says it was written when David feigned madness before Abimelech. The story about David feigning madness is in 1 Sam. 21:10–15 (also the subject of the heading for Psalm 56). But the Philistine king there is called Achish, not Abimelech (cf. Gen. 20; 26:1–16). Psalms 57 and 142 both refer to David being "in the cave." These may refer to the time when David hid from Saul in a cave (1 Samuel 24). But more likely they have in mind 1 Sam. 22:1, which says that David and his men took refuge in "the cave" near Adullam. But "cave" here is an error for "fortress," the two Hebrew words being similar. This shows that the headings of these two psalms were based on a late version of Samuel in which the original reading, "fortress" had already been mistaken as "cave."

Still others of these fourteen headings mention Doeg's report to Saul (Psalm 52 = 1 Sam. 21:7; 22:6–10), the betrayal of the Ziphites (Psalm 54 = 1 Sam. 23:15–23), some of David's wars (Psalm 60 = 2 Samuel 8 and 10), and his time in the wilderness (Psalm 63). In all these cases, one must be familiar with the story of David in Samuel in order to make sense of the headings. In other words, the headings were added by people who were trying to associate the psalms with known events in David's life. The psalms do not provide any independent information about those events.

The fourteen psalms listed above also show how the headings of the psalms are sometimes contradicted by their content. We saw that Psalm 3 refers to enemies and foes—plural—although its heading mentions only Absalom. The heading of Psalm 30 refers to it as a song at the dedication of the temple and a psalm of David. But David had been dead thirteen years when the temple was dedicated (1 Kings 7:1), so it is unlikely that he wrote a song for the occasion. Moreover, Psalm 30 expresses its author's gratitude for Yahweh's having saved him from some near-death experience. This hardly seems appropriate for the celebration at the temple's dedication. Psalm 51:18 assumes that the walls of Jerusalem have been destroyed and are in need of rebuilding. This reflects conditions during the exile, after 586 B.C.E., some 400 years after David lived in Jerusalem and had his affair with Bathsheba. In Ps. 63:3 the writer says he has looked upon God in the sanctuary—an allusion to the temple. But again, the temple was not built when David was in the wilderness of Judah where the psalm's heading sets it. The heading of Psalm 59 alludes to Saul's order to arrest David after his marriage to Michal (1 Sam. 19:11). This event took place on a single night, probably David's wedding night, since David escaped that night and ran away from Saul. But the psalm repeats the refrain that the enemies who seek the author's life return each evening like prowling dogs (vv. 6, 14). Although it is not one of the fourteen, even the famous 23rd Psalm does not fit its heading, "A psalm of David." Its last line says, "Surely goodness and mercy shall follow me all the days of my life, and I shall dwell in the house of Yahweh forever." The "house of Yahweh" is the temple in Jerusalem. Since it was built by Solomon after David's death, David himself could not have written this line and hence is probably not the author of this famous psalm.

Mentions of David's Name within the Psalms

18:50   [Yahweh] magnifies the victories of his king,
         and shows loyalty to his anointed,
         to David and his descendants forever.

72:20   The prayers of David son of Jesse are ended.

78:70—71 He chose David his servant
         and took him from the sheepfolds,
         from behind the nursing ewes he brought him,
         to shepherd Jacob his people
         and Israel his heritage.

89:3—4   I made a covenant with my chosen.
         I swore an oath to David my servant.
         I will establish your descendants forever
         and build your throne for all generations.
                 . . .

89:20   I found David my servant.
         With my holy oil I anointed him.
                 . . .

89:35—36 Once for all I swore by my holiness.
         I will not lie to David.
         His descendants will last forever
         and his throne will be like the sun before me.
                 . . .

89:49   Where is your loyalty, Lord,
         which you swore to David by your faithfulness?

122:5   For there [Jerusalem] are the thrones for judgement,
         the thrones of the house of David.

132:1   Remember, O Yahweh, for David
         all the afflictions he suffered.
                 . . .

132:10—13 For the sake of David your servant
         do not turn away the face of your anointed.
         Yahweh swore truthfully to David.
         He will not turn back from it.
         "From the fruit of your loins

> I will set [your son] on your throne.
> If your sons keep my covenant
> and my decrees which I teach them,
> then their sons forever
> will sit on your throne."
> . . .

132:17   There [Jerusalem] will I make a horn sprout up for David
> I will prepare a lamp for my anointed.

144:9–10   God, I will sing a new song to you,
> with a ten-string harp I will play for you,
> who gives victory to kings,
> who frees David his servant.

Of the 150 Psalms only these seven mention David's name within the psalm itself. Only two of these seven (18 and 144) are associated with David in their headings. Psalm 72:20 is not really part of Psalm 72 but marks the end of a section of the book of Psalms known as the "Prayers of David." The other six psalms above are concerned with David as the founder of the royal house of Judah rather than with him as an individual. None of them yields any information about David's life per se.

Psalms 89 and 132 both refer to the promise of an enduring or "eternal" Davidic dynasty. This promise arose as a way of explaining the dynasty's duration in Judah. It was an important element in the image people in Israel and Judah had of their great, ancestral king. It is also very important for Dtr's account of David (2 Samuel 7). These psalms show how David and his reign were interpreted by later writers, including Dtr. But they tell us nothing about the historical David.

Once the secondary ascriptions to David in the headings are removed from consideration, the book of Psalms contains very few references to him. Most of these references simply reproduce information from 1–2 Samuel. They contain little of significance for a biography of the man. However, like 1 Chronicles, the Psalms cannot be totally dismissed as a source of historical information about David. They can help to separate the details of his life from the traditions about him that developed later in Israel. They are especially important for any consideration of the divine promise about the endurance of David's dynasty.

The Bible and Biography

Writing David's biography is like looking for a peach seed. The peach itself is the story of David in the Deuteronomistic History. Other sources supply background (archaeology and anthropology) and add details (Chronicles and Psalms). But 1 Samuel 16–1 Kings 2 contains the basic historical core of David's life. I use a peach because its seed—the historical core—may be large. But to get to it, one must peel back the skin of Dtr's editing. Then there is the pulp of the "spin" placed on the story by David's apologists. One must dig through it to reach the seed. The analogy is not entirely appropriate, because unlike the peach, in historical or biographical research it is sometimes hard to tell the pulp from the seed; it is not always easy to decide which elements of the David story to peel away and which to keep as historical.

In this book, I will adopt two major principles as guidelines for accomplishing this task.[22] The first is the principle of skepticism. By this I mean that when some aspect of the biblical story fits a literary or ideological theme we should be skeptical about its historical value. We have seen that the biblical authors and editors were not interested in history for its own sake but used it as an instructional tool. But history is often molded or bent to accommodate the lesson that the writer wishes to teach. When some detail of the David story fits a clear theological agenda it does not necessarily mean that history has been revised. But we do well to be skeptical. In addition, we have seen that Dtr was a skillful and creative editor—a good storyteller.[23] Hence, we must also consider the role that literary themes and devices played in shaping Dtr's story of David. An example of both of these tendencies in the David story is the characterization of Saul. David's replacement of Saul and superiority over him is both a literary and a theological theme. This should make us skeptical about whether Saul was really as inept and unstable as 1–2 Samuel portray him.[24]

The second principle is what J. Maxwell Miller calls that of analogy.[25] It holds that the past was basically analogous to the present and to what is known of similar societies and circumstances. Another way of putting Miller's point is that people of all time have the same basic ambitions and instincts. This includes David. The principle of analogy addresses the question of the real motives behind David's actions in 1–2 Samuel. It asserts that David acted in accord with the customs and motives common among ancient Middle Eastern rulers and with general human tendencies in his acquisition and retention of power.

This principle calls into question any explanation of David's motives and deeds that appears to be apologetic. It assumes that "where there's smoke, there's fire." That is, the accusations against David that the History of David's Rise and Court History sought to explain away were probably historical. His execution of Saul's male heirs, for example, was certainly politically motivated despite the claims of 2 Samuel 21 to the contrary. It was common practice for a new ruler in the Middle East to wipe out the heirs of his predecessor in order to avoid the threat of overthrow later on. One sign of apology in the narrative has been called the technique of "overstress."[26] This is where the story repeatedly states David's innocence in regard to a particular accusation. The more the author protests, the more we suspect the charge was true.

Examining the biblical account of David by this principle requires what I like to call "reading against the grain." This means that we become aware of the way in which the writer is trying to promote or excuse David and then carefully study the biblical account for evidence to the contrary. An important technique for reading against the grain is the rule of *cui bono* (Latin for "For whose benefit?" or "To whose advantage?"). It holds that the person who benefited from a certain occurrence is most likely the one responsible for it. David benefited from the deaths of key individuals at crucial junctures in his career. The rule of *cui bono* suggests that he was responsible for those deaths. Another useful technique is looking for oddities or inconsistencies in the story that, when explored, suggest a historical reality different from the one recounted in the narrative.

A third technique that makes use of both the principle of skepticism and the principle of analogy is characterization. It involves simply paying close attention to any hints in the narratives about the character of David or any of the individuals who interact with him. Such hints appear in statements about a person's motives, intentions, or personality. They also occur in the reports of a person's thoughts and speeches or conversations. We will need to be skeptical of the intentions expressed by the writer. We will also need to "read between the lines" or "against the grain" with the principle of analogy in mind to discern what a historical person's true intentions might have been.

It is not just David's character we are interested in. It is also those of the people around him. The techniques used in the study of biblical characters

were developed by feminist scholars.[27] They were designed to correct a tendency to ignore the importance of the female characters and their roles in the
Bible. Women characters are especially significant in the David story. Several
of David's wives—Michal, Ahinoam, and Abigail—play crucial parts in his
rise to kingship. Other women in his life—Bathsheba, Tamar, Rizpah, and
Abishag—bring out his more human qualities. The more we know about the
characters around David, female and male, and their interactions with him,
the richer our understanding of him and his personality will be.

Obviously, these principles and techniques will yield a much less flatter-
ing portrait of David than if we take the Bible's account at face value. But
this portrait will be more realistic and therefore closer to the historical
David. In the end, I am claiming simply that King David was human and
had the same drives and ambitions as any powerful man. Our ultimate goal
is to understand as much as we can about David the man. We now turn to
that task.

3

Was David a Shepherd?

David's Origins and Youth

When Kingly David of his owne accord,
Though he were then th'anointed of the Lord,
And though his Sheephooke might his Scepter be,
This holy Youth so humble is, that he
Will back to th' fields his fathers flock to keepe
And make his subjects, (for a while) his Sheepe.

— Michael Drayton, "David and Goliath"

And I first played the tune all our sheep know, as, one after one,
So docile they come to the pen-door till folding be done.
They are white and untorn by the bushes, for lo, they have fed
Where the long grasses stifle the water within the stream's bed;
And now one after one seeks its lodging, as star follows star
Into eve and the blue far above us,— so blue and so far!

— Robert Browning, "Saul"

Shepherd as a Metaphor

Imagine rolling hills covered with thick grass under a glorious deep blue sky. Here and there the dark exclamation point of a tree punctuates the green carpet. The ribbon of a tiny brook meanders through the hills. Its steady gurgle is interrupted only by the occasional bleating of one of the cottony creatures lapping at its bank. An adolescent boy sits with his back to a tree beside the brook. His voice floats above the noises of the water and the sheep in clear, reverent tones. His hands strum a small harp cradled in his lap, while his eyes scan the horizon for any threat to his sheep.

David's boyhood is often depicted in Western art as just such an idyllic scene. Unfortunately, there is hardly an element of it that has any basis in historical reality. The landscape is European and comes from Renaissance painters who used their own countryside as the background for their studies of biblical figures. The area around Bethlehem is hilly but rocky and dry, and there is no brook. David's instrument was the lyre, smaller and simpler than the harps we know today.[1] Even the sheep raised in Palestine were a different species from those in Europe and America.[2] Most important, the entire idea that David was a humble, rural shepherd is questionable. It owes more to the 23rd Psalm than to 1–2 Samuel, where it is relatively rare. But as we saw in the previous chapter, Psalm 23 was probably not written by David.

References to David as a Shepherd in 1 Samuel 16–1 Kings 2

1. His anointing, 1 Sam. 16:11: "Samuel said to Jesse, 'Are all your sons here?' [Jesse] replied, 'There is still the youngest who is tending the sheep.'"
2. His summons to court, 1 Sam. 16:19: "Saul sent messengers to Jesse and said, 'Send me David, your son, who is with the sheep.'"
3. The story of David and Goliath, 1 Samuel 17: "David went back and forth from Saul to tend his father's sheep in Bethlehem. (v. 15) . . . When Eliab, [David's] oldest brother heard what he said to the men, Eliab became angry at David and said, 'Why did you come [here]? With whom did you leave those few sheep in the wilderness?' (v. 28) . . . David said to Saul, 'Your servant was a shepherd for his father's sheep' (v. 34) . . . David took his stick in his hand and chose from the dry stream bed five smooth stones, which he placed in his shepherd's bag." (v. 40)
4. Yahweh's promise of a dynasty, 2 Sam. 7:8: "Thus says Yahweh of hosts, 'I took you from the pasture, from behind the sheep, to be leader over my people Israel.'"

This well-known image of David's youth occurs in only four contexts in the Bible's main narrative about him. It is a literary creation in each of these contexts rather than a historical reality. The metaphor of the king as a shepherd is very common in ancient Middle Eastern countries. The pharaohs of Egypt, for example, are sculpted holding a shepherd's crook in one hand (*Fig. 7*). The metaphor also occurs frequently in the Bible. The prophets Ezekiel (chap. 34) and Zechariah (chap. 13), for example, use it to condemn Israel's unrighteous leaders for leading their "flock" astray. Micah prophesies the coming of a new shepherd, "who is to rule in Israel" (Mic. 5: 2–4). Even a foreign king like the Persian Cyrus can be called a shepherd (Isa. 44:28) because the people of Judah were his subjects and thus part of his flock. But most important for our purposes is the explicit use of this metaphor in the story of David. The elders of Israel quote Yahweh as telling David,

> It is you who shall shepherd my people Israel.
> It is you who shall be the ruler over Israel. (2 Sam. 5:2)

This metaphor has been adopted to explain David's origins. We have already seen that 16:1–13 is a secondary addition to Dtr's history. This becomes more apparent in the fact that the rest of 1–2 Samuel makes no reference to this anointing. David is anointed king twice more (2 Sam. 2:1–4; 5:1–5), first over Judah and then over Israel. Yet neither of these passages mentions or presupposes the anointing in 1 Sam. 16:1–13. More important, the purpose of this anointing story is patently theological. As a prelude to what follows, it makes the point that David was chosen by God to replace Saul. If there is any history here it is to be found in the remarkably candid admission that David was made king while Saul was still alive.

The second reference to David as a shepherd in 1 Sam. 16:19 follows an extraordinary description of David in verse 18. We will analyze this description shortly. Among other things, it refers to him as eloquent and an expert warrior. These are not qualities of a simple shepherd. They belong to someone with experience as a statesman and a soldier. It is unlikely that a man of such qualities and experience would be serving his father as a shepherd. This reference to David as a shepherd also has an important literary and theological function. It hints that this summons to the royal court is David's first step toward kingship. Thus, in taking him from tending his father's sheep, Saul sets David on the road to becoming the shepherd over Israel.

The famous tale of David's defeat of Goliath, which is the third place in 1 Samuel where David is described as a shepherd, is an independent legend. We will study it in detail in the next chapter. It was not an original part of the History of David's Rise but was combined with it, probably by Dtr. It contradicts the surrounding narrative at several points. The stories on either side of it depict David as a seasoned warrior before his encounter with Goliath. In 1 Sam. 16:18, he is described as a "man of war," and in 18:7 the women of Israel laud him for killing "his tens of thousands." Both of these texts contradict the picture of David the shepherd boy, fresh from the pasture, who slays his first and only enemy soldier. At the end of chapter 16, Saul and David have formed a close relationship, with David as Saul's beloved armor bearer (16:21). Yet at the end of the Goliath story (17:55–56) Saul does not know who David is.

Part of the explanation for these contradictions is the legendary character of the Goliath story. David may have defeated a large opponent like Goliath at some point in his career. But like all legends, the original story of that encounter has grown over time. The tendency in retelling the story was to enhance David's faith and courage as well as his youth and inexperience. The shepherd image is part of that enhancement. David's oldest brother scolds him for leaving his "few sheep" to come watch the battle. David himself expresses confidence in Yahweh's protection based on his experiences defending his sheep against wild animals. The shepherd image also hints at the future that awaits this exceptional youth as the ruler of his people.

Outside of 1 Samuel 16–17, David is referred to as a boy shepherd only in 2 Sam. 7:8, which was composed by Dtr. That it is playing on the metaphor of the ruler as shepherd is clear from the previous verse, which refers to Israel's previous leaders, "whom I commanded to shepherd my people Israel." Again, therefore, it is closely connected with the literary and theological motif of King David as the shepherd of his people Israel.

In line with the principles that guide our analysis of the David story, we must be skeptical about the historical validity of this depiction. It is certainly possible that David tended sheep as a boy; as we will see, his father was a prosperous sheep "rancher." But the Bible's claim that David was anointed king or came to Saul's attention as a shepherd boy is doubtful historically. It was not so much a claim about historical fact as a metaphor for

David's future position as king. Over time, as the stories were passed on, it became a popular part of the tradition about him.

A Kingly Description

Unlike modern novels, the Bible rarely describes either the physical appearance or the personality traits of its characters. Think about Moses and Jesus, for instance. The Bible says nothing about what they looked like. The portraits that readers form of biblical characters are usually based on incidental remarks made in the course of the plots of the stories. For David, however, there is one verse that contains a remarkable concentration of descriptive terms:

> I have seen a son of Jesse, the Bethlehemite, who knows how to play. He is a powerful nobleman, a warrior, eloquent, and a handsome man, and Yahweh is with him. (1 Sam. 16:18)

This verse is a kind of job recommendation. Saul is looking for a musician to soothe him on those occasions when the "evil spirit from Yahweh" torments him. One of Saul's servants recommends David for his musical ability and then goes into some detail describing him. The description stands out from its context because it does not fit with the image of David as a shepherd boy. It may, however, give us a glimpse of the historical David. And in any case, the qualities in this verse furnish a useful structure for examining David's early life. They also summarize the traits he exemplifies in the stories throughout 1 Samuel 16–1 Kings 2.

"A Son of Jesse the Bethlehemite"

All parents know what it is like to be recognized through their children: "You must be John's mother." "Hello, I'm Mary's father." Imagine how Jesse might feel! His name is found throughout the Bible because he was David's father. Thus, he is the source of the Davidic dynasty, which includes every king of Judah. Isaiah 11:1 refers to him as the stock from which the expected Messiah will emerge: "A shoot shall come out from the stump of Jesse." Matthew and Luke in the New Testament are at pains to describe Jesus' lineage from David, the son of Jesse (Matt. 1:5–6; Luke 3:31–32). Yet, despite the frequent mention of Jesse's name, we know next to nothing about him as an individual. He was famous not for own accomplishments but because of his son.

Still, the glimpses of Jesse in the Bible contain some hints about him and about David's background. The servant who recommended David to Saul called him "a son of Jesse the Bethlehemite" without any explanation as to who Jesse was. Even in the very first mention of Jesse in the Bible his name occurs without any introduction. Yahweh simply tells Samuel, "I will send you to Jesse the Bethlehemite" (1 Sam. 16:1). The abruptness of these references suggests that Jesse was a well-known figure not only in Bethlehem but also in the tribe of Judah, where Bethlehem is located, and perhaps even in Benjamin, Saul's tribe. First Samuel 16:5 says that Samuel commanded the elders to consecrate themselves. It then goes on to say that Samuel consecrated Jesse and his sons, indicating that Jesse was one of the elders or leaders of Bethlehem.

Bethlehem is in the area of Palestine known as the central highlands or hill country. This is a mountainous strip of land, running north and south through the region west of the Jordan River (*Map 2*). In it nestle several places that were important in David's life, including Gibeah and Jerusalem, the capitals of Saul and David, respectively. All three places are in close proximity. Bethlehem lies only about five and a half miles south of Jerusalem, which is about three miles south of Gibeah (*Map 1*). All three are within easy walking distance of each other. This means that Bethlehem was not as isolated as is sometimes imagined. David and his fellow townsfolk were very near to Saul's capital and likely well aware of what went on there, all the more since Jesse was an elder or official in Bethlehem.

The Bible gives sparse information about the other members of David's immediate family. His mother's name is never mentioned. Three different passages refer to his brothers, but they are not in complete agreement.

David and his Brothers

1 Sam. 16:6–10	1 Sam. 17:12–15	1 Chron. 2:13–15
1. Eliab	1. Eliab	1. Eliab
2. Abinadab	2. Abinadab	2. Abinadab
3. Shammah	3. Shammah	3. Shimea

4.	4.	4. Nethanel
5.	5.	5. Raddai
6.	6.	6. Ozem
7.	7.	7. David
8. David	8. David	

The difference between "Shammah" and "Shimea" is a matter of spelling and therefore inconsequential. Likewise, the name Elihu in 1 Chron. 27:18 is probably an error or a variant spelling for Eliab. The greatest difference in these lists is in their reckoning of the number of Jesse's sons. There are two crucial verses: "Jesse brought his seven sons (or "seven of his sons") before Samuel, but Samuel said, 'Yahweh has not chosen any of these'" (1 Sam. 16:10) and "David was the son of an Ephrathite from Bethlehem of Judah whose name was Jesse and who had eight sons" (1 Sam. 17:12).

First Chronicles 2:13–15 lists David as the last of seven sons. The idea that the seventh son is special and favored is common in ancient literature and probably lies behind the reference to David as the seventh son.[3] The notion that he was the eighth seems to have come from confusion between 1 Sam. 16:10 and 17:12. The writer of 16:10 probably meant to include David among Jesse's sons who all eventually came before Samuel. Unfortunately, by placing the statement in 16:10—before David arrives—this writer made it sound like David had seven brothers. This is how the writer of 17:12 interpreted it.

However, some scholars have offered another explanation. They suggest that the description of David as the eighth son is the author's way of emphasizing David's lowly beginnings.[4] Rather than being the seventh son, as one might expect in light of his future greatness, David was the eighth son, a nobody. His greatness is due to Yahweh's choosing him, not to his birth order.

Both of these positions, seventh and eighth, then, are possibly of literary and folkloric origin. Neither can be considered historically reliable. The stories in 1 Samuel mention only three of David's brothers by name: Eliab, Abinadab, and Shammah. So it may be that David had only three brothers instead of six or seven. The book of Chronicles gives a full list of Jesse's seven sons by name. But since Chronicles was written so much later than Samuel, it is impossible to know whether this list is historically reliable.

One thing all these lists agree on is that David was the youngest. This may also be to accommodate literary and theological considerations. The

book of Genesis, for instance, describes a series of important characters—
Isaac, Jacob, Rachel, and Joseph—as younger siblings. Its message is that
God prefers to work with the disadvantaged—the young, the weak, and
the poor. The story in 1 Sam. 16:1–13 stresses the choice of David despite
his youth and appearance because "Yahweh looks upon the heart" (v. 7).

But there is also surprising evidence about the society and environment
at David's time to indicate that his place as the youngest may have been a
consideration in his choice of career.[5] As mentioned in Chapter One, there
was an increase in the population of the central highlands about the time
David was born. The resulting scarcity of natural resources meant that
there was often not enough land to support all of the sons of a family with
their own families. The youngest, like David, were forced to strike out on
their own and find their livelihood in other pursuits. Later in this chapter,
we will explore how this affected David's career choices.

First Chronicles also identifies two sisters of David:

> Their sisters were Zeruiah and Abigail. The sons of Zeruiah were three:
> Abishai, Joab, and Asahel. Abigail bore Amasa, and the father of Amasa was
> Jether the Ishmaelite. (1 Chron. 2:16–17)

David's sisters are mentioned together only one other place in the Bible:

> Absalom appointed Amasa in the place of Joab over the army. Amasa was
> the son of a man named Ithra the Israelite who had had sexual relations
> with Abigail, the daughter of Nahash, the sister of Zeruiah, the mother of
> Joab. (2 Sam. 17:25)

There are several peculiar features about the references to these sisters.
Sons in ancient Israel were customarily known by their father's name rather
than their mother's. It might be that Joab and his brothers were known as
"the sons of Zeruiah" because she was David's sister. But she is identified
as his sister only once in the Bible—in 1 Chron. 2:16. Another possibility is
that Zeruiah was really the *father* of Abishai, Joab, and Asahel, and not their
mother.[6] It is also odd that the sons of Zeruiah play virtually no role in the
story of David until he becomes king of Judah. If they were really David's
nephews, one might expect them to appear earlier and to have a greater
involvement in his rise to the throne.

The reference to Abigail in 2 Sam. 17:25 is even more perplexing. It calls her the daughter of Nahash, not of Jesse. How, then, could she be David's sister? Again, there are several possibilities. This could simply be an error. The name Nahash, which occurs two verses later, may have been accidentally written by a scribe in place of "Jesse." Or perhaps Abigail was David's half sister; his mother could have married Nahash after Jesse died. It is also intriguing that only two women in the Bible are named Abigail, and both are related to David. This has led some scholars to suggest that the two women were one and the same.[7] Since the other Abigail was David's wife, this would mean that David married his own (half) sister.

These difficulties may have arisen because social relationships are often described in the Bible (and other ancient documents) as blood relationships. Thus, other army commanders besides Joab are also said to be related to their king. Abner is called Saul's cousin (1 Sam. 14:50) or uncle (1 Chron. 8:33; 9:36, 39). And Amasa is Absalom's cousin (2 Sam. 17:25). Joab may not have had a blood relationship to David. But their social relationship of king and commander led to his being known as David's nephew. This in turn could have led to Zeruiah being identified as David's sister. Zeruiah may actually have been Joab's father. But since his name did not appear in the lists of David's brothers, later tradition assumed that Zeruiah had to be David's sister and Joab's mother.

To judge from their first mention in the story (1 Sam. 26:6–9), the "sons of Zeruiah" joined David only after his marriage to Abigail (1 Samuel 25). As we will see, this marriage was a crucial political step for David. It placed him at the head of the Calebites, the most important clan in Judah. From there, it was a short step to kingship over all of Judah. Perhaps the sons of Zeruiah were kinfolk of Abigail and joined David because of his marriage to her. Because Joab was described as David's nephew, and Zeruiah and Abigail were related, Abigail had to be David's sister as well. In other words, it is possible that neither Abigail nor Zeruiah was really David's sister and that Zeruiah was not even a woman.

This solution is obviously speculative. The fact is, we do not know much about David's family. The few lists that are in the Bible are confused. What we know of the social and environmental conditions from the time supports the possibility that he was the youngest son of a fairly large family. Exactly how large, it is impossible to say. Social factors at work in the tradition have probably led to some who were not David's blood relatives being described as such.

"Who Knows How to Play"

According to 1 Sam. 16:14–23, David's musical talent is what first brought him to Saul's attention. It is ironic that David of all people should be Saul's comforter, since he is really the source of Saul's distress. Though Saul does not yet know it, David is his chosen replacement. As the story in 1 Samuel unfolds, Saul grows increasingly unstable and insanely jealous of David. This portrait of Saul is historically very dubious. The writer is obviously building a contrast between Saul and David and promoting the latter at the expense of the former. We have already seen how later tradition enhanced and exaggerated David's reputation as a psalmist by attributing both the temple music and most of the book of Psalms to him. Nevertheless, his musical ability may have a foundation in history, particularly if we understand its function.

Saul did not want music for entertainment. In the ancient world, music served more of a religious and magical function. It played an important role in the temple worship, as we have seen. It was also used to induce prophetic trances. Saul began prophesying when he met a band of prophets carrying musical instruments (1 Sam. 10:5–6, 10). Similarly, the prophet Elisha called for a musician and then prophesied while he played (2 Kings 3:15). David's strumming on the lyre was meant to relieve Saul from the tortures of the evil spirit sent from Yahweh. But this was not just because of its soothing sound. Music was believed to possess magical powers to keep away or exorcise demons and evil spirits.[8] David was a magician as much as a musician.

Once this function of the musician is understood, it casts a different light on David's initial presentation to Saul as a musician. Saul would have wanted a musician as a regular and necessary part of his entourage to ward off evil spirits and bring good fortune. The writers behind the biblical story, however, exploited this information against Saul and on behalf of David. They portrayed Saul as a man driven out of control by an evil spirit. This may have been an ancient way of referring to mental disease. Saul is certainly seen as irrational. Only David's music can calm him; and even it does not always work. David's playing, on the other hand, gave rise to the tradition that he was a psalmist and the one who arranged the temple music. Note, though, that this passage does not tout David's abilities as a singer or poet, but only as one who plays (literally "strums") the lyre.

We have no idea how the lyre (Hebrew *kinnɛr*) sounded, but we do know what it looked like. None has ever been found in Palestine, but there are examples from other countries. There is also a particularly nice drawing of one on a seal from Jerusalem (*Fig. 8*). The lyre typically consisted of a rectangular sound box and two unequal arms with a bar between them from which three to twelve strings were stretched. It was small enough to be cradled in one arm while the other hand strummed it. Lyres were expensive to make and were used mainly by the aristocracy. This does not fit well with the image of a poor shepherd. But it does agree with the other descriptive terms used for David in 1 Sam. 16:18, especially the next one.

"A Nobleman"

The literal meaning of this Hebrew expression is "a powerful man." Some English translations take it in a military sense: "a man of valor" (NRSV). But it is better understood here as a reference to social standing, for two reasons. First, virtually the same expression is used of Saul's father, Kish, and the NRSV translates it, "a man of wealth" (1 Sam. 9:1). Kish was a "business man" rather than a military figure. Second, the next item in the description of David calls him "a man of war." But this would be redundant if David's military ability had already been mentioned.

The attribution of wealth and status to David's family background again contrasts with the common portrait of him as a humble shepherd. But it provides another explanation for his being known as a shepherd. In ancient Israel there was no system of currency or banking. Wealth was measured in land and livestock. As a "powerful man," Jesse would have owned many sheep. David could have been a shepherd, not in the sense of the lone and lowly herdsman, but in the sense of an owner or "sheep rancher." Indeed, Mesha, the same king of Moab whose stele was discussed earlier, was a "sheep breeder" (2 Kings 3:4). However, this does not change the fact that the Bible's image of David as a shepherd was probably drawn from the metaphor for a king.

David's upper-class background fits with the clues we have seen that Jesse was a respected nobleman in Bethlehem and one of the city's elders. This background would have been an important item in the recommendation to Saul. It identified him as a young man of good upbringing. He was of the same social class as Saul and would know how to behave in the royal household. It would also have helped David in his later negotiations with the elders of Israel and Judah concerning the leadership of both peoples. In both cases he was dealing with people of his own social level. His social class did not pose a barrier to his being considered a king, as it might have if he had arisen from an inferior stratum of society. The judge Jephthah, for example, was driven out of his clan, despite his leadership qualities, because of his low social status (Judg. 11:1–3).

David's status as a noble is also supported by the book of Ruth. Its main characters, Ruth and Boaz, are identified as David's great-grandparents. Boaz was a wealthy landowner, who is described in Ruth with basically the same phrase as the one that we are now considering for David: "a prominent rich man" (NRSV). The genealogy connecting David with Boaz and Ruth may have been tacked on to their story, but it is essentially the same as the one given for David in Chronicles. Assuming it is genuine, it gives important information about David's family background.

David's Genealogy (Ruth 4:18–22 and 1 Chron. 2:4–15)

Judah

Perez

Hezron

Ram

Amminadab

Nahshon

Salma or Salmon

Boaz

Obed

Jesse

David

Both Ruth and Chronicles list women in David's ancestry. This is unusual, since lineage was typically traced through males. Comparable genealogies in the Bible do not mention any women. What makes these lists for David even more remarkable is that the women they mention were not Israelites. Ruth was from Moab; Tamar (mentioned in 1 Chron. 2:4) was Canaanite. The Gospel of Matthew (1:5) names a third woman among David's ancestors, Rahab, also a Canaanite.

The stories about these women in the Bible are not of the sort that one expects to find for the line of Israel's most renowned king. Tamar seduced her father-in-law, Judah, and bore his twin sons. Rahab was a prostitute by profession. Ruth "uncovered the feet" of Boaz before they were married— an idiom for exposing (at least) the genitals. But these women also displayed other, extraordinary qualities. Tamar was more righteous than Judah by his own admission (Gen. 38:26). Ruth exemplified loyalty, and Rahab faith. All three were courageous, resourceful, and independent. The preservation of their stories as part of David's background may reflect an effort to counter the narrow nationalism of some Jews at a later period. But David's Canaanite heritage could well be historical, and his connection with the Moabites may be too. If so, Israel's greatest king was not of pure Israelite stock!

"A Warrior"

Literally, "a man of war," this item refers to someone with considerable experience and success on the battlefield. It therefore contrasts markedly with the stories that portray David as a shepherd boy with no military training or experience; before the battle with Goliath he is so unaccustomed to a soldier's armor that when he tries it on for the first time he cannot move (17:38–39).

First Samuel 16:18 does not explain how David acquired his expertise as a warrior. It only lists this as one of the attributes he brought with him to Saul's court. The statement goes together with the notice that Saul took into his service every warrior or valiant man he saw (14:52). But archaeology provides a clue about this aspect of David's life and career. As we have mentioned, the evidence shows that there was a population increase in the central highlands a little before 1000 B.C.E. This had a devastating impact on the natural resources of the area and consequently on the livelihood of its inhabitants. There were more people and less fertile land to support them. A new social class of landless people emerged. Some of them attached themselves to existing institutions as mercenaries, priests, or "squires" to the wealthy. Others lived as outlaws in competition with the established institutions.[9]

David became a member of this class. For part of his career, according to the biblical stories, he was attached to Saul as a musician and squire.

Later he was a mercenary pursued by Saul and employed by the Philistines. He became the commander of a small army of persons who were discontent with or refugees from structured society (1 Sam. 22:2). We have seen that David's place as the youngest son may have been a factor that drove him into this new social class. As each of David's brothers married and fathered his own children, more demand was placed on Jesse's estate. By the time David came of marriageable age, there was not enough land available to sustain him with a family of his own. Thus, despite his noble and affluent origins, David referred to himself as a poor man who could not afford the bride price for the king's daughter (1 Sam. 18:23).

Away from the prosperity of his family, David learned to live by his wits and his arms. His skill as a warrior was the single most important attribute in his rise to power. He quickly became Saul's armor bearer (1 Sam. 16:21). His later success in the army, first as a soldier and then as a commander, eventually brought him into conflict with Saul himself. He gathered a band of outlaws around him and became their chief in direct rivalry to Saul. They lived on what they could plunder and hired themselves out to the Philistines as mercenaries. When David became king, he continued his military triumphs. He consolidated Israel and Judah into a nation and held them together by strength of arms. He even subjugated surrounding clans and built a small empire in Palestine and its immediate environs. Thus, David's skill as a warrior is a key ingredient in the Bible's description and probably in the career of the historical person as well.

"Eloquent"

There are several dimensions to this expression. Literally it means "clever of word." It indicates David's familiarity with proper protocol among the upper class. It also suggests his shrewdness and intelligence as well as his facility with words. The speeches attributed to David play an important role in the effort to justify his actions and present him favorably. They portray him as remarkably pious and faithful, as in his reply to Goliath:

> You come to me with sword and spear and javelin; but I come to you in the name of Yahweh of hosts, the God of the ranks of Israel, whom you have defied. This very day Yahweh will deliver you into my hand, and I will strike

you down and cut off your head; and I will give the corpses of the Philistine army this very day to the birds of the air and the wild animals of the earth, so that all the earth may know that there is a God in Israel and that all this assembly may know that Yahweh does not save by sword and spear; for the battle is Yahweh's and he will give you into our hand. (1 Sam. 17:45–47)

David's confidence is not in his own expertise but in Yahweh. And the reason he can be so confident is that the Philistine has openly defied Yahweh.

In other speeches, David's piety is mingled with humility and respect toward Saul, even though Saul is seeking his life. There is no trace of any political ambition on David's part. On two occasions the tables are turned, and David has an opportunity to kill Saul (1 Samuel 24; 26). But he refuses, saying that he cannot extend his hand against "Yahweh's anointed" (24:6; 26:9–11). He then confronts Saul with proof that he spared the king's life out of loyalty. He addresses Saul respectfully as "my lord" and "my father." At points he is even more self-effacing: "Against whom has the king of Israel marched out? Whom do you pursue?—a dead dog, a single flea!" (24:14). The dog metaphor is common in royal settings in the ancient Middle East[10] and again attests David's nobility as well as his eloquence.

Other features of this speech are intended to show David's cleverness in speech. He does not blame Saul directly but deflects the blame to nameless others: "Why do you listen to the words of those who say 'David seeks to do you harm?'" (24:9). He levels a curse not at Saul, but at those people who have moved Saul against him. The reason for the curse is that they have driven him away from Yahweh:

If Yahweh has incited you against me, let him accept an offering, but if mortals, let them be cursed before Yahweh, because they have driven me out today from sharing in Yahweh's heritage, saying, "Go serve other gods." (26:19)

At the same time, the speech may have a subtle edge to it. David's question is ambiguous: if Saul thinks he is pursuing a mere flea, he is mistaken. The flea is quick and hard to catch, and its pursuer soon becomes its victim; the flea bites.[11]

David's dealings with the Philistines in 1 Samuel also illustrate his cleverness. Here, he is more devious, though no less admirable as far as an Israelite reader would be concerned. In his dealings with the Philistine

King Achish, David and his men raid settlements and bring the plunder to Achish (1 Samuel 27). But they lie to the king and tell him that the plunder was taken from clans in Israel or Judah. The text makes it clear that David did not actually attack any settlements of Israel or Judah but only told Achish this to deceive him. And Achish falls for it. He comes to trust David implicitly, in the belief that he had betrayed his own people. Thus, when war erupts between Israel and the Philistines, Achish expects David and his men to fight on the side of the Philistines: "You and your men must march out to battle with me" (28:1). David's reply is duplicitous: "Then you will learn what your servant does." What David does, of course, is to feign loyalty to Achish and the Philistines. So his invitation to Achish masks a threat, clear to the reader but not to Achish. In the heat of battle, David will turn against the Philistines.

Fortunately for Achish, the other Philistine leaders know David only through his reputation as a killer of Philistines. They do not share Achish's enthusiasm for having David join them in war. They demand instead that he dismiss David and his mercenaries. David responds with genuine disappointment and reaffirms his desire to "fight against the enemies of my lord the king" (29:8). But it is Saul, not Achish, who is David's true lord and king. The real enemies against whom David wishes to fight are Achish and the Philistines.

These speeches obviously fit the pro-Davidic purpose behind 1–2 Samuel. They do not tell much about the historical figure. But David's "cleverness of speech" hints at his personal charm and political savvy, which may well have been qualities of the historical man. In 1–2 Samuel, David's success at attracting leading people to his side is phenomenal. In the beginning, Saul himself is quite taken with David and "loved him greatly" (1 Sam. 16:21). The same is true of Saul's children, Jonathan (1 Sam. 18:1; 19:1) and Michal (18:20). Both of them help David flee from their father after Saul's own affection turns to rage. David acquires the support of the leading citizens in the kingdom, such as the priests and prophets. And of course he is very popular with the people at large.

One must take these reports with the proverbial grain of salt, because they reflect the writer's desire to elevate David and alienate Saul. Nevertheless, David's popularity is realistic, and there is no reason to believe that the royal family was immune to his charm. Even aside from these stories, the portrait of David remains that of a skillful politician and a persuasive diplomat. He gathered followers in part with promises of rewards for their service. This is implied in a speech by Saul to his own men: "Will the son of Jesse give any of you fields and vineyards? Will he make any of you commanders of thousands or commanders of hundreds?" (1 Sam. 22:7).

Before Saul was dead, David began moving toward the throne of Judah, courting the elders with gifts from his conquests: "Here is a present for you from the plunder of the enemies of Yahweh" (1 Sam. 30:26). As king of Judah, he set his sights on the crown of Israel. His diplomatic skills are apparent in his letter to the citizens of Jabesh–Gilead, strong supporters of Saul:

> May you be blessed by Yahweh because you showed this loyalty to Saul your lord and buried him. Now may Yahweh treat you loyally and faithfully. I also will reward you because you have done this thing. Now, let your hands be strong, and you be valiant, for your lord Saul is dead, and the house of Judah has anointed me king over them (2 Sam. 2:5–7).

David congratulates the people of Jabesh for their loyalty to Saul and subtly invites them now to cast their support behind him. For the people of Jabesh this would mean turning against Saul's heir and successor. But David suggests that their debt to Saul has been paid, and now that he is dead they owe nothing to his son.

David consolidated and enlarged his domain not only by military means but also through treaties with the surrounding peoples. He negotiated at least some of these treaties before he was crowned king, when, as a rising chieftain vying for power, he needed the help of other rulers. They were happy to lend aid to a known rival of their enemy, Saul. Later, as king, David was able to renegotiate the treaties from a position of greater strength. His political and diplomatic skill as much as his military strength brought him the kingdom and held it together while he worked to build an empire.

"A Handsome Man"

This designation for David, literally a "man of form," tells us very little about his actual appearance. It may simply be a literary motif for a king. Saul was also said to be handsome—strikingly so: "[Kish] had a son named Saul, a handsome young man. No one among the sons of Israel was more handsome than he. He stood head and shoulders above all the people" (1 Sam. 9:2).

Saul looked like a king should look. So did David's oldest brother, Eliab. At least Samuel thought so: "Surely," he thought, "Yahweh's anointed stands before him!" (1 Sam. 16:6). But Yahweh rebukes Samuel: "Do not regard his appearance or his stature, for I have rejected him. For God does not see as humans see. Humans see the face, but God sees the heart" (1 Sam. 16:7). The obvious point of this verse is to contrast David with Saul. Still, it raises the question of David's physical appearance by hinting that outwardly he did not seem very kingly.

So what did David look like? In the absence of a detailed description, we can only make guesses from a few hints in the stories. First, the contrast between Saul and David suggests that David was short. Saul stood "head and shoulders" above everyone in Israel. David's brother must also have been tall because Samuel was told not to look on his stature. David was the youngest or "smallest" (the same word in Hebrew can have both meanings) of the brothers. The contrast is even more exaggerated when he faces Goliath.

The writer obviously has a special interest in stressing the contrasts between David and Saul. However, David's small stature also is suggested in other stories where this interest does not seem to be in focus. On one occasion, David's wife, Michal, fools Saul's messengers by placing a household idol in bed under the covers and telling them that David is ill (1 Sam. 19:16). In order for Michal's ruse to work the idol would have to be about the same size as David. In a story in Genesis, Rachel is able to hide more than one of these idols (same Hebrew word) under the saddle of her camel (Gen. 31:19, 30, 34–35). Surely the idol in the David story was not this small. But it was probably not life-size if Michal was easily able to move it about. It may have been able to serve as a convincing substitute for David precisely because he was a small man.

To complete the ruse deceiving her father's guards, Michal placed a tangle of goat's hair at the head of the idol in the bed (1 Sam. 19:13). The clump of goat's hair would have to resemble David's own hair for the trick to work. This suggests that his hair was thick and wild, and probably curly. There are other hints at the color of David's hair and his complexion. When Samuel first saw David "he was ruddy and attractive, handsome to the eye and of good appearance" (1 Sam. 16:12).[12] Similarly, against Goliath

(17:42) he is described as "ruddy and handsome in appearance." The word "ruddy" in Hebrew, as in English, means "reddish" as for Esau in Gen. 25:24: "The first came out reddish all over."

Obviously, this is all quite speculative. But to the extent that the Bible says anything about his physical appearance, we may imagine David as a short man with a ruddy complexion and thick, reddish-brown, uncontrollable hair. That is the way he will appear in my portrait.

"Yahweh is with him"

In the mouth of the servant who recommended David to Saul this expression may have meant nothing more than that he was successful or had promise. He might have been saying that David was lucky and "fortune smiled on him." This would have been important for a musician whose playing was supposed to bring fortune and drive out evil spirits. But in 1–2 Samuel, the statement takes on theological significance. Together with David's trust in Yahweh, it forms the overriding message of these books.

In Samuel, David is the "man after God's own heart," chosen by Yahweh to replace Saul as king. Yahweh defeated the lion, the bear, and the Philistine by David's hand (17:34–37), and gave him victory over all his enemies (18:13, 16). Saul feared David because Yahweh was with him (18:12, 15). Saul's plots against David all backfired. David became increasingly successful and popular. Yahweh's prophets and priests helped protect David and guide him away from Saul (1 Samuel 19; 21–22). When Saul had David trapped (23:24–28) he was "providentially" forced to withdraw at the last minute. Yahweh even gave David opportunities, which he piously declined, to kill Saul (1 Samuel 24; 26). After Saul died, Yahweh led the new king to victory over the Philistines (2 Sam. 5:19–20, 23–25) and wherever he went (2 Sam. 8:14). Yahweh promised him a continuing dynasty (2 Samuel 7). Even in his troubles, Yahweh did not abandon David but restored him to the throne, according to his hopes (2 Sam. 15:25; cf. 16:12).

David's attitude toward Yahweh, in turn, is consistently depicted as one of trust and obedience. In flight from Saul he constantly divined the will of Yahweh. He refused to kill "Yahweh's anointed" (1 Sam. 24:6, 10; 26:9). He complained that Saul had forced him to leave Yahweh's land and tempted him to worship other gods (26:19). In time of crisis, David "strengthened himself in Yahweh his God" (1 Sam. 30:6). He divided the spoil equally among his men because it came to them from Yahweh (1 Sam. 30:23–25). Yahweh guided David to Hebron where he was made king (2 Sam. 2:1). King David then brought the ark up to Jerusalem (2 Samuel 6) and desired to build the temple (2 Sam. 7:2). In flight from Absalom, he was concerned for the ark (2 Sam. 16:24–29). Even in suffering, he saw himself as being in Yahweh's hands (2 Sam. 15:25–26). His execution of Saul's descendants was a pious act, which he was forced to carry out in order to remove bloodguilt from Israel (2 Samuel 21). In another act of piety (2 Sam. 24:18–25), he erected an altar and sacrificed to Yahweh in order to turn a plague away from Jerusalem. He insisted on buying the property and the animals for the sacrifice, refusing to offer to Yahweh what had cost him nothing. Finally, on his deathbed in 1 Kings 2:1–4, David charged Solomon to follow his example of righteous obedience to the word of Yahweh. As the psalm in 2 Samuel 22 neatly puts it: "Yahweh rewarded me according to my righteousness" (vv. 21, 25).

Yahweh's presence with David, of course, is not verifiable, historical reality. A historian might affirm that David had remarkable success in his military and political endeavors but would attribute it to other factors such as David's tactical military skill and political astuteness. Neither can David's faith and piety be verified historically. The Bible clearly exaggerates them in its glorified image of David. But, it is safe to assume that he was religious according to the standards of his day. Like other ancient Middle Eastern kings, he would have guarded sacred objects and sites carefully to avoid divine wrath. He would have practiced divination through priests and prophets to determine the will of Yahweh in various circumstances. He would have wanted to build a temple to Yahweh both as a sign of his devotion and as a perpetual testament that God was on his side. David no doubt saw himself as a faithful servant of Yahweh who was rewarding him in kind. As we survey the events of his life in the following chapters and try to uncover the true motives for his actions, it will be important to judge him by the religious ideals of his day, not ours.

Summary

Our biographical portrait of David's background and early life, then, is built around the description in 1 Sam. 16:18. Physically, we envision him as a short man, redheaded and fair complected. He came from a prominent, upper-class family. David may have spent time as a boy tending some of his father's many sheep. But that is not the origin of the Bible's image of him as a shepherd. That image reflects a common metaphor for rulers and alludes to David's future as king.

David was forced by economic pressures on his family to make his own way in life and developed a variety of skills. He may originally have attached himself to Saul's household as a musician. It was a common superstition of the day that music could ward off the constant threat of evil spirits. However, 1 Sam. 16:18 says he was already a formidable warrior. So his main reason for joining Saul may have been military service. Once there, he quickly became Saul's armor bearer. This was just the first step in an accelerated military career. David already displayed a keen political sense and shrewd diplomatic and negotiating skills. These qualities guaranteed that he would advance quickly.

4

Who Killed Whom?

The Goliath Story and David's Career
as a Soldier in Saul's Army

Valiant—the word and up he rose—
The fight—he triumph'd o'er the foes,
Whom God's just laws abhor,
And arm'd in gallant faith he took
Against the boaster, from the brook,
The weapons of the war.

—Christopher Smart, "A Song to David"

And now the youth the forceful pebble flung,
Philistia trembled as it whizz'd along:
In his dread forehead, where the helmet ends,
Just o'er the brows the well-aim'd stone descends,
It pierc'd the skull, and shatter'd all the brain,
Prone on his face he tumbled to the plain:
Goliath's fall no smaller terror yields
Than riving thunders in aerial fields:
The soul still ling'red in its lov'd abode,
Till conq'ring David o'er the giant strode:
Goliath's sword then laid its master dead,
And from the body hew'd the ghastly head;
The blood in gushing torrents drench'd the plains,
The soul found passage through the spouting veins.

—Phillis Wheatley, "Goliath of Gath"

Frankly, the way I saw it, Goliath didn't stand a chance.

—Joseph Heller, *God Knows*

David and Goliath

Just before halftime during the broadcast of Superbowl XXIX in 1995, an adolescent with shoulder-length hair and a simple white smock appeared on the TV screen. A leather sling dangled from his left hand and he was leaning on a shepherd's crook. Facing him was a line of burly men with thick beards, clad in bronze armor with crested helmets and clutching swords and spears. The men were all mocking and ridiculing the boy. The tallest among them began to threaten him.

Unshaken, the boy silently and deliberately loaded a stone in the pocket of his sling and started whirling it overhead. The camera focused in on the sling; the picture blurred with its increasing speed. Suddenly, the sling stopped, and the camera shifted to the giant's stunned face, the stone now embedded in his forehead. The giant fell forward to the ground, and the boy knelt to retrieve the stone. He looked at it and smiled approvingly, then held it up to reveal the logo of a famous sporting goods manufacturer.

The advertisers never mentioned the names of the characters. They didn't need to. Whether you have read the Bible or not, you know the story. It is the quintessential triumph of the underdog. But is it historical? That is a difficult question to answer. As we shall see, the biblical story holds quite a few surprises for the careful reader. All of them have a bearing on the story's historical credibility.

Two Stories in One

We have already noted several contradictions between the Goliath story and the description of David's arrival at court in 1 Sam. 16:14–23. In the latter, David is a warrior and Saul's beloved armor bearer. But in the Goliath story, he is a young shepherd boy carrying food and messages back and forth between his father at home and his brothers in the army. He has no battle experience and has never worn armor. Saul does not even know him and asks Abner, "Whose son is this?" (17:55), a Hebrew idiom for "Who is this?" Yet, Saul had earlier sent a messenger to Jesse (16:22), showing that he knew all about David and his home. These contradictions exist because the story of David and Goliath was an independent tale that Dtr inserted into the History of David's Rise, even though the two documents did not entirely agree.

Dtr's version of the Goliath story was much shorter than the one now in the Bible, however. The story as it now stands in the Hebrew Bible (known as the Masoretic text) is a combination of different versions. The ancient Greek translation of the Hebrew Bible known as the Septuagint (LXX) preserves the original version of the story, which included only verses 1–11, 32–49, 51–54.[1] Stories of this nature tend to grow over time, and that is what has happened here. The other verses (12–31, 50, 55–58) were added to the Hebrew text sometime after the LXX translation was produced (ca. 200 B.C.E.). These additions increase the legendary flavor of the story. This situation spills over into chapter 18, where vv. 1–5, 10–11, 17–19, 29b–30 are additional, that is, absent from the LXX but included in the Hebrew Bible.

The Older Version of the David and Goliath Story (Preserved in the LXX)

[1]The Philistines gathered their camps for war and assembled themselves at Socoh, which belongs to Judah. They camped between Socoh and Azekah at Ephes-dammim. [2]Saul and the men of Israel had gathered together and camped in Terebinth Valley; they prepared to meet the Philistines in battle. [3]The Philistines stood on the hill on one side and Israel stood on the opposite hill with the valley between them. [4]A representative [exact meaning uncertain] emerged from the Philistine camps. Goliath was his name, from Gath. He was six cubits and a span tall. [5]A bronze helmet was on his head and he wore plated body armor, which weighed 5000 bronze shekels. [6]Bronze greaves were on his legs and a bronze scimitar hung between his shoulders. [7]The shaft of his spear was like the rod on a weavers' loom; its blade weighed 600 iron shekels. And a shield carrier walked in front of him. [8]He stood and called out to the ranks of Israel saying to them, "Why do you come out in battle array? I am a Philistine, am I not? And you are Saul's servants, are you not? Choose for yourselves a man to come down to me. [9]If he prevails fighting with me and kills me, we will be your slaves. But if I pre-

vail against him and kill him, then you will be our slaves and will serve us."
¹⁰The Philistine continued, "I defy the ranks of Israel today, give me a man
and let us fight together." ¹¹When Saul and all Israel heard these words of
the Philistine they were dismayed and terrified. ³²But David said to Saul,
"Don't be disheartened, my lord. I, your servant, will go and fight with this
Philistine." ³³But Saul said to David, "You can't go to fight against this
Philistine! You are a youth and he has been a warrior since his youth."
³⁴David answered Saul, "Your servant was a shepherd among the sheep, and
whenever a lion or bear would come and take a sheep from the flock, ³⁵I
would go out after it, knock it down, and save the sheep from its mouth. Then
if it attacked me I would grab its beard, strike it down, and kill it. ³⁶Your servant has killed both lions and bears, and this uncircumcized Philistine will be
like one of them because he has defied the ranks of the living God. ³⁷Yahweh,
who saved me from both lion and bear will save me from this Philistine." So
Saul said to David, "Go. Yahweh will be with you." ³⁸Saul then dressed David
in a uniform with a bronze helmet on his head ³⁹and Saul's own sword on
top of the uniform. After David tried a time or two to walk, he said to Saul,
"I can't walk in these because I'm not used to them." So they took them off
of him. ⁴⁰Then [David] took his stick in his hand and choosing five smooth
stones from the wadi, he put them into the pouch (his shepherd's bag), and
with his sling in his hand he approached the Philistine. ⁴¹The Philistine
drew closer and closer to David, his shield carrier in front of him. ⁴²When
the Philistine looked closely and saw David, he disdained him because he
was a youth. ⁴³The Philistine said to David, "Am I a dog that you come to
me with a stick?" And the Philistine cursed David by his gods. ⁴⁴Then the
Philistine said to David, "Come to me so I can give your flesh to the birds
of the sky and the beasts of the field." ⁴⁵David replied to the Philistine,
"You come against me with sword, spear, and scimitar, but I come against
you in the name of Yahweh of hosts, the God of the ranks of Israel, whom
you have defied. ⁴⁶Yahweh will hand you over to me today. I will kill you,
cut off your head, and leave your corpse and the corpses of the Philistine
camp for the birds of the sky and the beasts of the field. Then all the earth
will know that Israel has a God, ⁴⁷and all those gathered here will know that
it is not by sword or spear that Yahweh gives victory. Rather, the battle
belongs to Yahweh, and he will hand you over to us." ⁴⁸Then as the Philistine approached David, David also ran quickly toward the battle line to
meet the Philistine. ⁴⁹David reached into the bag, took out a stone, and
slung it, hitting the Philistine in the forehead. The stone sank into his fore-

head, and he fell face forward to the ground. [51]Then David ran and stood over the Philistine. Unsheathing his sword, he killed him, cutting off his head with it. When the Philistines saw that their champion was dead, they fled. [52]Then the men of Israel and Judah arose with a shout and pursued the Philistines as far as Gath and the gates of Ekron. The Philistine wounded fell along the Shaarim road all the way to Gath and Ekron. [53]When the Israelites returned from pursuing the Philistines they plundered their camps. [54]And David took the Philistine's head and brought it to Jerusalem, but he put his weapons in his own tent.

The additions to chapter 17 (vv. 12–31, 50, 55–58) are sometimes in tension with the original story. For example, v. 51 says that after David had injured the Philistine with the sling, he finished him off by beheading him with his own sword. But v. 50 disagrees. According to it, David killed the giant with the sling, and there was no sword in his hand. As the Hebrew (Masoretic) text now reads, therefore, David kills Goliath twice—once with the sling stone and then again with a sword. In the original version, therefore, David beheaded his enemy. The difference between these two verses is reinforced by Psalm 151, the LXX's addition to the book of Psalms. It says that David beheaded Goliath with his own sword, and it does not even mention his famous sling! Its author was familiar with the version of the story in the LXX but not with the secondary additions to it in the Masoretic text.

As mentioned, the additions enhanced the legendary nature of the Goliath story. The main section of the addition, verses 12–31, emphasizes David's youth and inexperience. He is a mere boy running errands between his father and brothers. He gets excited at the prospect of witnessing a battle. His youthful faith is offended at the giant's defiance of Yahweh, so he volunteers to serve as Israel's champion. He goes in the name of Yahweh, the God of Israel. It is the legendary aspects of the story that have made it so popular over the centuries. And its popularity in turn caused the legend to grow. David became younger and more inexperienced. His faith and the size of the giant increased proportionately.

Not-So-Gigantic Goliath

It turns out on closer inspection of the text that Goliath was not all that big. According to the Masoretic text he stood six cubits and a span (v. 4).

A cubit was about eighteen inches and a span about six, making the Philistine an impressive nine and a half feet tall! But there is textual evidence that this unrealistic figure is inflated. The LXX and a Dead Sea Scroll fragment of Samuel (4QSam^a) for this verse read *"four* cubits and a span." This would put Goliath's height at about six and a half feet—still tall but hardly extraordinary by today's standards. He would be just tall enough to play guard or maybe small forward in the NBA! Since the tendency in a story like this is always toward exaggeration, the smaller number must be considered more original. Besides, the word "six" in Hebrew occurs just a few lines later (v. 7). It could have come into v. 4 by accident if a copyist's eye unintentionally skipped ahead. A man six and a half feet tall might have been considered a giant in David's day, when people were generally shorter than today, without being out of the realm of possibility.

It used to be thought that the description of Goliath (vv. 5–7) genuinely reflected Philistine armor and weaponry of the time.[2] His arms were compared to those of the Greeks and other inhabitants of the western Mediterranean where the Philistines came from.[3] The practice of individual combat was also taken to be Philistine and compared with the fight of Hector and Achilles in the *Iliad*.[4] It is now recognized, however, that Goliath is accoutered with a sampling of weapons from different parts of the ancient Middle East at a later date.[5] They do not match the depictions of Philistine warriors in Egyptian reliefs, who are shown wearing feathered headdresses rather than bronze helmets and do not have the body armor or greaves (shin guards) of Goliath (*Fig. 9*). There never was a soldier equipped quite like Goliath. His outfit is drawn from the writer's knowledge of different kinds of weaponry in his (the writer's) day. Its function in the story is literary rather than historical. It serves to impress upon the reader the fearsomeness and apparent invincibility of the Philistine in contrast to David, whose principal armor and weapon is his faith. Thus, the writer stresses not only the diversity of the giant's armor but also its weight. His coat of mail weighs more than 125 pounds, and his iron spear tip more than 15. The humorous interlude where David tries on Saul's armor and cannot move (17:38–39) reinforces the contrast between him and the giant.

Two pieces of Goliath's armor deserve special attention. The first is his spear. The Bible says it was "like a weaver's beam" (17:7). Some have suggested that this was an Aegean-style javelin.[6] Such javelins had a loop or thong in the middle to increase leverage and therefore hurling distance. It was this loop that supposedly made Goliath's spear "like a weaver's beam." But weaver's shuttles have many more than one loop. The reason for the comparison of Goliath's spear to a weaver's beam seems to be size, especially considering the next statement about the weight of its tip. Six hundred shekels of bronze is conservatively estimated to be about fifteen pounds, which indicates that the weapon was not intended for hurling.

The second interesting item is Goliath's helmet. How could David's stone have hit him in the forehead if he was wearing a helmet? The LXX translation reflects an awareness of this difficulty. After it tells how the stone sank into the Philistine's forehead, the LXX adds, "through the helmet" (v. 49). One modern scholar who was also bothered by this question made the unique suggestion that the stone actually hit the Philistine in the knee where his leg guards or greaves left a space for bending. The stone disabled him long enough for David to come and decapitate him. The suggestion is supported by the similarity between the Hebrew words for "forehead" (mēṣaḥ) and "greaves" (mishāh).[7] Although clever, this explanation seems a little far-fetched.

There is another, simpler solution that also has to do with the nature of the equipment. The copyist or translator responsible for adding the explanatory phrase in the LXX was probably thinking of the Greek helmets of his day with their nose guards. But the helmet that the writer of 1 Samuel 17 had in mind was more likely a conical helmet like those worn by the Assyrians (*Fig. 10*). This kind of helmet has no nose guard; it leaves an open space at the top of the nose, between the eyes. It was that spot that the writer had in mind as the target of David's stone.

The motif of individual combat also serves a literary purpose. Goliath is so intimidating that the entire Israelite army stands in awe of him. Only David, moved by righteous indignation and faith, steps forward. The Philistine's defiance of Israel provides an opportunity for David to distinguish himself from the rest of his countrymen. From here on he will be the focus of the narrative.

A Case of Mistaken Identity

"Then there was another battle with the Philistines at Gob; and Elhanan son of Jaareoregim, the Bethlehemite, killed Goliath the Gittite, the shaft of whose spear was like a weaver's beam" (2 Sam. 21:19, NRSV).

According to this verse, it was not David who killed Goliath but a man named Elhanan from Bethlehem! There have, of course, been attempts to explain away the contradiction between this verse and 1 Samuel 17. Some have suggested that there was more than one large Philistine warrior from Gath (= "the Gittite") named Goliath. But this is improbable given that the same description of the shaft of his spear occurs in both cases. Another explanation is that Elhanan was David's real name. However, other than the fact that they are both from Bethlehem, there is no connection between them in the Bible.

The biblical writers themselves felt uneasy about the contradiction. The Chronicles parallel to this verse reads: "Again there was war with the Philistines; and Elhanan, son of Jair, killed Lahmi, the brother of Goliath the Gittite, the shaft of whose spear was like a weaver's beam" (1 Chron. 20:5, NRSV). According to this verse, Elhanan killed not Goliath but his brother, Lahmi. The name Lahmi is actually the second part of the word "Bethlehemite" (Hebrew: *beth-lahmi*). The Chronicler's solution to the contradiction, therefore, was to invent a brother for Goliath. He then made up a name for him out of the word "Bethlehemite" from 2 Sam. 19:21.

The reason the contradiction exists in the first place is that some of the details from the notice of Elhanan's victory have been appropriated into the more famous tale of David's victory. In addition to the description of the spear being like a weaver's beam, the name "Goliath" itself is one of those details. It is not Hebrew but a genuine Philistine name. But it is not original to the story in 1 Samuel 17. It occurs only twice in the entire chapter (vv. 4 and 23). Most of the time, the text refers to David's enemy simply as "the Philistine." It is original to the mention of Elhanan and not to the story of David. Thus, David did not kill Goliath! The oldest version of the story does not preserve the name of the giant Philistine whom David vanquished.

A Historical Kernel

The conflation of two versions of the story, the magnification of Goliath's size, even the identification of his name and weaponry are all the results of the way in which this tale has become enlarged over time. Nevertheless, the basic story is quite plausible—especially considering the nature of the weapons and battle tactics involved. Indeed, the great Israeli general, Moshe

Dayan, once wrote an article showing how David's victory was a master-piece of military strategy.[8] David had the advantage of mobility. He could not defeat the Philistine at close quarters in hand-to-hand combat, but he could elude him indefinitely. Saul's effort to get David to wear armor reflected a clear failure to understand this advantage.

David also had the advantage of being able to strike from a distance. Missing from the Philistine's arsenal was a bow or other long-range weapon. Even with his spear, as heavy as it was, he was basically limited to close-range fighting. But David had a sling. Modern readers tend to think of the sling as a toy for children, especially in rural settings. But in the ancient Middle East, the sling was a standard military weapon wielded by entire divisions of armies (*Fig. 10*). It could be very effective in war. Sling stones, about the size of tennis balls and carved out of flint, are a common find at ancient battle sites. David had no ready sling stones. He used a stick (often misinterpreted as a shepherd's staff) to rake the ground in search of stones. It was this stick that the Philistine noticed as David approached, and he taunted him about it: "Am I a dog that you come to me with a stick?" (v. 43). He did not mention the sling. This suggests a third advantage of David's weapon—it could be easily concealed. All of these tactics combined—David's mobility, his ability to conceal his weapon and then to attack from a distance—would have given him something of an advantage over the Philistine.

Does this story, then, have a basis in history? We will probably never know for certain because over the centuries it has taken on the properties of a legend, as such stories often do, through exaggeration and accretion. In the process, it also attracted elements from other, lesser-known stories—including the name and description of Goliath. Still, many elements of the story are quite believable. David could well have distinguished himself early in his career by defeating a formidable Philistine opponent. In any case, the older version of 1 Samuel 17 agrees with 16:18 and the surrounding context in describing the young David as a skillful and clever warrior.

The Conflict Between Saul and David

1 Samuel 18–20

According to these chapters, the same victory that brought David such fame also sparked the controversy with Saul that would lead to open conflict between the two of them. Not surprisingly, the narrative places the blame for the controversy entirely upon Saul. The problem arose when the Israelite women, emerging from their villages to greet the returning army, chanted,

> Saul has slain his thousands
> and David his ten thousands (1 Sam. 18:7).

Saul was overcome with jealousy.[9] The next verse ominously reports that he watched (literally, "eyed") David suspiciously from then on.

Saul's reactions to David are part of the characterization of him as inept and unstable. They follow on the heels of the description of him as tormented by an evil spirit from Yahweh (16:14–23). Saul's jealousy, says the writer in effect, is irrational, even insane; David is completely blameless. He is, in fact, Saul's most valuable asset, though Saul is blind to this fact. In short, David succeeded in all that he did, and Saul stood in fear and awe of him (1 Sam. 18:12–16).

The women's victory song has some interesting features. The numbers "thousands" and "ten thousands" cannot be taken literally. They are standard poetic variants for large numbers. The insult to Saul lies in comparing him, the king, with one of his servants and even crediting the servant with greater accomplishments.

Since the numbers are poetic hyperbole, they must be interpreted with caution. But the women's song suggests that David had slain many more than one Philistine. This may be because Dtr chose to replace many battles with the Philistines that David took part in while in Saul's army with the more legendary and theologically potent tale of his triumph over "Goliath."[10] In any case, though the depiction of Saul as insanely jealous and David as completely innocent reflects the writer's pro-Davidic bias, the source of the conflict between the two was likely what the writer portrayed it to be: David's military prowess. His success on the battlefield and accompanying popularity at home made tension with Saul inevitable.

Outline of 1 Samuel 18–20 in the Masoretic Text

18:1–5	Jonathan makes a covenant of friendship with David
18:6–9	Saul's jealousy is aroused at the song of the women

18:10–11	Saul tries twice to pin David to the wall with his spear
18:12–16	David is a successful and beloved military leader
18:17–19	Saul promises his daughter Merab to David but reneges
18:20–30	David marries Saul's other daughter, Michal
19:1–7	Saul orders his servants to kill David; Jonathan intercedes
19:8–10	Saul tries again to kill David with a spear
19:11–17	Michal helps David escape
19:18–24	David flees to Samuel at Ramah
20:1–42	David and Jonathan make a covenant of friendship

Saul's suspicion and mistrust moved him to plot against David's life. These chapters describe a series of plans by Saul to rid himself of David by more or less secret means. In each case, the plan "backfires" so that David gains even more power and prestige than he had before. With each plan Saul's action against David grows more overt. Finally he is forced to devote himself openly to David's destruction.

This neatly escalating sequence of violence and overtness is obscured by the present order of episodes in the Masoretic text. This is a continuation of the same phenomenon seen in chapter 17. Just as the Masoretic text of the "David and Goliath" story combines different versions, chapter 18 in the Hebrew text contains a handful of additions that are lacking in the LXX. The principal additions are as follows.

1. 18:1–5 describes an encounter between Saul's son Jonathan and David immediately after David's victory over "Goliath." These verses presuppose the passage of an extended period of time, saying that Saul kept David in his service, that David's military success continued, and that Saul therefore made him commander of the army. This long interlude breaks the continuity between David's victory and the celebration of that victory, which took place "as they were coming home when David returned from killing the Philistine" (18:6). The disruptive character of 18:1–5 is another indication, besides their absence from the LXX, that these verses are not original here. In addition, the picture of Jonathan in these verses is unre-

alistic. We read that Jonathan loved David instantly (v. 1), that he made a covenant with him (v. 3), and that he gave him his own armor, robe, and weapons (v. 4). This gift symbolizes Jonathan's relinquishing his place as crown prince to David.[11] The two may have been friends. But it is hard to believe that Jonathan would give up his future as king to someone he had just met.

2. 18:10–11 contains another version, besides the one in 19:9–10, of Saul's attempt to kill David with his spear. The repetition is a sign that one of the versions is secondary, and comparison with the LXX confirms that 18:10–11 is a later addition.

3. 18:17–19 has Saul offering his older daughter, Merab, to David in marriage. The episode is similar to 18:20–27 where he gives his other daughter, Michal, to David. Saul's offer here has often been related to his promise that the slayer of the Philistine giant would be given his daughter (17:25). However, this connection is not made in the text itself; Merab's hand is a reward for future gallantry, not for past deeds (18:17). In fact, Saul's promise is within one of the additions to the Masoretic text in chapter 17 not found in the LXX.

4. 18:29b–30 reiterates David's military success especially against the Philistines (compare 18:14–16). Like the other additions it is repetitive and unnecessary.

Once these later additions are removed, the story line emerges clearly:

1. Saul first made David a commander of a thousand (18:12–16), ostensibly as a promotion in reward for heroism. His real motivation, though, was fear. The text expresses it ironically—Saul was afraid because Yahweh was with David. So Saul "removed him from his presence" (v. 13). In doing so he hoped also to remove David and his accomplishments from the national spotlight. But his main hope was more sinister. As a commander out in the field David might be killed in battle, thus solving all of Saul's problems. He would be rid of David forever without having to lift a finger against him. But Saul's plan backfired. David's military success continued (v. 14), and his popularity grew until all Israel and Judah loved him (v. 16).

2. The king's second stratagem was only slightly more direct (18:20–29a). Saul offered David the chance to become his son-in-law by marrying

his daughter Michal. His motive was "that she may be a snare for him and that the hand of the Philistines may be against him." David expressed interest in the proposal but lamented that he was poor and could not afford the bride price for the king's daughter (v. 23). This allowed Saul to lure David into the trap represented by an unwitting Michal. The only bride price required by the king was a hundred Philistine foreskins. Once more, Saul was hoping that his foreign enemies would do his dirty work for him.

But again his plan backfired. David accomplished the mission and delivered the foreskins. (The Masoretic text reports that David brought two hundred foreskins—twice the number demanded by Saul—but the LXX reading of one hundred is the better one.) David's success compelled Saul to go forward with the marriage to Michal. This, in turn, brought David back into Saul's presence and also gave him an indirect claim to the throne. What is more, David's completion of this task could only have increased his popularity in Israel. Not only did he kill Israel's enemies, he mutilated them, symbolically making Israelites of them. It was a classic case of adding insult to injury.

3. Both of Saul's attempts to use the Philistines against David having backfired, he now acted more directly through his own servants. His next move is out of sequence in the book of 1 Samuel. The story that appears in 19:11–17 takes place on David's wedding night and should follow directly after the account of the marriage in 18:20–25. Saul stationed men around the couple's home intending to arrest David in the morning. But Michal learned of Saul's plan and warned her new husband (19:11). She then helped him escape by lowering him from the window of their house. Apparently, the house was built into the wall of the city (like Rahab's in Josh. 2:15) so that David was able to leave unobserved.

Michal then deceived her father's messengers, placing a household idol in David's bed with a tangle of goat hair at the head, and telling them that he was sick. She later told Saul (v. 17) that David had threatened her if she did not help him. But this was clearly a lie. Her deception of Saul's messengers with the idol and the goat hair was her own doing, after David had gone. So it could not have been motivated by a threat from him. Saul's failure to arrest David on this occasion taught him an important and heartbreaking lesson. His own daughter had demonstrated that her devotion to David was greater than her loyalty to her father.

4. Not only Michal, but also Jonathan, the crown prince, sided with David. In his next initiative against David (19:1–7), Saul tried to persuade his servants to kill David (v. 1). But Jonathan warned David and told him to remain hidden until he (Jonathan) could speak with his father and determine the source of his hostility. This presupposes that David was already in hiding from Saul and thus this passage must originally have come after the story of David's flight (19:11–17).

    When Jonathan met with Saul he spoke in David's defense and eventually persuaded Saul to retract the death warrant. David came out of hiding, and he and Saul were reconciled (v. 7). It was an uneasy reconciliation, however, and destined to be short-lived. But it had an important and enduring result: Jonathan would never again be privy to his father's machinations against David, for Saul had learned where Jonathan's sympathies lay.

5. The brief reconciliation between Saul and David was broken the next time there was war (19:8–10). As usual, David fought loyally in the service of his king. But his heroics aroused Saul's envy. Upon returning from the battle, Saul sought comfort in David's lyre from the torments of Yahweh's spirit. But his jealous rage overcame him, and he tried to kill David with his spear. This episode marks the decisive break in David's relationship with Saul in 1 Samuel. Saul had now made a personal, conspicuous attempt on David's life. His hostility was out in the open. There was no more need for secretive plots.

6. The last two episodes in this section illustrate the finality of David's break with Saul. The story of David's trek to Ramah (19:18–24) confirms Saul's open aggression against David. He not only tried to kill David but also set out in open pursuit of him. A glance at a map shows the historical unlikelihood of this episode (Map 1). Ramah was probably located directly north of Gibeah. But David's ultimate destination was south, in Bethlehem, his hometown, and the Judean wilderness beyond. It would have made no sense for David to flee north from Saul. The story serves a purely apologetic purpose. It reintroduces Samuel and makes clear his support and that of the prophets for David.[12] It also shows Yahweh's support for David

against Saul. The prophetic ecstasy from Yahweh that falls first upon Saul's messengers and then upon Saul prevents him from harming David at Ramah. In a degrading spectacle, the king loses control of himself and lies naked on the ground all night "prophesying."[13]

7. Finally, the test devised by David and Jonathan in chapter 20 proves that reconciliation between David and Saul was not possible. Following the episode in Ramah, David sought out Jonathan in Gibeah for help (20:1). Jonathan did not know that Saul had tried to kill David. Apparently believing that things were not as bad as David was painting them, he agreed to test his father's resolve to destroy David. The test took place at a feast where David was expected and Saul had plans to arrest or kill him. When David did not show up and Jonathan defended him, Saul became furious and aimed his spear at his own son (v. 33). Humiliated and convinced that further lobbying was futile, Jonathan left the table to warn David according to a prearranged signal (vv. 34–39). Saul and David would be at odds from this point on until one of them died.[14]

The Historical Value of the Account

The Bible's presentation of this period of David's life is dominated by theological and literary themes. These themes serve the apologetic interests of the writers. Following the guidelines we have established, therefore, we must be skeptical about the historical validity of these stories. However, there are still some useful insights into this stage of David's career that emerge from a careful reading.

The main point of this section is the contrast between Saul and David. Saul is depicted as insanely jealous, while David is innocent of even the thought of replacing Saul as king. The fact that everyone else loves David is proof of Saul's paranoia. The army, the common people, the prophets, the priests (in 1 Samuel 21), and even the king's own daughter and son are admiring supporters. Only Saul fears him, and Saul is irrational.

This picture is certainly exaggerated, to say the least. If support for David had been this widespread, Saul would not have been able to drive him out or lead the troops against him. We have already seen that the story of David's support from the prophets at Ramah (19:18–24) is unhistorical and a later addition. But what about the other relationships David has in the story and his popularity in general? Did he actually marry Michal and become Saul's son-in-law? Was Jonathan's devotion to David as strong as the narrative depicts? Just how widespread was David's support in Israel?

The relationships between Saul, David, Michal, and Jonathan form a complex web at the literary level.[15] Both brother and sister love David; both risk their lives for him. David returns his affection but not hers. Yet his official relationship through marriage is to her. As crown prince, Jonathan is an obstacle to David's becoming king. But Michal is the means through which he lays claim to the throne.

From a historical perspective, though, David's relationships with both Michal and Jonathan are questionable. His marriage to Michal has such political significance that it must be regarded skeptically. Almost all of David's marriages were politically motivated. But none of the others had the same propaganda value as this one (cf. 2 Sam. 3:13). This marriage makes David Saul's son-in-law and gives him a legitimate, though indirect claim to the kingdom. In other words, Michal transforms David from a usurper into an heir. But in 2 Samuel we will see evidence that David took Michal only after Saul's death. We will also see that he had another reason for bringing her to Jerusalem in addition to the claim to Saul's crown that she represented.

Jonathan's relationship to David in the narrative establishes two important apologetic points. First, their covenant of friendship demonstrates David's faithfulness to his friend. His promise not to cut off Jonathan's "house" (20:15, 42) looks forward to 2 Samuel 9, which describes his care for Jonathan's remaining son, "Mephibosheth." It is remarkable that King David allows this son to live, and this may reflect a genuine sense of affection on David's part for Jonathan.

Second, Jonathan's "love" for David has political overtones. Love in this context is political loyalty.[16] Jonathan is willing to step aside to let David become king (18:1–5; 23:15–18). The writer even casts David as Jonathan's brother or alter-ego. Unlike Saul, Jonathan is always viewed positively. In chapter 14 especially, he is clever, strong, and brave, and most of all, he trusts in Yahweh. In short, he is much like David. So when Jonathan volunteers to abdicate the throne for David, he is really just acting on behalf of another version of himself.

The exaggeration in this relationship is obvious. It is hard to imagine Jonathan joining with David in a conspiracy against his father. And it is simply beyond belief that the crown prince would surrender his right to the throne in deference to David. Moreover, the larger picture sheds a different light on the friendship between Jonathan and David. While the two of them may have been friends once, David's break with Saul was a break with Jonathan as well. Jonathan did not leave his father's household to flee with David into the wilderness. And in the end, he died in battle with his father.

It is sometimes suggested that David and Jonathan were more than friends, that they were homosexual lovers. This is based on David's lament for Saul and Jonathan, which reads "your love to me was wonderful, surpassing the love of women" (2 Sam. 1:26). There are two issues involved here: the meaning of this verse and the historical relationship of David and Jonathan. As we have seen, the stress on the relationship between Jonathan and David is part of the apology for David. Their historical relationship was not as close as it is depicted in 1 Samuel. It is also far from certain that David was really the author of this lament.

As for the meaning of this poetic line, it is extremely unlikely that it is intended to describe a homosexual relationship.[17] It is, rather, hyperbole. Homosexual acts were condemned in Israelite law (Lev. 20:13). So David's apologist would hardly have described him as homosexual or included a piece that described him that way. This line in v. 26 illustrates a cultural difference. Middle Easterners still speak of and display affection between members of the same sex much more readily than do Westerners. Such displays do not imply homosexual attraction. By contrast, public displays of affection between men and women are regarded as scandalous in the Middle East.

Apart from David's relationships with Saul's family members, the general perspective on David in this section of 1 Samuel is historically credible. The description of David's success in Saul's army is believable, although we do well to think in terms of a militia rather than a real army. According to the Bible the standing army was a new creation under Saul (1 Samuel 11; 13:2). Still, David may well have served as Saul's armor bearer and, later on, his commander. He was successful in battle against the Philistines. There are indications, which we will see later on, that he was a brilliant military tactician. His victories would have made him a popular figure in Saul's "army," even if not to the extent that 1 Samuel would have us believe. His personal charm, added to his prowess as a soldier, probably made him well-liked in Saul's inner circle. In short, if we overlook the Bible's exaggeration, there is no reason to doubt that at one time Saul regarded David highly or that David and Jonathan were friends.

An Attempted Coup?

If David once had the favor of Saul as the Bible indicates, what was it that poisoned their relationship and turned them into enemies? First Samuel blames this entirely on Saul, who is portrayed as paranoid and unbalanced. But this explanation is questionable to say the least. Not only is the writer of 1 Samuel obviously biased in favor of David and against Saul, but he voices Saul's thoughts and intentions, which he could not have known. Saul's jealousy can hardly have been the whole story.

There are several elements in the story that suggest a different answer to this question. The first is Saul's fear. The narrative mentions more than once that Saul was afraid of David (18:12, 15, 29). Exactly what was it that he feared? The answer is clear from Saul's words to Jonathan, "As long as the son of Jesse is alive upon the earth, you will not establish your king-ship" (20:31). Saul fears that David will thwart him from establishing a dynasty by preventing Jonathan from becoming king. The way David would do this is to become king himself. But there is more. The stories make it clear that Saul is not just afraid for his heir but for himself. In other words, his fear is that David will lead a revolt and overthrow him as king.

Was Saul's fear reasonable? It is clear from the biblical story that David had both the capability and the desire to lead a revolt. Saul's authority was based on military leadership; he was acclaimed king after a military victory (1 Samuel 11). Control of the kingdom depended on control of the mili-tary. Thus, kings and other rulers in the Middle East were (and are) often toppled by their own generals. David was a very successful and popular military commander. The Bible says that all Israel and Judah loved him (1 Sam. 18:16). This is even more significant than appears at first.

The word "love" is well attested in ancient Middle Eastern literature as a term for political loyalty. One of the clearest examples is 2 Sam. 19:6. Here Joab scolds David for not congratulating his troops because he is pre-occupied with mourning for Absalom. He says David loves those who hate him and hates those who love him. Absalom "hated" David because he rebelled against him. But David's troops "love" him because they remained loyal. When the Bible states that all Israel and Judah loved David (1 Sam. 18:16), it is saying that the people of Israel and Judah were loyal to him. The reason for their loyalty is that he "went out and came in before them" (v. 13). This is an idiom for military success. David "had success in all his undertakings" (v. 14). He had won the devotion of the army as a war hero by his victories over their enemies. In other words, the verse is saying that the army's primary loyalty was to David. The claim that all Israel and Judah were loyal to David is an exaggeration. But the verse admits that David had acquired the power to rival Saul.

The story of David's marriage to Michal suggests that David also had the political ambition to lead a coup. Saul took a great risk in endorsing the marriage. He obviously did not expect David to succeed against the Philistines. If the marriage went forward it would place David very close to Saul's person and give him some legitimacy as a claimant to the throne. But David also took an awful risk. He placed his life on the line. What could motivate him to take such a gamble? The answer was entry into the royal family, by which he moved a giant step closer to the power he craved. Saul spoke of Michal being a "snare" for David (v. 21). But it was not Michal who was the real lure; it was the position of son-in-law to the king. This marriage was not about love. It was about political status. We are told that Michal loved David (v. 20) but not that her love was reciprocated. Both Saul and David speak not of his marrying Michal but of his becoming the king's son-in-law. Michal is not consulted, nor are her feelings ever considered. David is driven not by feelings for her but by ambition. To be raised to a position proximate to the throne is worth risking his life for. His ambition is obvious. And the Philistine foreskins attest his ruthlessness. Saul has good reason to be afraid (18:29).

The stories in 1 Samuel 18–20 urge strongly that David was innocent of any intention to overthrow Saul. The modern reader "against the grain" is compelled by their "overstress" on this point to suppose precisely the opposite.[18] I would speculate that the ultimate reason for Saul's pursuit of David was a failed coup attempt. All the ingredients were present. David had the power and the ambition to try to overthrow Saul. The biblical story admits that he was suspected of plotting to do just that. The apology protests so much against this accusation that one can hardly avoid the suspicion that there is something to it. Saul drove David out and sought to kill him because David had tried to overthrow Saul. This is a radical suggestion, and impossible to prove. But it would account for the events the Bible describes as well as the vehemence of its apologetic denial of such a charge.

Summary

The conclusions reached in this chapter fill out the portrait of David in several surprising ways. First, the famous "David and Goliath" story as we have it is legendary. However, David did distinguish himself in battle against the Philistines, exhibiting exceptional skill and judgment in combat. Saul was pleased with him and promoted him to be one of the commanders of his developing army. His continued military success brought him a significant following among Saul's subjects, though the extent of his success and popularity have been exaggerated in the Bible.

David's popularity owed as much to his personal charm as to his victories on the battlefield. He endeared himself to Saul's own household. Again, this has doubtless been exaggerated in the Bible. He was probably not married to Michal—at least not yet. Nor was his friendship with Jonathan as close as the Bible depicts it. But his advancement in Saul's army indicates that there was a period of amicable relations between them.

Saul soon came to fear that David would try to overthrow him. The fear was reasonable. David was very ambitious. His growing power and popularity supplied him with the tools to act on his ambitions. The threat Saul sensed was real. The story protests David's innocence strongly—maybe too strongly. I suspect that David was actually involved in a plot to usurp the kingship. Saul was forced to go on the offensive while he still had the upper hand. But before Saul could have him arrested him and executed, David escaped.

5

Holy Terrorist

David and His Outlaw Band

I do not believe that the highly gifted, bold, ambitious ones are good
fortune for the world.

—Grete Weil, *The Bride Price*

In 1985, Paramount Studios released *King David*. In the film,
Richard Gere played a politically correct and ultramodern David who
believed that the one true God accepted people of all nations. This David
defied the prophets and the law, refusing to attack foreigners within the
land of Israel. He advocated following the feelings of one's heart instead of
the principles of the law or the instructions of some "holy man." It was
through the heart, he said, that God really speaks to people. This portrayal
of David was ahistorical in many ways (David is essentially non-violent!).
But the movie was right about one thing. On his way to be king David
treated people of all ethnic backgrounds the same. He had a common goal
for everyone—subjugation.

The Fugitive

With his flight from Saul, David's social status changed again. He was now
an outlaw. The rest of 1 Samuel reports how he went south to the wilderness area of Judah. Its rugged terrain had afforded good hiding places to
fugitives from the authorities since time immemorial. David no doubt

knew the land well and could count on help from his kinfolk, some of whom joined him. He quickly became the leader of a band of renegades. Like others before and after them who hid out in this area, David and his men did what they had to do to survive. They raided and pillaged settlements in the vicinity.

The biblical stories about this period of David's life are episodic and loosely bound. They fall into two main sections. First Samuel 21–23 is transitional. It continues the theme of David's support among the leading citizens of Saul's realm, focusing on the priests. The material in 1 Samuel 24–2 Samuel 1 is then concerned with Saul's death. It advocates David's innocence by disassociating him from the battle in which Saul was killed. The themes of Yahweh's protection of David and Saul's instability continue throughout this section.

The principal story in this first section is the one about the priests of Nob. It is recounted in three scenes separated by other material, as the following outline shows.

Outline of 1 Samuel 21–23

21:1–9[1]	Scene I: David flees to the priestly city of Nob
21:10–15	David feigns madness before King Achish of Gath
22:1–2	David gathers an army of 400 at Adullam
22:3–5	David takes his parents to Moab for safety
22:6–10	Scene II: Saul learns that the priests at Nob helped David
22:11–23	Scene III: Saul slaughters the priests of Nob
23:1–14	David liberates the town of Keilah from the Philistines
23:15–18	Jonathan comes to David and encourages him
23:19–28	David is trapped by Saul and narrowly escapes

The Priests of Nob

In the first scene (21:1–9), David stops briefly for provisions in the town of Nob. He does not tell the priests who live there that he is fleeing from Saul. Instead, he invents a story about being on a secret mission for the king

(21:2). Ahimelech, the leading priest, gives David food and the "sword of Goliath" (v. 9). He also divines for him (22:10, 13).

After several intervening episodes, the story of the priests of Nob continues in 22:6–23. In the second scene (22:6–10), Saul finds out from an Edomite servant named Doeg that the priests have aided David. Then in the final scene (22:11–23) Saul acts on what he has learned. He has the priests brought to Gibeah and accuses them of treason. He dismisses Ahimelech's claim to know nothing of the rift with David. Then Saul orders the execution of the priests and the annihilation of their village.

This story is filled with irony and with themes of special interest to the writer. It graphically depicts Saul's insane jealousy and shows the lengths to which it drove him against David. It also brings out the animosity between Saul and Yahweh and blames it on Saul. Ahimelech's defense (22:14) eloquently expresses the author's own view: "Who among all your servants is as faithful as David, the king's son-in-law, the commander[2] of your bodyguard, who is honored in your household?" These reminders serve only to infuriate Saul all the more. The story depicts him as attempting to destroy the worship of Yahweh in Israel by killing all of Yahweh's priests. By taking in Abiathar, the one surviving priest, David rescues the worship of Yahweh from extinction.[3]

Abiathar's survival is especially important to the theme of Yahweh's protection of David because he brings the ephod with him. This was a garment worn only by priests, and it contained special implements used for divining Yahweh's will. Through it, David is able to inquire of Yahweh and receive guidance that keeps him one step ahead of Saul's pursuit. This is the point of the stories about David's movements and near escapes following the arrival of Abiathar (1 Samuel 23).[4] Of all the players in the tragedy in Nob, David is the only one who came out ahead. The priests lost their lives; Abiathar lost his family; Saul lost any hope of reconciliation with Yahweh. But David gained special access to Yahweh through Abiathar and the ephod.

The predominance of these literary and theological themes raises doubts about the historicity of the Nob episode. We have already seen that the depiction of Saul as insane is historically dubious. This story of his slaughter of the priests is the most extreme example of that characterization. It serves an important function in the narrative by showing how dangerous and unstable Saul has become. This in turn justifies all of David's subsequent efforts to get away from him. The fact is that Saul was as much a worshiper of Yahweh as David. He would not have tried to wipe out the worship of Yahweh in Israel. He could hardly have killed the priests at Nob without grave repercussions from his other subjects.

This story has more to do with events in Dtr's day than in David's. Dtr used it to explain how the clan of priests in Jerusalem, known as the "Zadokites," came to replace the priests of the outlying areas. First Samuel 2:27–36 contains a prophecy written by Dtr about the destruction of the house of Eli, the priest who was Samuel's mentor. The prophecy stated that at some time in the future there would be only one member of Eli's household left. "I will spare you one man at my altar to wear out his eyes and use up his strength, but all the rest of your house will die by human swords."[5]

The priests at Nob were Eli's descendants, and their destruction was the fulfillment of this prophecy. Abiathar was the prophesied single survivor. The prophecy also foretold the rise of a "faithful priest" (2:35) who would replace Eli. "I will raise up a faithful priest for myself. He will act according to what is in my heart and in my mind. I will build a secure [literally "faithful"] house for him, and he will go before my anointed one forever." Later on, Zadok would join Abiathar as David's priest. Later still, Solomon would banish Abiathar, leaving Zadok and his heirs as the only priests in Jerusalem. The actual process by which the Zadokites in Jerusalem came to prominence must have been more complex than these stories indicate and took place long after David. But the point is that the story of the annihilation of Nob was meant to explain this development rather than historical events from the time of David.

Other Episodes in Chapters 21–23

The three episodes that come between the first and second scenes of the Nob story deserve comment. The first (21:10–15) tells how David pretends to be insane in order to escape from Achish, king of the Philistine city of Gath. The name "Achish" is not Hebrew but a real "Philistine" name of Indo-European origin. It is apparently the same name (though not the same person) as that of Anchises, father of Aeneas, the legendary founder of Rome.[6] This encounter contradicts the later, more detailed account of David's service under the Philistines (chap. 27 and 29). Achish would hardly have accepted David into his service (27:2–3) if he had believed from earlier experience that David was insane.

The story in chapter 21 parodies the Philistines. It depicts them as gullible and unable to distinguish reason from insanity. It also lauds David for his cleverness in dealing with Israel's enemies. Finally, it contributes to the contrast between David and Saul. Saul is insane. David's feigned insanity is only a clever ploy for tricking the Philistines. In short, despite some genuine elements, the historical value of this story is quite doubtful.

The other two episodes, however, may well contain historical information. The picture of David as an outlaw leader collecting a small army of the disgruntled and indebted (22:1–2) fits well with what we have learned about him. As a fugitive from Saul, David now shared these people's social status. His background in Saul's court made him the ideal candidate to lead them.

The transfer of his parents to the king of Moab for safekeeping (22:3–5) is connected with the Moabite lineage for David at the end of the book of Ruth. This kinship would explain why David chose Moab as a refuge for his parents. At the same time, David's concern for his parents' safety is another positive reflection on his character. Portraying David as a solicitous son certainly fits well with the intent of this literature to promote him as an exemplary figure.

The main point of the stories of David's narrow escapes is theological. They show Yahweh's presence with him and against Saul, especially in light of the arrival of Abiathar with the ephod. Still, even these stories hint at some details that are historically valuable. The account in 23:1–14 affords insight into the way in which divination, through the ephod and other means, was practiced. Note that all the questions David asks of Yahweh can be answered yes or no: "Shall I go attack those Philistines?" (v. 2), "Will Saul come?" (v. 11), "Will the men of Keilah hand me over?" (v. 12). The process of divining was mechanical, something like flipping a coin. It did not impart detailed predictions. These two stories also reveal something of David's method of dealing with towns like Keilah and Ziph. We will explore this in more detail later in this chapter. For the moment, it is worth noting that these two towns in Judah are quite willing to turn their fellow tribesman David over to Saul. They do not exhibit the loyalty one would expect to find if David had indeed freed them from oppression and plundering.

Finally, the account of the last interview of David with Jonathan (23:15–18), like the earlier ones, is not historical. The crown prince would hardly visit an outlaw who was being pursued by his father. (How did Jonathan find David when Saul could not?) And it is simply unbelievable that he would turn over the crown to him: "You shall be king over Israel, and I shall be second to you" (v. 17). This is the most obvious example of the effort in 1 Samuel to depict Jonathan as David's supporter and to stress the covenant between them (v. 18).

Briefly, then, the stories in 1 Samuel 21–23 are concerned primarily with building the contrast between David and Saul. Except for a glimpse or two at David's outlaw activities in the wilderness, this material is not very useful for purposes of historical reconstruction.

David's Innocence in Saul's Death

With chapter 24, the story of David in 1 Samuel begins to prepare for Saul's death. The subsequent narrative consists of three subsections, each with its own point to make regarding David's non-involvement in the death of Saul.

Outline of 1 Samuel 24–2 Samuel 1

Subsection I: David did not kill Saul when he had the chance

23:29–24:22[7]	David has a chance to kill Saul in a cave at En-Gedi
25:1–42	Death of Nabal and marriage of David to Abigail
25:43–44	Notice about other marriages of David
26:1–25	David's second chance to kill Saul

Subsection II: David was far away from the battlefield where Saul died

27:1–28:3	Achish of Gath grants David asylum and the city of Ziklag
28:4–25	Saul consults Samuel's ghost through a medium at En-dor
29:1–11	The Philistine lords refuse to let David go to war with them
30:1–31	David and his men pursue the raiders who burned Ziklag

1 Samuel 24–26

This first subsection contains two versions of the same story (chap. 24 and 26). It is not clear whether one was written on the basis of the other or each is a separate version of a common tradition.[8] But they have a common structure. David finds himself with an opportunity to kill Saul. But he refuses to take advantage of it because he will not "extend his hand against Yahweh's anointed." Instead, he takes something of Saul's to prove that he was close by. Then, when Saul is again at a distance, David calls to him and shows him the items he has taken as proof that he is innocent of any plot to harm Saul. At the end of each story Saul acknowledges that David is in the right. Both stories make the point that because David did not take advantage of earlier opportunities to kill Saul, he must not have been involved in his fall on Mount Gilboa.

The speeches in these two stories are strongly apologetic nature. In the second story, Abishai stands over the sleeping Saul begging for the privilege of pinning him to the ground with a single stroke of his own spear (26:8)—apparently the same spear Saul cast at David earlier. But David forbids Abishai, "Do not destroy him. For who can extend his hand against Yahweh's anointed and be guiltless? . . . Yahweh forbid that I should extend my hand against Yahweh's anointed" (26:9, 11).

By making off with Saul's spear and water jug David proves that he intends the king no harm (26:13–16). Saul is chasing him without reason. David curses those who have stirred Saul up against him because they have driven David away from Yahweh. By this, David means that they have forced him to leave the land of Israel (26:18–20). Saul is moved by David's words to confess his wrong (v. 21). He blesses David, saying he will succeed in whatever he does (v. 25). In this way he looks forward to David's kingly future.

The first story is more blatant. In a particularly degrading depiction, Saul enters a cave to defecate (literally "cover his feet"). Unknown to him, David and his men are hiding in the cave. While Saul is crouching, defenseless, David sneaks up behind him and cuts off a piece of his robe. This may have been understood by the ancient audience as a symbolic emasculation. When David's men want him to kill Saul, he responds, "Yahweh forbid that I should do this thing to my lord, Yahweh's anointed, to extend my hand against him, for he is Yahweh's anointed" (24:6). Saul leaves the cave, and David, following closely behind, calls to Saul and offers him the bit of hem cut from his robe as proof that "there is no evil or conspiracy in my hand" (v. 11). "This day your eyes have seen how Yahweh gave you into my power [literally, "hand"] in the cave . . . . But I thought, 'I will not extend my hand against my lord, for he is Yahweh's anointed'" (v. 10).

As in the other story, David is again self-effacing:

> After whom has the king of Israel marched out?
> After whom are you chasing?
> After a dead dog? After a single flea? (24:14)

However, David's question here could also be taken as an assertion of power with a veiled threat—if Saul thinks he is pursuing a mere dog or a flea he is badly mistaken. Still, the story emphasizes that David does not try to take vengeance himself but calls upon Yahweh to judge between him and Saul. The verdict is obvious to everyone—including Saul! Saul even admits that David will become king: "I know that you will surely be king and that the kingdom of Israel will be established in your power" (24:20). These speeches are thus designed to show not only David's reverence for Yahweh's anointed but also Saul's recognition of David as his successor.

It goes without saying, in light of their apologetic nature, that the value of these two chapters for historical reconstruction is virtually nil. It is extremely unlikely that David ever found himself with any such advantage over Saul. Indeed, the historical David would doubtless have taken advantage of the opportunity to kill Saul had it been presented to him.

Sandwiched between these two versions of David's opportunity to kill Saul is one of the most extraordinary texts in the Bible. The story about Nabal and Abigail (1 Samuel 25) is a literary masterpiece that seems also to contain valuable historical information.[9] While it may seem out of place initially, its setting between chapters 24 and 26 is intentional and reinforces their message about David's leaving vengeance to Yahweh. What makes the story in chapter 25 remarkable, however, is its depiction of David as fully intent on avenging himself. He is prevented from doing so only by Abigail, who was sent by Yahweh (v. 32). She alone keeps him from shedding innocent blood (v. 33), which would have tainted his future kingship (vv. 30–31).

Nabal, David's nemesis in this story, is very much like Saul in some respects. He is rich as a king (v. 2) and, judging from his wealth, was probably the chief of the Calebites (v. 3), the leading clan in the tribe of Judah. So Nabal was an important political figure, the closest thing there was at the time to the king of Judah. He is portrayed as a most unsavory character—brutish and mean (v. 3). The Hebrew word *nābāl* itself means "fool" or "criminal." This was not, however, the man's real name (who would give such a name to a child?). His real name may have been Jether or Ithra. This conjecture is based on two passages found elsewhere. First Chronicles 2:17 refers to Jether as the father of Abigail's son, Amasa. And 2 Sam. 17:25 names Ithra the Ishmaelite as the husband of David's sister, Abigail. Jether and Ithra are variant spellings of the same name.

"Nabal" infuriated David with an insulting refusal of David's request for provisions. The request really amounted to extortion—"protection money" paid to a mafioso. David makes it clear that he could take what he wanted from Nabal's shepherds at any time (v. 7). The peace he wished to Nabal was contingent on Nabal's payment of the "gift." The ten men whom David sent furnished a good idea of the size of gift he was looking for. But at least David's message was couched in polite language. He referred to his men as Nabal's servants and to himself as the older man's "son" (v. 8). Nabal, in contrast, replied with an insult:

> Who is David? Who is the son of Jesse? Today there are many slaves who break away from their masters. So should I take my bread and my water and the meat I have butchered for my sheepshearers and give them to men who come from I don't know where? (vv. 10–11)

It was not that Nabal actually did not know who David was. He knew all too well. It is as if Nabal is playing on his own name by saying, "Only a fool would give his hard-earned income to a nobody vagabond like David."[10]

Insulting David by calling him a runaway slave and a beggar turns out to be a very foolish thing to do. David is furious when he hears Nabal's reply, and he sets out to avenge the insult. He is about to do to Nabal what he wisely resisted doing to Saul. He plans to obliterate Nabal's entire household. But even if Nabal deserves a violent death, the others in his household are not to blame for his acts. So David is not only about to take vengeance for himself, a task he should leave to Yahweh, but he is also on his way to shedding innocent blood. Abigail saves him from himself. Using an idiom meaning "males" (rendered literally in the King James Version as "one who pisseth on the wall"), David's oath of vengeance (v. 22) spells out his intention to kill every male pertaining to Nabal. This is very important; because she is a woman, Abigail alone can save the day. A male would be killed on sight, but the woman Abigail is allowed to approach David (v. 23) and intercede.

Abigail's speech and demeanor are models of diplomacy. She is obviously a person of refinement and sophistication. We would recognize immediately that she is very different from Nabal even if the story did not say so (v. 3). The servants are aware of the difference. They go to her when they realize the trouble their master has brought upon them (vv. 14–17). She instantly comprehends the danger of the situation and acts decisively (v. 18). She rides out to meet David herself, knowing that no mere messenger will do. When she sees him, she throws herself at his feet. In her speech she consistently refers to him as "my lord" and to herself as "your servant." Whether she is sincerely approaching David as a future king or is merely using flattery to soothe an explosive male,[11] her speech is persuasive.

> [24]Upon me alone, my lord, be the guilt; please let your servant speak in your ears, and hear the words of your servant. [25]My lord, do not take seriously this ill-natured fellow Nabal; for as his name is, so is he; Nabal is his name, and folly is with him; but I, your servant, did not see the young men of my lord, whom you sent. [26]Now then, my lord, as the LORD lives, and as you yourself live, since the LORD has restrained you from bloodguilt and from taking vengeance with your own hand, now let your enemies and those who seek to do evil to my lord be like Nabal. [27]And now let this present that your servant has brought to my lord be given to the young men who follow my lord. [28]Please forgive the trespass of your servant; for the LORD will certainly make my lord a sure house, because my lord is fighting the battles of the LORD; and evil shall not be found in you so long as you live. [29]If anyone should rise up to pursue you and to seek your life, the life of my lord shall be bound in the bundle of the living under the care of the LORD your God;

but the lives of your enemies he shall sling out as from the hollow of a sling.
[30]When the LORD has done to my lord according to all the good that he has
spoken concerning you, and has appointed you prince over Israel, [31]my lord
shall have no cause of grief, or pangs of conscience, for having shed blood
without cause or for having saved himself. And when the LORD has dealt
well with my lord, then remember your servant. (NRSV)

Abigail's acceptance of responsibility for David's displeasure is mere
politeness. She is not to blame for Nabal's misdeeds (25:24–25). Nabal is a
scoundrel who should not be taken seriously (v. 26). She asks David to
accept the gift she has brought, never implying that it has been in any way
coerced (v. 27). Then, politely asking forgiveness for speaking further (v.
28), she refers flatteringly to David's bright future under Yahweh's blessing.
Her point, made very gently, is that taking innocent lives could cause David
grief as king. Her words hint that his vengeance might even hinder his
ascent to the throne. Her speech alludes to Saul as David's pursuer and
enemy (v. 29). In the context of chapters 24–26 the message is clear. David
has refused to harm Saul and has left it to Yahweh to judge him. He should
also leave the task of revenge toward Nabal to Yahweh. That way he can
accede to the throne without bloodguilt.

Abigail's mission is successful. David aborts the attack on Nabal, leaving it
to Yahweh to exact vengeance. Yahweh promptly does just that. When Nabal
learns of his narrow escape he falls into a coma and dies a few days later (vv.
37–38). Duly impressed with Abigail's wisdom and charm, David has Abigail
brought to him, and they wed (vv. 39–42). Part of the purpose of telling
about their encounter is to show that the two of them are ideally suited for
each other. This marriage was a very important step in David's political
career. Through Abigail he assumed Jether's (a.k.a. Nabal) wealth and status
as leader of the Calebites. It was a short step from there to the kingship over
all Judah. Thus, when David entered Hebron, the Calebite capital, to be
crowned king over Judah, he did so with Abigail on his arm (2 Sam. 2:2).

The benefit of this marriage for David's career is an element of the
story that is historical. This raises doubts, however, about the claim that
David had nothing to do with Nabal's death. In fact, this story is a sort of
ancient "Whodunit," a murder mystery. The pattern of events surrounding
Nabal's death will become familiar in the rest of 1–2 Samuel as David's
typical *modus operandi*: an enemy of David's dies at a time that is very conve-

nient for his political ascent. What sets Nabal's death apart from the deaths of Saul, Abner, Ishbaal, and Amasa is that Nabal dies not at the hand of Joab or another human agent but is killed by Yahweh. This could be a theological explanation of a more "natural" cause for death, such as heart attack or even overindulgence in the wine that he refused to give to David. (The name Nabal is also very similar to the Hebrew word *nēbel* meaning "bottle" or "wineskin.") But the writer's perspective is that Yahweh caused Nabal to die. Still, the parallel with other stories suggests a more sinister cause—murder—plotted by David but carried out by someone else (Nabal is also similar to the Hebrew word *n'bēlāh*, meaning corpse!). In this case, the prime suspect has to be Abigail. She alone had direct access to Nabal. She also had motive; David offered her liberation from a bad marriage and the prospect of greater prosperity and status in the future.

Abigail is subtly implicated by hints in her speech. She wishes that all David's enemies and those who seek to do him harm will be like Nabal (v. 26). The statement presupposes Nabal's death before it occurs. Some commentators even conclude that the verse is out of place,[12] although there is no manuscript evidence to this effect. As the story stands, Abigail is portrayed as having knowledge beforehand of the disaster that is about to strike her husband. She also wishes that Yahweh would sling David's enemies away with a sling (v. 29—who could miss the allusion to David's weapon of choice?), and the story reports that Nabal's heart died inside of him and became "like a stone" (v. 37). Abigail thus appears to know the form Nabal's death will take before he dies. This would be impossible unless she is responsible for it.

Abigail's closing remark contains a suggestive double meaning: "When Yahweh has dealt well with my lord, then remember your servant" (v. 31). The first half of the statement can be interpreted in two ways: (1.) "When Yahweh has rewarded my lord David with kingship" or (2.) "When Yahweh has given my husband (Nabal) his just deserts." It is difficult to decide between these two interpretations, and perhaps the sentence is deliberately ambiguous. But the unfolding of the story favors the second interpretation. Abigail's request that David "remember" her is a thinly veiled marriage proposal. David "remembers" her when he sends for her to take her as his wife (vv. 39–42). This happens after Nabal is dead but before David becomes king— that is, when Yahweh has "done well" with Nabal but not yet with David.

Abigail, then, appears to be a much more developed character than first meets the eye. Intelligent, charming, and eloquent, she shares many traits attributed to David. She also appears like David in other ways that are not immediately apparent in the story. Ruthless, or at least desperate, she was willing to conspire with David to murder her husband in order to forward his career and secure her own future. Her similarity to David may be another reason why she comes to be known as his sister (see Chapter Three).

Returning to the idea of this story as a murder mystery, if we ask who had motive, that is, who benefited from Nabal's death, the first answer is David. It is hard to overstate how important this episode was for him. He got the dead man's wife, property, and position. Overnight he became the richest and most powerful man in Judah. As mentioned, the same *modus operandi* will appear several more times in the David story—an important figure who stands in his way dies under questionable circumstances.

But Abigail benefited by being freed from a terrible marriage and positioned to become the wife of Judah's and Israel's rising star—and therefore herself a future queen. She seemed to know about the crime beforehand, and she had opportunity. David was behind Nabal's death, but the biblical story suggests it was a conspiracy.

1 Samuel 27–30

This subsection describes the events leading up to Saul's death in battle. Its purpose is to show that David was far away tending to other matters when Saul died and therefore could not possibly have had a hand in his fall. It begins by describing how David served the Philistines and was even the bodyguard of Achish, king of the Philistine city of Gath (28:2). This is an astonishing admission given that the Philistines were Israel's main enemy! But it is an excellent example of the nature of the apology for David. The writer admits David's collaboration with the Philistines but offers extenuating circumstances. In fact, the writer blames Saul, because it was his relentless pursuit that drove David to seek asylum among the Philistines (27:1).

The story also explains how David deceived Achish into believing that he had become a traitor to his own people. David told Achish that the plunder he brought him came from Judah or one of its clans (27:10). But that was just to fool him. In reality, says the writer, David never attacked Judah or Israel (27:8). The reason Achish never discovered the truth was

that David killed everybody in the villages he plundered (v. 9). No one survived to report to Achish. As a result, Achish came to trust David implicitly. He thought David had no choice but to be loyal to him since he had
"burned his bridges" in Israel and Judah.

David also hid the truth from Achish behind clever words, as we have
seen. When war again broke out between Israel and the Philistines (28:1)—
the war in which Saul would die—Achish assumed that David would join
him. David expressed his willingness: "Then you will know what your servant does" (28:2), but the attentive reader recognizes a veiled threat and
David's true intent. In the heat of battle Achish would learn that David's
loyalty remained with Israel. As gullible here as when David feigned madness (21:10–15), Achish took David's statement as an indication of his
eagerness to avenge himself on Saul. He even made him his bodyguard
without the slightest inkling of the danger in which he was putting himself.

The story of David and Achish is continued in chapter 29. The intervening story of Saul's seance (28:3–25) is a later addition.[13] Although
intrusive, the episode fits well with the theme of this subsection. In it, Saul
is clearly portrayed as no longer fit to be king. He is desperate, frantic for
some word from Yahweh, with whom he long ago severed relations. In his
desperation he consults a medium, an occupation which he himself out-
lawed. A ghost is called up. In the present version of the story, the ghost is
identified as Samuel, who announces that Saul and his sons will be "with
me" the next day. Saul's fate has been sealed. His death has been decreed by
Yahweh. Thus, as in the case of Nabal, it is not David who brings about
Saul's death but Yahweh. The next set of stories will show that David is
nowhere near at the time.

With chapter 29 the scene shifts back to David and Achish. The Philistine army is gathering for war against Israel. The Philistine commanders are
not as happy about the presence of David and his men as is Achish. They
recall that "Saul has slain his thousands and David his ten thousands." The
question of how Philistines would have known the victory chant of
Israelite women does not detain the narrator. For these Philistines, David is
inseparably linked with Saul as an enemy. Wiser than Achish, they fear that
he may attempt to regain Saul's favor at the price of their lives. They
demand that Achish send David and his men away.

Achish is disappointed. His regretful dismissal of David again shows
how blind he is to David's true actions and loyalties. "As Yahweh lives," he

swears (by the God of Israel!), "you are honest" (29:6–7). Then, "you are as good in my opinion as an angel of God" (v. 9). David responds that he wishes to "fight against the enemies of my lord the king." His words again have double meaning. The reader understands what Achish does not. The Philistine commanders were right. David's loyalty remains with Saul. Fortunately for Achish, he must acquiesce to the wishes of the commanders. He sends David with his men back to Ziklag early the next morning. The story makes clear that before Saul's final battle begins David is well on his way back south to Ziklag, far away from the battlefield on Mount Gilboa.

The last episode of this subsection recounts David's retrieval of the people and property taken from Ziklag. It places David a great distance away from where Saul was killed. In fact, it took David and his men three days just to reach Ziklag (30:1). And what they encountered there took them even farther from the battlefield where Saul was dying. Ziklag had been burned, and all their families taken away.

David's capable handling of this crisis contrasts with Saul's utter collapse. David's men were distraught at the loss of their families. They blamed him and threatened to mutiny (30:6). But David "strengthened himself in Yahweh his God." He consulted Yahweh through Abiathar and the ephod and then set out in pursuit of the raiding party. On the way, they "happened" upon an Egyptian slave who had been left to die in the desert. The Egyptian led them straight to the raiding party that had attacked Ziklag. They turned out to be Amalekites. Their presence contradicts 1 Samuel 15, where Saul reportedly annihilated the Amalekites. This contradiction confirms the suspicion that chapter 15 is secondary. In the final form of this literature, however, the Amalekites become a subtheme. As the people whom Saul failed to annihilate, they symbolize his rejection as king and continue to plague his reign. It is David who completes the task upon which Saul founders.

David led his men in a surprise attack. They slaughtered most of the Amalekites, recovering their own families and property and a great treasure of loot stolen from elsewhere. When a dispute arose among the men about the division of the plunder, David again showed his leadership capability. He issued a decree: all will share alike (30:25). The writer notes that this decision became a (royal) statute and ordinance for Israel. Though not yet king, David is already acting the part.

Historically, there is little reason to doubt that David spent time as a mercenary for the Philistines. A pro-Davidic author would not invent such a charge. It makes sense that he and his men were given the city of Ziklag. The Philistines cannot have been as gullible as Achish is pictured, and they had their own best interests at heart. Ziklag was an outpost on the edge of the southernmost region known as the Negev (*Map 2*). David was stationed there to protect the southern flank of Philistine territory. From there, he could conduct raids on surrounding areas.

David and his men survived on what they were able to plunder from others. The claim that they never attacked settlements inhabited by Israelite or Judahite people is not historical. These ethnic distinctions were not clear-cut, and David would not have had time to check them anyway. Besides, he and his men were concerned with survival. Their targets were chosen based on economic considerations, not ethnic ones.

The story of the Amalekite raid on Ziklag and David's counterattack is historically plausible. It is the timing of these events that is questionable. According to 1 Samuel they occurred at the same time as the battle in which Saul was killed. The reason for this is evident. David could not have fought against Saul because he was far away chasing Amalekites at the time. It is the apologetic nature of this presentation that makes it doubtful historically. The more the writer denies David's participation in Saul's downfall, the more a critical reader suspects it.

1 Samuel 31–2 Samuel 1

The last chapter of 1 Samuel and the first chapter of 2 Samuel offer different accounts of how Saul died. In 1 Samuel 31 Saul was badly wounded by arrows. To avoid humiliation and death at the hands of his enemies, he committed suicide. The Philistines found his corpse along with those of Jonathan and Saul's two other sons. They mutilated and displayed all four of them on the city wall of Beth-shan. But the men of Jabesh-Gilead retrieved the bodies and took them to their city for burial. This version is paralleled by 1 Chronicles 10, which adds nothing of historical value.

The second version in 2 Samuel 1 shares the general setting of battle on Mount Gilboa but is significantly different in its details. It comes from the mouth of an Amalekite who brought Saul's crown and bracelets to David. The Amalekite claimed to have found himself on Mount Gilboa when the Philistines were closing in on Saul. As in the first version, Saul was badly wounded. But here the Amalekite takes credit for finishing him off, though at Saul's request.

These two accounts are not real variants. The Amalekite's story does not ring true, and one must conclude that he is lying. What was he doing strolling around Mount Gilboa in the heat of battle? The characterization of Amalekites as scavengers (cf. 1 Samuel 30) suggests that this man went to the battleground ahead of the Philistines to rob the dead and dying (1 Sam. 31:8 says the Philistines arrived the next day). There, he found Saul's royal insignia on his already dead body and took them to David in anticipation of a reward.

The two stories have different functions in the overall narrative. The first explains how Saul died, by his own hand, far from David. The second describes how David learned of Saul's death and reports his reaction. It also continues the theme of the sanctity of Yahweh's anointed. The Amalekite was a resident alien (Hebrew: *gēr*) and therefore subject to the same laws and customs as a citizen of Israel (1:13). Therefore David asks him accusingly why he was not afraid to destroy Yahweh's anointed (v. 14). The Amalekite had condemned himself by claiming to have taken Saul's life. There can be only one punishment for such a grievous crime—death. Besides, after his recent experience (chap. 30), one less Amalekite in the world could hardly have troubled David. The reference to an Amalekite here again contradicts 1 Samuel 15, where the Amalekites were supposedly obliterated. But also again the insertion of that chapter provides an intriguing irony. Since Saul's offense was in failing to destroy the Amalekites, his death is in a sense his own responsibility. Once more, it is left to David to complete the task that Saul had failed to perform.

In addition to executing the Amalekite, David and his men mourned the death of Saul and Jonathan, fasting, weeping, and tearing their clothes (2 Sam. 1:11–12). The eulogy over Saul and Jonathan (2 Sam. 1:19–27) is attributed to David as his composition for the occasion. There is no way of knowing whether David really wrote it, but it serves an apologetic purpose. The lament and the fact that David ordered that it be taught throughout all Judah (v. 18) are intended to assure the reader of David's sincere grief at the passing of Israel's two great heroes. Surely the poet who expressed such affection for Saul and Jonathan could not have assassinated them.

Historical Assessment of 1 Samuel 24–2 Samuel 1

In the Wilderness

Now that we have identified the more apologetic and literary elements of this material, we can piece together what remains into a historically viable portrait of this portion of David's life. As his speeches in chapters 24 and 26 recount, Saul's efforts to kill him forced David to flee south into the rugged Judean wilderness. He was no doubt familiar with this terrain because Bethlehem was not far away. He may even have spent time here before coming to Saul's court. The region was a traditional haven for outlaws and fugitives, and David's leadership skills quickly attracted a following among them. Those who came after him were debtors and people disgruntled with the status quo (1 Sam. 22:1–2). One of the tactics David used to attract them is indicated by Saul's words to his own men: "Listen, you Benjaminites. Will the son of Jesse give any of you fields and vineyards? Will he appoint any of you commanders of hundreds or commanders of thousands? Is that why all of you have conspired against me?" (22:7–8).

Saul accuses his fellow Benjaminites of betraying him. Assuming there was some validity to the charge, what would have motivated them to support David over their own tribesman? Saul's own words provide an answer. They indicate that David had been making promises of land and promotions to his adherents. This means that his eyes were already fixed on the crown, for only the king could grant lands and make such appointments. These "campaign promises" were part of his efforts to build a groundswell of support that he could ride to the throne. Saul's words further indicate that the bulk of David's support came from his own people in Judah. First Samuel 22:1 also mentions David's kinfolk. Most of his fellow renegades in the wilderness probably came from Judah and felt threatened by the Benjaminite king Saul. David thus made use of sectional rivalries and suspicions to set himself against Saul as a better leader for his own people of Judah. David's own son Absalom would later use the same tactics against him.

David organized his followers into a small "army" or a raiding band. They were bandits. Today we might even call them terrorists, considering the political nature of David's agenda (see below). This band survived by pillaging settlements in the area. The Bible denies that they ever conducted raids against settlements of Judah (1 Sam. 27:8–12). David only claimed to attack Judah so as to deceive the Philistines into believing that he had become a traitor to his people. But this denial is part of the apology for David. Even in it one sees something of David's ruthless nature. He kept the Philistines from finding out what he was really doing by slaughtering all the inhabitants of the villages he and his men raided. But if the Philistines could not tell the ethnic affiliation of the victims from their property how could David know the identity of every individual or village he destroyed? And was he really that careful?

Other stories suggest that David was not so discriminating. For example, the inhabitants of Keilah and of the Wilderness of Ziph both betrayed David to Saul, according to 1 Samuel 23. The people of Keilah evidently found life under David's "liberation" no less oppressive than it had been under the Philistines. The Ziphites also seemed eager to turn David over to Saul. In both cases, the Judahite settlers in the region saw themselves as potential prey for David as much as any other people. The story in 1 Samuel 25 is the best illustration of David's operation. When the inhabitants of the area, like the chieftain "Nabal," resisted his demand for provisions, David moved to attack and take what he wanted. The composite picture, then, indicates that David's band survived in the wilderness by terrorizing the local population. They made no real allowances for any ethnic or tribal group except, perhaps, for David's immediate clan. Everyone was fair game.

David's band had no political allegiance. They were an army for hire—mercenaries. This may be the meaning of the term "Hebrews," used by the Philistines for David and his men in 1 Sam. 29:3. At that time, the word may have designated a social class rather than an ethnic group.[14] David fought for the Philistines just as he had fought for Saul. This was a great embarrassment to the writer of David's apology, who explained that David had fooled the Philistines. But David's ties with the Philistines continued into his reign. Even after David had become king of Israel, an important segment of his army continued to be made up of Philistines (2 Sam. 15:19–23).

For their part, the Philistines were happy to lend aid to an enemy of Saul. David the outlaw was as much a thorn in their side as in Saul's. They were willing to give him Ziklag because it was more convenient than trying to root him out of the notoriously rugged terrain in which he was ensconced and which he controlled. Besides, at Ziklag he and his men could serve as guardians of the southern Philistine frontier.

Political Ascendancy and Saul's Death

David and his band were good at what they did. They soon became a force to be reckoned with both militarily and politically. The single most important step in David's political rise was his removal of the Calebite chief whom the Bible calls Nabal. By marrying his widow Abigail, David appropriated not only his wealth but also his social and political position. This also significantly enhanced his power base. From there it was a short way to the throne of Judah. It is no accident that David was anointed king of Judah in the Calebite capital of Hebron, or that Abigail accompanied him there.

As chief of the Calebites, David could no longer be regarded simply as an outlaw. His relationship with the Philistines must have changed. This is speculation, but it fits well with the sequence of events described in the Bible. Combining the territory where he had conducted his outlaw raids with the holdings of the former Calebite chief, David now controlled the Negev bordering both Saul's domain and that of the Philistines. His political strength is suggested by the Philistines' reference to him as "the king of the land" (1 Sam. 21:12). This text is set long before David became king of Judah, so it does not refer to his position as king of Judah or as king of Israel. It does, however, show that David became a significant force in the Negev, one that neither the Philistines nor Saul could ignore. But they chose to deal with him in different ways. The Philistines bargained with David, while Saul sought his life.

By all indications, Saul was a strong military leader. He fought against Israel's enemies in every direction and defeated most of them (1 Sam. 14:47–48). His strategy against the Philistines was well-planned and effective. Samuel tells of several triumphs over the Philistines by Israel under Saul. His only recorded loss in battle was the one on Mount Gilboa. What brought about this sudden and devastating loss? The answer may be David, or more precisely, the league between David and the Philistines. Saul was prepared to confront the Philistines on his west, as they encroached from the coast. But he did not anticipate that a formidable enemy would threaten him from the south. David forced Saul to defend two fronts. This weakened his resistance to the Philistines and eventually brought about his collapse. David, therefore, was more than a mere outlaw who was a thorn in Saul's southern flank. He challenged Saul's dominion in Judah and then formed the crucial part of the coalition that destroyed him. In that sense, David was the one ultimately responsible for toppling Saul.

There is reason, moreover, to believe that David's involvement in Saul's death on the battlefield was more direct.[15] The strenuous defense of David in 1 Samuel 24–2 Samuel 1 is enough to raise suspicions. The more forcefully the writer denies David's participation in Saul's last battle, the more we suspect it. There are also some peculiarities about the accounts of Saul's death (1 Samuel 31; 2 Samuel 1) that fuel such suspicions. For example, the location of the battle on Mount Gilboa does not make much sense historically. It is too far north of the territory of both Saul and the Philistines. Why would both armies go so far out of their way to fight? This setting for the battle seems fictional. It may be due to the author's attempt once more to distance David from Saul's death. David occupied the south, so the writer moved the battle in which Saul was killed far away to the north.

Even more important is the function of the story in 2 Samuel 1. The Amalekite's story and David's reactions to it are designed to deflect speculation away from the significance of Saul's crown and bracelets. These were the very symbols of Saul's power. The Amalekite recognized this and brought them to David hoping for a reward. His actions bespeak a widespread understanding that Saul was David's enemy and that David wished to be king. The apology tries to show that this understanding was mistaken because it did not take David's character into consideration. We are told that David acted properly toward Saul, despite the friction between them. But the story also indicates that David ended up with the tangible symbols of Saul's royal authority. This is strongly incriminating evidence! We may never know for sure exactly how or where Saul died. But we must at least suspect that David was involved.

There is yet one more indication of this. Much later, during David's reign, 2 Samuel tells how David's son Absalom revolted against him and succeeded in briefly deposing him. As David fled Jerusalem before the charge of his son, he was greeted by a Benjaminite named Shimei who cursed him and jeered at him. Shimei told David, "Yahweh has requited you for all the blood of the house of Saul, in whose place you have become king, by handing the kingdom over to Absalom, your son" (2 Sam. 16:8).

Shimei obviously saw David as a usurper who had stolen the throne from Saul in the same way that Absalom was now stealing it from him. No doubt Shimei was expressing a widely held viewpoint and one that may well have a basis in history. The young man David, who, if my suggestion is correct, had failed years earlier to overthrow Saul, finally succeeded with the help of the Philistines.

Summary

We have now added the following scenes to the biographical portrait we are painting. David fled from Saul to the wilderness of Judah. There he gathered a substantial following of men who were also outlaws. He organized them into a raiding band that terrorized the inhabitants of the Negev and pillaged their settlements. The writer of the apology for David has tried very hard to cover up and explain his activities in the wilderness but with only limited success. Contrary to the apology, there is no indication that the band discriminated between ethnic Judahites and people of other origins, assuming there was really a difference between them.

David's most important single conquest in this period was that of the Calebite chief, "Nabal" (Jether?). Nabal's wife Abigail may have been David's own sister or half-sister. The two of them conspired to have Nabal killed, and then David married her. He took over both Nabal's wealth and his leadership position. This effectively gave David control over Judah and the Negev. He thus became a force to be reckoned with. The Philistines dealt with him by treaty. They hired David and his men as mercenaries and made them the guardians of their southern frontier.

The alliance of David's forces with the Philistines proved too much for Saul, who was killed in battle against the coalition. David may have taken part in the battle, although the apology has covered up his participation. David, therefore, finally succeeded in bringing Saul down. Next, he would move toward taking Saul's place as king.

Fig. 1. Michelangelo's *David.* (COURTESY OF THE ACCADEMIA MUSEUM, FLORENCE, ITALY)

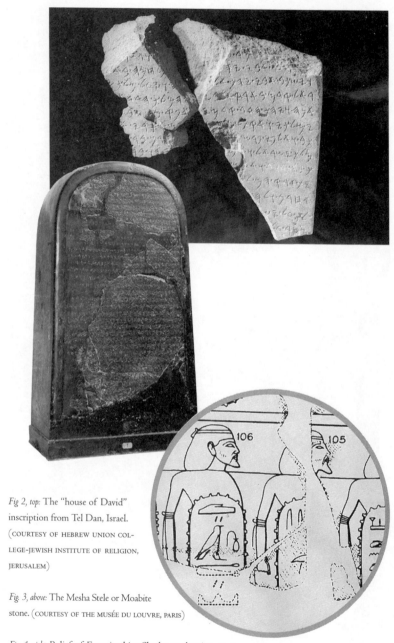

Fig 2, top: The "house of David" inscription from Tel Dan, Israel. (COURTESY OF HEBREW UNION COL-LEGE-JEWISH INSTITUTE OF RELIGION, JERUSALEM)

Fig. 3, above: The Mesha Stele or Moabite stone. (COURTESY OF THE MUSÉE DU LOUVRE, PARIS)

Fig. 4, right: Relief of Egyptian king Sheshonq, showing name rings where Kitchen reads "David" (D-w-t). (SOURCE: HERSCHEL SHANKS, "HAS DAVID BEEN FOUND IN EGYPT" BIBLICAL ARCHAEOLOGY REVIEW 25, 1 [JANUARY/FEBRUARY, 1999], P. 35)

Fig. 5, above: Modern Jerusalem showing the "City of David" and the temple mount. (COURTESY OF WILLIAM G. DEVER)

Fig. 6, left: The "stepped stone structure" in the "City of David."

Fig. 7. Canopic coffin from the tomb of Tutankhamun. (COURTESY OF THE CAIRO MUSEUM, EGYPT)

Fig. 8. Depictions of lyres from the ancient Near East.

(SOURCE: NAHMAN AVIGAD, "THE KING'S DAUGHTER AND THE LYRE," ISRAEL EXPLORATION JOURNAL 28

(1978), PP. 146 AND 148; COURTESY OF THE ISRAEL EXPLORATION SOCIETY)

Fig. 9, above: Relief depicting Philistines with feather head-dresses from Medinet Habu, Egypt. (PHOTOGRAPH BY ERICH LESSING)

Fig. 10, right: Relief depicting the attack on Lachish from Sennacherib's palace in Ninevah, showing Assyrian soldiers with conical helmets and slings (PHOTOGRAPH BY ERICH LESSING)

6

Assassin

David's Reign as King of Judah

Notes by Ethan ben Hoshaiah which he wrote down in haste during
the next part of the deposition of the princess Michal: two assassinations closely upon one another by which Abner removed and also Ishbosheth the only two men still obstructing David's grasp for power over
all Israel/query: by hand of God or hand of David/common traits

—Stefan Heym, *The King David Report*

"What is the nature of the Lord?" Bathsheba asked.
"He is like me," said King David.

—Torgny Lindgren, *Bathsheba*

Like Samuel, I hate to say this, but like Samuel, most of my life, I have
had no difficulty in persuading myself that my will is, by a stroke of
great good fortune, the Almighty's. And it may have been. I can't be sure
it wasn't. The successes I've had, my recoveries from the depths, they
make me believe, at the right moment, that I am indeed the Chosen of
the Lord, here to enact His will. Which I can only interpret as my own.

—Allan Massie, *King David*

Juan Bosch combined careers as Roman Catholic priest, statesman, professor of political science, and author. He worked for years in his

native Dominican Republic against an oppressive dictatorship and was finally elected president in 1963 by a huge majority. After only nine months in office, though, he was forced into exile by rebels. While in exile he wrote *David: The Biography of a King.*

Bosch probably understood better than anyone else who has studied David the kinds of dangers faced by public officials—especially in a government in transition. It is interesting, therefore, that in writing about the assassination of Abner (2 Samuel 3), Bosch raised the question of David's involvement.[1] He did not expand on this other than to say that the question remained unanswered. In this chapter I wish to propose a more definite answer.

The Throne of Judah

Following the deaths of Saul and Jonathan, the kingship of Israel might appear to have been David's for the taking. But things were not so simple. Second Samuel 2 reports that David's accession to the kingship of Judah was immediate but that it was another seven and a half years before he was crowned king over Israel. Those years witnessed a bitter civil war between the "house of David" and the "house of Saul" that culminated in the assassinations of the two leading figures in Israel, Abner and Ishbaal. The early chapters of 2 Samuel skim over those years quickly. But even they indicate that this was a difficult period. The actual historical circumstances were even more complicated.

Outline of 2 Samuel 2:1–5:5

2:1–4a	David anointed king of Judah in Hebron
2:4b–7	David's letter to Jabesh-Gilead
2:8–11	Abner makes Ishbaal king of Israel
2:12–32	War between David and Ishbaal; Abner kills Asahel
3:1	Notice that David's side is gradually winning the war
3:2–5	List of David's sons born in Hebron.
3:6–39	Abner's defection to David and murder by Joab
4:1–12	The assassination of Ishbaal
5:1–5	David anointed king of Israel in Hebron

According to the Bible (2 Sam. 2:1–4), David did not seek the throne but had it thrust under him. It was at Yahweh's order that he moved to Judah, specifically to Hebron. Once there, he was anointed king by the elders of Judah at their initiative. We have already seen that Hebron was the capital of the Calebites, Judah's most powerful clan. It was, therefore, the logical dwelling place of the king of Judah. Yet there is no hint in this text that David's motives were at all political. He did not go to Hebron in search of the kingship but because Yahweh commanded it.

The historical David no doubt actively pursued kingship. His anointing as king first over Judah and then over Israel was the culmination of a series of carefully calculated steps designed to bring him to power. We hinted at some of these steps previously. We can now discuss them in more detail and relate them to each other. The order of these steps is not certain. The steps themselves, moreover, should be understood as tentative.

Steps That Led to David's Anointing over Judah

1. Became leader of raiding band of outlaws in Judean desert
2. Served Philistines as mercenary
3. Married Ahinoam of Jezreel (Saul's wife?)
4. Had "Nabal" killed and married Abigail, became chief of the Calebites
5. Sent gifts from raids to elders of Judah
6. Anointed "king" by elders of Judah in recognition of his *de facto* control

1. David became the chief of an outlaw band in the wilderness of Judah (1 Sam. 22:2). We noted that, if Saul's words to his servants in 22:7 are taken seriously, David was already "campaigning" at this early stage by promising land and promotions to those who would serve him. Since only a monarch could grant such favors, David had already set his sights on the throne.

2. Saul pursued David into the wilderness. His pursuit may have been motivated by an attempted coup led by David. According to 27:1–4, it was Saul's pursuit that first drove David to seek help from the Philistines. As Saul's enemy, they welcomed him. David served the Philistines as a mercenary (2 Samuel 27). They profited from

him in two ways. First, they placed him and his men in Ziklag to guard their southern frontier. Second, from Ziklag David and his men continued to conduct their raids on the inhabitants of the Negev and to share the plunder with their Philistine patrons. While it is historically doubtful that David maintained his loyalty to Saul, as the Bible claims, it does seem likely that he fooled the Philistines in a sense. His raids enriched Philistine coffers. But they also established and expanded the territory that David himself, not the Philistines, controlled and that would serve as a base for his further acquisition of power.

3. and 4. David's marriages were an essential part of his claim to royal power. As far as the people of Judah were concerned (2 Sam. 2:2–4), his most important marriage was to Abigail because of her status among the Calebites. But his other marriages also supplied him with other important credentials. Although the marriage to Michal in 1 Samuel 18 is probably not historical, David may have taken another woman from Saul's household, namely Saul's wife Ahinoam. Both Saul (1 Sam. 14:50) and David (1 Sam. 25:43) had wives named Ahinoam, and the name does not occur anywhere else in the Bible. As with Abigail, this seems likely to be more than a coincidence, especially in light of 2 Sam. 12:8, where Nathan refers to David having Saul's wives in his harem. Only Ahinoam is mentioned as wife to both Saul and David. Thus, it could well be that "David swaggered into Hebron with the wife of a Calebite chieftain on one arm and that of the Israelite king on the other."[2]

We do not know the details of Ahinoam's identity or of her marriage to David. She is said to be from Jezreel. It is not clear which of two places this refers to. It could have been a site in the same region of Judah as Abigail's Carmel (Josh. 15:56). This would explain why Ahinoam is consistently referred to in tandem with Abigail (1 Sam. 25:43; 27:3; 30:5; 2 Sam. 2:2) and why the two women are an important element in David's claim to sovereignty over the Calebites and Judah (2 Sam. 2:2). Or it could be a reference to the Jezreel valley at the northern edge of Saul's kingdom. Either way, the marriage was clearly political.

5. When David and his men rescued their property from the Amalekites, they also took the loot that had been plundered from other cities.

David distributed part of this booty among the elders of Judah (1 Sam. 30:26–31). These were the leaders of the various city-states in Judah. This may not have been the first time that David sent gifts to them. It comes as no surprise, therefore, to read that these same elders chose David to rule over them (2 Samuel 2); he had stacked the deck in his favor. If they had forgotten the effectiveness he had shown as a military commander under Saul, his command of the band of raiders in the wilderness of Judah reminded them. This reminder was two-pronged. David's domination and annihilation of villages in the wilderness suggested that failing to choose him as king could be perilous, while being his subjects could bring rewards.

6. When David arrived in Hebron, therefore, it was a foregone conclusion that he would be crowned king. The elders of Judah were quite aware of both the positive and negative potential of his military capabilities. His marriages gave him royal pedigree and experience as a statesman. There was no other option.

As we will see in the next chapter, it might be more accurate to call David "chief" over Judah rather than "king." Judah was not yet a true nation. But David's leadership was an important step in that direction. Under his central authority the individual clans and the territory they controlled were brought together for the first time.

The Kingship over Judah and Saul's Death

There was always a distinction between Israel and Judah—even during the "United Monarchy" of Saul, David, and Solomon. David and Solomon treated them differently, as we will see. They are mentioned separately in the Bible's account of Saul's reign: "all Israel and Judah loved David" (1 Sam. 18:16). And David ruled over Judah alone before he became king over Israel. Saul probably never had a firm hold on Judah at all. The stories in 1 Samuel 13–15 indicate that his kingdom encompassed primarily the highlands of Benjamin and Ephraim. Once David surfaced as his rival, whatever hold Saul may have had on Judah disappeared in short order.

As a separate entity, Judah's political development was not necessarily tied to that of Israel. David's rise to king in Judah did not depend on Saul's vacating his throne. Second Samuel 2 relates that David's anointing over Judah took place *after* the death of Saul. But the figures it gives for David's reign suggest that he actually rose to that position *beforehand*. It says that David ruled over Judah from Hebron for seven and a half years (v. 11) but also that Ishbaal (=Ishbosheth), Saul's son and successor, reigned only two years over Israel (v. 10). This indicates that during the final five and a half years of Saul's reign David was ruling over Judah. The story of David's anointing in 1 Sam. 16:1–13 agrees. Even though this story is likely a later addition it is remarkably frank in its admission that David was anointed king long before Saul died.

One reason for David's success as king of Judah was his relationship with the Philistines. There is no indication in the Bible of any friction with them during his reign over Judah. So, we must assume that the affiliation he had established with them as a mercenary continued with his assumption of larger leadership roles over the Calebites and Judah. The affiliation may have become formalized. I have suggested that David had an agreement, perhaps even a treaty, with the Philistines that united them in opposition to Saul. No longer their "employee," he dealt with them as a sort of head of state. He employed Philistines as his personal guard; they were among his most loyal soldiers during his reign over Israel (2 Sam. 15:18–22). Nor was it with the Philistines alone that David made such arrangements. David sent envoys to the new king of the Ammonites promising to "deal loyally" with him as he had with his father, Nahash (2 Sam. 10:1–2). This language implies that there was a treaty or covenant between David and Nahash. But Nahash was Saul's enemy, indeed the enemy who, in a sense, launched Saul's career (1 Sam. 10:27b–11:15).

Together, David and the Philistines and perhaps others like the Ammonites represented a coalition against Saul. This coalition was what toppled Saul by forcing him to fight on two fronts. I have suggested that David's involvement in Saul's fall was more direct than the Bible indicates. He was an active participant at least in the planning if not in the fighting of the battle in which Saul and his sons lost their lives. This was what David had wanted all along and what he probably tried earlier in his career to accomplish. Saul's throne was left for him to claim. That claiming process would take an additional seven years.

From the Throne of Judah to the Throne of Israel

But Saul's throne was not quite vacant yet. Two members of the house of Saul remained in the way of David's ultimate goal: Abner, the commander of Saul's army, and Ishbaal, Saul's son and successor. Both were assassinated at opportune moments for David, and both deaths brought important political gains his way. Following the now-familiar pattern, the book of 2 Samuel denies that David had anything to do with the two assassinations and plays down his ambition to be king. But historical analysis will again produce a very different and much more realistic picture of David.[3]

The Assassination of Abner

With Saul gone, the most powerful man in Israel was Abner. It was he who placed Ishbaal on the throne (2 Sam. 2:8–10). Why Abner did not take the throne himself is not clear. Perhaps, because he was not an heir, he feared this would divide what few subjects were left. In any case, however, Abner was the real obstacle standing in the way of David becoming king over both Israel and Judah. As soon as Ishbaal had seated himself on the throne, civil war broke out between the "house of David" and the "house of Saul." The cause for this war was David's aggression spurred by his ambition to annex Israel. We will see how the biblical story reveals this after we explore Abner's murder.

Abner's assassination is the focus of 2 Samuel 2–3, which recounts two important episodes as background. The first is the initial battle of the civil war (2:12–32). The battle was fierce, but David's forces, under Joab, carried the day. Among the casualties was Joab's youngest brother, Asahel. According to the story (2:18–23) it was Abner who killed him, though hardly out of malice. As Abner was retreating with his army, Asahel pursued him, intent on making a name for himself by slaying the enemy commander. Despite being repeatedly warned, he refused to give up the chase, until Abner in self-defense struck him down. The battle ended before Asahel's brothers, Joab and Abishai, could exact revenge (2:24). But Joab particularly bore a grudge against Abner.

The second background scene concerns Abner and Ishbaal (3:6–11). It presupposes an important principle about monarchy that surfaces repeatedly in the David story, namely that sleeping with a member of the royal harem is tantamount to staking a claim on the throne. Thus, when Ishbaal accused Abner of sleeping with Saul's former concubine Rizpah (3:8), he was not concerned with matters of morality or propriety but with a challenge to his kingship. Rizpah was in the harem, and Abner's affair with her was an affront to Ishbaal's authority.

Abner did not deny the charge but contemptuously expressed his annoyance at Ishbaal for bringing it up. His response to Ishbaal, in effect, was, "How dare you charge me with a crime when I have the power to make or break you" (cf. v. 8). He further announced that he would transfer the kingdom to David (v. 10). The note in 3:1 that the "house of Saul" was losing the civil war suggests that Abner had another motive. He was anxious to avoid defeat and keep his military command. Whatever his real motive, he contacted David with an extraordinary offer. Abner would bring "all Israel" over to David. This would mean the final defeat of Ishbaal. It was exactly what David had been waiting and fighting for. Second Samuel 3:17–19 also reports that Abner spoke with the elders of Israel and his fellow Benjaminites about making David their king. He therefore came to Hebron ready to offer the kingship over Israel to David.

Several facets of this episode make it historically suspect. Private conversations such as the one between Ishbaal and Abner are, of course, of dubious historical worth. How could the writer know what was said? Ishbaal's accusation and Abner's actions are also somewhat hard to believe. Both of them would have understood the implications of the affair with Rizpah. But it is unlikely that Abner was covertly trying to replace Ishbaal, since he had the power to do so openly at any time. It would also be very foolish of Ishbaal to accuse Abner of treason knowing that he actually controlled the power of the kingship. If Abner was annoyed with Ishbaal, why not remove him and seize the throne personally? This entire story may have been contrived as a way of attributing to Abner the initiation of the parley with David. We may suspect that the historical situation was otherwise and that David lured Abner to the negotiation session in order to have him assassinated.

An earlier verse had explained that Saul had given Michal in marriage to another man after David's flight from Gibeah (1 Sam. 25:44). David now demanded that Abner restore Michal to him (3:13) before he would agree to meet for negotiation. Michal's husband, Palti(el) ben-Laish, felt genuine affection for Michal and went running after her as Abner carted her away (2 Sam. 3:16). But she was important to David for different reasons. In all the time they had been apart David had never once tried to get her back. But now, with Abner's defection, Saul's throne was in sight, almost in David's grasp. As Saul's son-in-law through his marriage to Michal, David was a member of the royal family with a legitimate claim to the crown. Michal was a political asset.

Strikingly, 2 Sam. 3:14–15 says that it was Ishbaal, not Abner, who acceded to David's demand and retrieved Michal from Paltiel. Ishbaal's intervention on David's behalf appears very odd considering their adversarial relationship, not to mention Michal's political benefit to David. It may be that Ishbaal was under some kind of legal obligation to return Michal[4] or that he was trying to curry favor with David, whom he recognized as the imminent victor in their conflict. But the apologetic nature of this material leads us to regard this detail as an indication that the story of David's marriage to Michal was contrived. In other words, David had Michal brought to him for the first time at this point as a way of solidifying his claim on the crown. This would mean that Palti(el) was Michal's original husband. Michal was taken from him and brought to David. It explains why David did not have her brought to him during his time in the wilderness. He was not married to her then and was in no position to demand her. It may be, in fact, that David took Michal only after he had become king of Israel.

With respect to Abner's murder, the writer goes to great lengths to show that Joab acted purely on his own. In the first place, David had no incentive to kill Abner. Abner came to Hebron offering to end the war and hand the kingship of Israel over to David. This was everything David had been working toward. Killing Abner would only have jeopardized David's position. The text states three times that Abner left his meeting with David "in peace" (vv. 21, 22, 23). It also says explicitly that David knew nothing of Joab's summons of Abner (v. 26) and that he found out about the murder only after it had happened (v. 28). It even hints that David was aware of Joab's grudge against Abner and tried to avoid any confrontation by sending Joab out on a raid when Abner was due to visit (3:22–25).

When Joab returned he was furious to learn that his enemy had come and gone peacefully. He immediately recalled Abner and, pretending to have private business with him, murdered him in cold blood (3:27). Joab's main motive was revenge for Asahel. But the story also suggests another motive. David evidently had made Abner his new army commander. That explains why Abner speaks to David as "my lord the king" in 3:21. He asks permission of his new commander-in-chief to go rally "all Israel" behind David. This new post would naturally place Abner in direct conflict with Joab, giving Joab all the more incentive for murder. This is no doubt an impression the writer wishes to create.

David's innocence is further indicated in his reaction to Abner's murder. He is described as distraught and terribly upset with Joab. He announces immediately that he and his kingdom are innocent of Abner's blood (v. 28). He places the guilt squarely on Joab and curses his family with disease and suffering as retribution (vv. 28–29). He distances himself from the "sons of Zeruiah," who are too violent for him. He also composes a eulogy for Abner (vv. 33–34) and calls him "a prince and a great man in Israel" (v. 38). He mourns bitterly for him with fasting (v. 33) and commands Joab and the army also to mourn (v. 31). The end result, reports the writer, is that everyone was pleased with David's actions and understood that he had no part in Abner's death (v. 37).

However, the very fervency with which David's innocence in this matter is asserted can lead a historian to suspect his complicity. A closer consideration of certain details of the story augments this suspicion. To begin with, David had incentive to get rid of Abner. Abner would have been a constant source of worry for David if he had lived. He was obviously very influential—in the story he persuades both the army and the elders of Israel to go over to David. His dealings with Ishbaal demonstrated that he was independent and would be difficult to control. Moreover, he was a Benjaminite and would always be inclined to keep the kingship within that tribe rather than letting it become the property of David and Judah. Most of all, the Bible makes very clear that Abner was the power in Israel. Whether he actually brought an agreement from the elders of Israel to make David king or the allegiance of the Israelite army is uncertain—and irrelevant. With Abner gone, dominion over Benjamin and Israel would be there for the taking, and David would be without challengers. But Abner's removal had to be explained in such a way that David could claim innocence and ignorance of the deed. Enter Joab.

The apology for David describes Joab's motive as personal—vengeance for the death of his brother Asahel. The other brother, Abishai, is also named as an accomplice: "So Joab and his brother Abishai murdered Abner because he had killed their brother Asahel in the battle at Gibeon" (2 Sam. 3:30). Verse 39 also implies Abishai's involvement when it mentions the "sons of Zeruiah." But the story itself records no role for Abishai in the murder. The inclusion of his name, therefore, is probably meant to emphasize the writer's point that Joab's deed was an act of familial blood vengeance rather than a political murder.

Though supposedly the occasion for Joab's vengeance, Asahel's fall in 2 Sam. 2:1–23 has some peculiar features that call its historical veracity into question. Again, private conversations between the two men on the battlefield could not have been known and are likely invented by the author. In addition, the portrait of Asahel here stands in tension with his inclusion in the list of David's "mighty men" (2 Sam. 23:18–19). The story in 2 Samuel 2 ascribes to Asahel the attributes of youth and inexperience in battle. He was "swift of foot" and rashly ignored the old soldier's warnings, intent on bolstering his reputation in imitation of his older brothers. By contrast, the list of "mighty men" describes Asahel as the commander (literally "head") of the honor guard known simply as "the Thirty." (Some manuscripts have "the Three," making Asahel a member of an even more elite honor guard.) The list also tells of Asahel's great expertise in battle that earned him a place as commander of the Thirty. Ironically, it was the way he wielded his *spear* against three hundred opponents that brought him renown! This Asahel is an experienced and valiant warrior and not the ambitious youth who naïvely falls victim to the butt of Abner's spear. It is also curious that Asahel appears on the honor roll for David's army when he supposedly had died before David even became king of Israel.

The story of Asahel's death serves an important literary function in the context of the apology for David. Abner himself hints at the function of the story in his speech to Asahel: "Turn away from following me; why should I strike you to the ground? How then could I show my face to your brother Joab?" (2 Sam. 2:22). The story provides a motive for Joab to kill Abner, which is important for the claim that Joab acted alone and for reasons of personal revenge. But the dissonance with the image of Asahel in the list of mighty men indicates that the earlier story about his death is not historical but an invention of the apologist to explain why Joab would have wanted to kill Abner and to deflect suspicion from David. This in turn would mean that the murder was not a personal vendetta but was otherwise motivated. It is logical to assume that Joab acted on orders from David, who was the chief beneficiary of Abner's death.

There are several indications that David's profuse display of grief at the news of Abner's death (3:31–39) was not entirely sincere. First, Abner's death fits a pattern that we have witnessed before in the deaths of Nabal and Saul. One prominent person after another dies under questionable circumstances, and David's career benefits enormously. Despite (and partly because of) the biblical writer's strenuous efforts to deny David's culpability, key elements in each instance point to him as the leading suspect. The comparison between Abner's death and Nabal's is made more overtly in 2 Sam. 3:33. The opening line of David's lament over Abner asks, "Should Abner die as a *fool* dies?" The word "fool" is *nābāl*, the same as the alias of Abigail's former husband. So one could translate, "Should Abner die as Nabal dies?" It should probably be translated as a noun rather than a name, but the allusion to Abigail's former husband is unmistakable. This comparison also seems to confirm that Nabal's death too was murder. David has to be a prime suspect in both cases, and his quest for power the motive.

Finally, despite the condemnations and curses that David heaps on Joab in the story, he does not punish him. This is a strong indication that he sanctioned Abner's death. It is true that on his death bed David ordered Solomon to execute Joab as punishment for his murders of Abner and Amasa. But this episode is not historical. It is part of an apology for Solomon in 1 Kings 2 defending him for the bloodbath that accompanied his accession to the throne. The real reason for Joab's execution is that he supported Adonijah as David's successor instead of Solomon. Besides, the events in 1 Kings 2 take place thirty-three years later according to the chronology of 2 Samuel, when Joab is an old man. The punishment is meaningless after so long a time. As it is, Joab gets away with murder. So does David.

The Assassination of Ishbaal

Abner's placement of Ishbaal on the throne of Israel illustrates the principle of dynastic succession. As Saul's son, Ishbaal had a right to the throne that Abner could not or would not claim. This explains why David and his apologist sought to claim heritage from Saul through marriage. It will also explain David's treatment of Saul's natural heirs.

Readers may be confused by the name Ishbaal. The book of 2 Samuel calls him "Ishbosheth." This is because scribes who copied the book found the presence of "Baal" in an Israelite name offensive, so they replaced it with the word *bōsheth*, which means "abomination" or "shame" in Hebrew.[5] Other scribes were not so scrupulous. So, 1 Chron. 8:33 and 9:39 retain the -*baal* element and give this name as "Eshbaal." This -*baal* element probably did not originally refer to the Canaanite god, Baal. The word means "lord" or "master" and could also be used for Yahweh.

Ishbaal's name does not occur in previous lists of Saul's sons in 1 Samuel. Furthermore, when 1 Samuel 31 relates the deaths of Saul and his three sons, Jonathan, Abinadab, and Malchishua, the implication is that these are Saul's only sons. The parallel in 1 Chron. 10:6 clearly interprets it this way, stating that "Saul and his three sons and all his house died together." The simplest solution to this problem is to identify Ishbaal with Ishvi, whose name is found in one list of Saul's sons (1 Sam. 14:49). The two names could be variant spellings of the same original.[6]

Ishbaal is characterized in 2 Samuel as nothing more than a puppet in the hands of Abner. The fact that Abner places him on the throne suggests that he was a youth. Second Samuel 2:10 says he was forty years old. But forty is a round number for a generation in the Hebrew Bible, so the figure is suspect.[7] Another sign of Ishbaal's youth is his ineptitude. The brief description of his reign makes clear that Abner was in charge. The few decisions Ishbaal undertakes on his own demonstrate his incompetence. Even with Abner behind him he was no match for David, and once he had alienated Abner, his downfall was imminent.

Abner brought Ishbaal to Mahanaim and made him king over "Gilead, the Geshurites,[8] Jezreel, Ephraim, Benjamin, and all Israel" (2 Sam. 2:8–9). These verses assign a large geographical area to Ishbaal, including regions on both sides of the Jordan. This list is clearly an ideal. Ishbaal never came close to controlling all this territory. This is the same domain claimed in the narrative for Saul, and the writer has simply transferred the claim to his son. And even Saul's control of anything beyond Benjamin and Ephraim was tenuous. These same verses make clear that Ishbaal had no real hold on all this land when they say that Abner brought Ishbaal to Mahanaim to install him as king. This is very strange, since Saul's capital had been at Gibeah. Further, Mahanaim was east of the Jordan River (Map 1), while the bulk of Ishbaal's kingdom was west of it. The reason for this move was the Philistines. They had captured nearly all of Israel's territory in their defeat of Saul, so that Ishbaal was no longer secure even in Gibeah. Abner moved east of the Jordan to regroup his forces for an attempt to regain the lost territory. In the meantime, Ishbaal ruled his "kingdom" from its fringe and exercised no control over most of the land he claimed.

It was David who provoked the war with Ishbaal. He did so by challenging Ishbaal's claim even of the land east of the Jordan where Abner had brought him. The challenge appears subtly in the letter David wrote to

Jabesh-Gilead (2 Sam. 2:5–7). The region of Gilead north of Mahanaim was one of the areas claimed by Ishbaal (2 Sam. 2:9). The city of Jabesh in Gilead had a tradition of support for Saul, perhaps because of ties of kinship with Gibeah, Saul's hometown (cf. Judg. 21:1–15). The Jabeshites also had a special affection for Saul, who had first proved himself as king by rescuing them from the Ammonites (1 Samuel 11). It was gratitude for their rescue that motivated the Jabeshites to risk their lives to retrieve Saul's and his sons' corpses for burial (1 Sam. 31:11–13).

David wrote his letter to the Jabeshites in his capacity as king of Judah. He congratulated them for their act of loyalty toward Saul (2 Sam. 2:4–7). But this letter was much more than a gesture of friendship or a formality of state. It was an outright political overture: "Let your hands be strong and be courageous. For Saul, your lord, is dead, and it is I whom the house of Judah has anointed king over them." David was telling the Jabeshites that their debt to Saul was paid in full. They were not obligated in any way to Ishbaal but were free to support David. The letter was, in effect, an invitation to the Jabeshites to establish a treaty with David against Ishbaal. The letter was an assault on the very heart of the constituency that Ishbaal had inherited from his father. It implied that David was Saul's successor. Ishbaal was not even mentioned.

To make matters worse for Ishbaal, David had already made a treaty with the king of Geshur. This was another area north of Mahanaim in the present-day Golan Heights that was also claimed by Ishbaal. The treaty is indicated by David's marriage to Maacah, the daughter of the king of Geshur and the mother of Absalom (2 Sam. 3:3). Such marriages among royalty in the ancient Middle East were typical ways of sealing treaties between states. David's maneuverings in international relations, therefore, had Ishbaal hemmed in. David was in Judah, south of Ishbaal. The Philistines were west, and the Geshurites, with whom David also had an alliance, were north. And now, with his letter to the Jabeshites, David was attempting to entice Ishbaal's remaining supporters away from him. Ishbaal had no choice but to attack.

Since Ishbaal was the aggressor on the battlefield, David could choose the site for the first battle and wait for Ishbaal's forces to arrive. He shrewdly chose the city of Gibeon. The Gibeonites bore a grudge against Saul, according to 2 Sam. 21:1–19, because he had executed some of them. The historical authenticity of this passage is questionable because it provides a justification for David's execution of Saul's heirs. But if the Gibeonites did indeed harbor animosity toward Saul for some reason they would have assisted David against Saul's son Ishbaal.

Only one battle of the entire civil war between David and Ishbaal is reported in the Bible (2 Samuel 2). The war itself dragged on for the entire duration of Ishbaal's two-year reign (2:10). It must have been bitterly exhausting for both sides. The Bible reports that Abner and his troops were gradually losing (3:1, 6). This would have provided additional incentive for Abner to negotiate with David. It made it that much easier to lure Abner into the trap that cost him his life.

With Abner gone, Ishbaal was powerless. He was left without an army and without subjects, since the elders of Israel had agreed to make David king (2 Sam. 3:17–21). Naturally, this picture is exaggerated. A later verse (4:1) says that "all Israel" was dismayed to learn of Abner's death, so it is unlikely that everyone in Benjamin, much less Israel, was ready to embrace David as king. It is safe to say, though, that with Abner out of the picture Ishbaal was not a serious obstacle for David. Ishbaal must have known that his days were numbered.

Even though he wielded no power and posed no real threat, he was Saul's heir and therefore would always be a source of concern for the usurper, David. Second Samuel 4 tells how two of Ishbaal's own captains assassinated him as he slept and brought his head to David. We are told that these two men were brothers and, like Abner, Benjaminites. There was thus opposition to Ishbaal within his own forces, especially after Abner's departure. There may even have been a faction within Israel that favored David over Ishbaal as Saul's successor. In any case, Ishbaal's captains perceived that his end was near, even if he did not. They hoped that by hastening the inevitable they could reap a reward. Like the Amalekite in 2 Samuel 1, their actions appear to reflect a widespread understanding that David was the enemy of Ishbaal and would soon be king in his place.

As with the earlier killings, the writer claims that David was unaware of and uninvolved in this assassination. The story says David had the two assassins summarily executed and their dismembered corpses displayed in Hebron to show his displeasure at their crime. Once again, however, this contention is difficult to believe. Ishbaal's death came at an extremely convenient time for David, since he represented the last obstacle between David and the throne of Israel. Also, as with Saul's death, David ended up with the incriminating evidence in his possession. Just as the Amalekite's story in 2 Samuel 1 may be designed to explain how David got Saul's diadem and bracelets, so this story explains how he came to have Ishbaal's head!

With Abner and Ishbaal gone, the elders of Israel (probably leaders of the highland city-states) had no alternative but to make David their king (2 Sam. 5:1–5). There was no one else to whom they could turn. David was in control of the army. The Israelite elders' anointing of David was as much a capitulation to his *de facto* power and position as it was an invitation for him to lead.

The list of steps taken by David in his ascent to the kingship of Judah may now be extended to include the stages by which he finally came to rule Israel.

Steps By Which David Came to Rule Israel

7. Hemmed in Ishbaal by treaties with Philistines and Geshur (2 Sam. 3:3)
8. Provoked war with the overture to Jabesh-Gilead (2 Sam. 2:4–7)
9. Lured Abner into a trap and had him assassinated (2 Sam. 3:22–30)
10. Had Ishbaal assassinated (2 Sam. 4:1–12).
11. Anointed king over Israel in Hebron (2 Sam. 5:1–5)

Summary

The David who has emerged in our biographical portrait was a shrewd politician. His assumption of Saul's position was the result of several calculated moves. Astute political maneuvering involving mercenary agreements with the Philistines, usurpation of Calebite chieftaincy, key mar- riages, and gifts (not to say bribes) to local leaders made David the natural choice to be king over Judah. Indeed, the local leaders had no other real option, because the guerrilla tactics of David's outlaw band gave him control of the Negev and of Judah.

David's reign as king of Judah overlapped with the last five and a half years of Saul's life. In this new role, David may have formalized his agreement with the Philistines. In any case, the combination of David's growing power and the Philistine threat eventually proved too much even for Saul's considerable military prowess, and he perished in battle against the Philistines. David immediately provoked war with Saul's successor, Ishbaal. The war lasted the two years of Ishbaal's reign. The Bible claims that David's forces were gradually triumphing, and this may be true. However, the war came to an abrupt end when David engineered the assassinations of both Abner and Ishbaal. David then laid claim to Saul's throne.

The elders of Israel, like the elders of Judah before them, had no choice but to accept David as their king. He was in command of the army of Judah, and there was no one to rally the Israelites against him. His rule over the territory that had been Saul's domain was still nominal. It remained for him to take control of it. Consolidating his new kingdom was his first priority. In the next chapter we will explore how David went about this, and we will see exactly what kind of king he was.

7

The Cost of Kingship

The Policies and Changes of David's Administration

These will be the ways of the king who will reign over you: he will take your sons and appoint them to his chariots and to be his horsemen, and to run before his chariots; and he will appoint for himself commanders of thousands and commanders of fifties, and some to plow his ground and to reap his harvest, and to make his implements of war and the equipment of his chariots. He will take your daughters to be perfumers and cooks and bakers. He will take the best of your fields and vineyards and olive orchards and give them to his courtiers. He will take one-tenth of your grain and of your vineyards and give it to his officers and his courtiers. He will take your male and female slaves, and the best of your cattle and donkeys and put them to his work. He will take one-tenth of your flocks, and you shall be his slaves.

—1 Sam. 8:11–17

The Bible says the people of Israel wanted a king to protect them from their enemies and make them like the other nations. "We will have a king over us. Then we also will be like all the nations. Our king will rule us and will go out before us to fight our battles" (1 Sam. 8:19–20). In Dtr's judgment this demand bespoke a lack of faith in Yahweh. Historical research can neither confirm nor deny this interpretation, but it can supplement it by pointing to other factors that contributed to the appointment of a king. Parallels with other societies indicate that the establishment of a monarchy was a complex process. Anthropologists have sometimes referred to three stages of development: segmented or tribal society, chiefdom, and kingdom. In Israel the segmented society was the time of the judges. Saul was chief over the central highlands. David became the first real king of the nation of Israel.[1]

This three-part scheme is not ideal.[2] It is oversimplified, for one thing. In each of David's roles described in the Bible—mercenary and guerrilla captain, leader of the Calebites, and "king" of Judah, as well as in the first part of his reign over Israel—David could be designated a "chieftain" in anthropological terms. Moreover, the three categories are not found in the Bible, which uses only the term "king" or "king designate" (*nāgîd*) to refer to Saul and David. It is probably better, therefore, to think of Saul and David as representing different stages in the formation of a monarchical nation or state.[3] Whatever terminology we adopt, it is important to recognize that David's reign was a much fuller development of kingship than Saul's. In this chapter I will trace the differences that the Bible describes between the reigns of Saul and David. Then I will survey the innovations David introduced as king and the impact they had on his subjects.

Consolidating the Kingdom

The Bible's account of David's reign in 2 Samuel is not chronological. Dtr's organizational principle was topical rather than chronological. Hence, for example, he lists David's sons born in Jerusalem as a group (5:13–16) rather than supplying a notice for each at the time of his birth. David's wars with the Philistines (5:17–25) are recounted separately from his battles with other surrounding peoples (8:1–14). And the victories over individual Philistines, which must have occurred during the Philistine wars, are described in yet another place (21:15–22). Again, 6:1–13 tells of both attempts to install the ark in Jerusalem together without giving details about what happened in the interval between them.

Outline of 2 Samuel 5–10

5:1–5	David anointed king of Israel in Hebron
5:6–10	Conquest of Jerusalem

5:11–12	Hiram of Tyre sends builders and supplies for David's palace
5:13–16	List of David's sons born in Jerusalem
5:17–25	Victories over the Philistines
6:1–15	The ark is installed in Jerusalem
6:16–23	Michal confronts David
7:1–29	Yahweh promises to build David an enduring dynasty
8:1–14	David's victories over the surrounding nations
8:15–18	David's cabinet
9:1–13	Mephibaal brought to David's court
10:1–19	David's defeat of the Aramaean-Ammonite coalition

While the exact order of these events is uncertain, four of them concern matters that would have demanded the immediate attention of the new king.

The Philistines

David's old allies now became his enemies. If we follow the order of 2 Samuel, the Philistines did not attack until after David had taken Jerusalem (5:6–10), begun work on his palace (5:11–12), and fathered at least eleven more children (5:13–16). But historically the Philistines made themselves the first item on David's royal agenda. This is clear from 2 Sam. 5:17, which says that the Philistines marched out in search of David as soon as they learned of his anointing over Israel.

As he had done with Ishbaal, David provoked the Philistines to attack. They perceived his move to unite Israel and Judah as a threat, which it was. David's kingdom would hem them in and pin them against the Mediterranean Sea. Ironically, Saul had been the Philistines' best protection against the ambitious David. They had been content with David's rule over Judah in opposition to Saul. But they were desperate to prevent him from unifying Israel and Judah.

The Bible indicates that David's wars with the Philistines took place in two segments. The first, as just mentioned, was at the very beginning of his reign (2 Sam. 5:17–25). The two battles recounted here are both set in the central highlands west and southwest of Jerusalem. This is because the Philistines were attempting to block David's passage to and commerce with the north by which he could effect the union of Israel and Judah. We do not know how long this part of the war lasted. It may not have involved any more than these two battles. The extent of the territory David gained by his victories was limited, encompassing only the area "from Geba all the way to Gezer" (v. 25), in other words, the central highlands where the Philistines had their blockade. David was content to leave the Philistines along the coast alone for the time being as long as they did not encroach on Israelite territory. In fact, the Philistines were probably not a unified group but consisted rather of rival city-states, so that David never fought the entire "Philistine people" all at once.[4] His enemies in these battles may have been only those Philistines living on the western edge of Philistine territory, next to the central hills.

David's victories in the first segment of his wars with the Philistines cleared the way for him to unite his kingdom in Judah with what had been Saul's domain in Benjamin. The second segment took place later in his reign when he began extending his rule beyond these two areas to include all of traditional Israel and Judah and even territory beyond. I will discuss this segment later in this chapter.

Establishing a Capital

Once the Philistines were confined to their own territory, the central hills again belonged to Israel and Judah. It was only then that David was free to make an assault on Jerusalem. Previously, he would have had to deal with the Philistines before he could even get to Jerusalem. Dtr describes David's conquest of Jerusalem as his first royal act (2 Sam. 5:6–10) because of the city's religious importance as the future site of the temple. There may also have been a gap in time between David's conquest of Jerusalem and his actual move to make it his capital.

Biblical scholars have long pointed to David's establishment of his capital in Jerusalem as a sign of his political brilliance. Had he maintained the capital at Hebron or moved it to Bethlehem, David would have alienated the people of Israel. But moving it to Gibeah or some other site in Israel would have caused equal feelings of alienation in Judah. Jerusalem, however, was neutral both politically and geographically. As a Jebusite city, it had never been under either Israelite or Judahite control. It was roughly on the border of Israel (Benjamin) and Judah, between Gibeah and Bethlehem.

Taking the city was not easy, for it was very well fortified and eminently defensible. The fact that David was willing to undertake such a risky venture suggests that he felt a pressing need to find a neutral capital. This may indicate serious tension between Israel and Judah even at the beginning of his rule.

The account of David's conquest of Jerusalem (2 Sam. 5:6–8) is very difficult to understand. English translations vary widely. Consider the following two samples.

> The king and his men marched to Jerusalem against the Jebusites, the inhabitants of the land, who said to David, "You will not come in here, even the blind and the lame will turn you back"—thinking, "David cannot come in here." Nevertheless David took the stronghold of Zion, which is now the city of David. David had said on that day, "Whoever would strike down the Jebusites, let him get up the water shaft to attack the lame and the blind, those whom David hates." Therefore it is said, "The blind and the lame shall not come into the house." (NRSV)

> Then the king and his men went to Jerusalem, to the Jebusites, the inhabitants of the region; but they told David, "You shall not come in here!" (For the blind and the lame had incited them, saying, "David shall not come in here!") So David seized the stronghold of Zion, which is now the City of David, and [he] said at that time, "Whoever smites a Jebusite, let him strike at the windpipe, for David hates the lame and the blind!" This is the reason it is said, "No one who is blind or lame shall come into the temple." (McCarter, *II Samuel*)

There are two major problems in this passage. The first is with the Jebusites' speech. The point of the speech in the NRSV translation seems clear. The Jebusites have such confidence in their defenses that they boast that even the blind and lame can keep David away. McCarter's translation is different partly because it is based on the Dead Sea Scroll fragments for Samuel. But what does it mean that the blind and the lame incited the Jebusites? McCarter understands this as a later editor's attempt to explain why David hated the blind and lame—because they were the ones who incited the Jebusites against him.[5]

The second problem has to do with David's instructions to his men. Most English translations have something similar to the NRSV. They take

David's words as instructions about how to enter the stronghold, namely by going up the tunnel by which its inhabitants drew water from an underground spring. Some modern interpreters have even gone so far as to identify this tunnel with the enlarged fissure known as "Warren's shaft," as we saw in Chapter One. But this interpretation does not explain the connection between David's instructions and the blind and lame. Hence, McCarter suggests that the word usually translated "water tunnel" (*ṣinnōr*) refers instead to an individual's windpipe or throat. In this case, David is telling his men to kill the Jebusite defenders rather than maim them.

The meaning of these verses was obscure even before the Bible was completed. The Chronicler, writing at a time much closer to the author of Samuel than we are, did not know what to make of them. He completely omitted any mention of the blind and lame in his version of David's conquest of Jerusalem and used the account instead to explain how Joab became David's army commander:

> David and all Israel marched to Jerusalem, that is Jebus, where the Jebusites were, the inhabitants of the land. The inhabitants of Jebus said to David, "You will not come in here." Nevertheless David took the stronghold of Zion, now the city of David. David had said, "Whoever attacks the Jebusites first shall be head and commander." And Joab son of Zeruiah went up first, so he became the head. (1 Chron. 11:4–6)

After David had acquired Jerusalem, he followed a standard practice of Middle Eastern kings by renaming it for himself—the City of David (2 Sam. 5:9). As Israel's capital, Jerusalem would change enormously, though not right away. Daily life in Jerusalem under David probably continued much as it always had with the same basic population and social structures. David did not drive out the inhabitants of the city or demolish it in order to start over. Jebusites like Araunah (2 Sam. 24:16) continued to live in and around the city and to own property.

The city of Jerusalem changed only gradually as David took over its citadel and enlarged it. The Jebusite citizens of Jerusalem seemed content with the change in leadership as it did not affect their lives greatly, at least not immediately. If anything, it may have made them more prosperous. Over time, the population of Jerusalem changed as people who identified themselves as Israelites or Judahites moved into the city. However, exactly what the ethnic distinction was between these newcomers and the older Jebusite residents is no longer clear, if it ever was. In the long run, Jerusalem was as much absorbed as it was conquered.

Bringing up the Ark

David's transfer of the ark to Jerusalem was part of his dedication of the city as his new capital. It was also likely another shrewd political move effected by David early in his reign.[6] He could only have done it after his conquest of the city and after his defeat of the Philistines whose control of the land blocked his access to the ark.

The ark was a symbol of Yahweh's presence. It was particularly associated with the tribe of Ephraim, according to 1 Samuel 1–7. By bringing the ark up to his new capital, David showed his respect for the religious traditions of the northern tribes and people. At the same time, the presence of the ark in Jerusalem strongly suggested that the God whom the northerners worshiped and who was represented by the ark supported David's reign. The fact that the Philistines had destroyed the ark's previous home, Shiloh (1 Samuel 4), proved to be very convenient for David, for he could now legitimately transfer it to a new shrine.[7]

David's effort to placate the people of Israel by bringing the ark to Jerusalem may have caused him problems with Judah. Hebron, where David had reigned over Judah for seven years, was a center for the worship of Yahweh. Thus Absalom asked permission to fulfill a vow to "Yahweh in Hebron"—in other words, to the local manifestation of Yahweh in Hebron (2 Sam. 15:7–8). But Jerusalem, as a Jebusite city, did not worship Yahweh as its primary deity. David's move to Jerusalem must have raised some religious eyebrows in Judah, especially in Hebron. His transfer of the ark to the city would only have exacerbated the problem. The people of Judah would have resented the favoritism toward the north's religious traditions. Such resentment may have been one of the sources of discontent that fueled Absalom's revolt. It is striking that he began the revolt against David from Hebron.

Dealing with Saul's Heirs

David's next immediate concern was to consolidate his hold on power in the face of Saul's legacy. As long as there were living male descendants of

Saul there would be claimants to the throne of Israel. David devised a final solution to this problem. I have proposed that he had a hand in the deaths of Saul and three of his sons in battle against the Philistines and in the assassination of Ishbaal. Two other texts describe further actions taken by David to deal with Saul's remaining male heirs.

Second Samuel 21:1–14 tells how David had seven of Saul's heirs (two sons and five grandsons) executed at the request of the Gibeonites. According to the narrative, David learned from Yahweh that a three-year famine in his kingdom was retribution for bloodguilt incurred by Saul for slaughtering Gibeonites. The background to this story is found in Joshua 9. There, the people of the Canaanite city of Gibeon tricked the Israelites into making a treaty with them. As part of the treaty, the Israelites swore not to kill the Gibeonites (Josh. 9:18–21). But 2 Samuel 21 says that Saul broke that treaty by executing some Gibeonites. The remaining Gibeonites insisted that the crime could be expiated only by blood. However, there is no reference in Samuel or anywhere else in the Bible to Saul's execution of Gibeonites. It is possible that the Gibeonites held a grudge against Saul for some act of his during his reign that went unrecorded. But the story in 2 Samuel 21 is a thinly disguised excuse for the bloodbath by which David secured his hold on the throne.

Again, the words of Shimei, the Benjaminite who cast ridicule and stones at David as he fled Jerusalem from Absalom, ring in confirmation:

> Get out, get out, you murderer, you fiend! Yahweh has requited you for all the blood of the house of Saul, in whose place you have become king, by handing the kingdom over to Absalom, your son. You are in this evil predicament because you are a murderer. (2 Sam. 16:7–8)

Shimei twice calls David a murderer (literally, "man of blood"). He mentions specifically the blood of the house of Saul. So he obviously has in mind the members of Saul's household, whom David has executed, and perhaps even Saul himself. What is more, Shimei mentions David's true motives for these executions—David was seeking to take Saul's place as king and, of course, to hold onto it.

Second Samuel 9 originally followed 2 Sam. 21:1–14. It describes David's treatment of the last remaining male in Saul's line. David's question in 9:1, "Is there anyone still left of the house of Saul . . . ?" makes sense only after the execution of the other members of Saul's house in chapter 21. The sole survivor was Jonathan's son, Meribbaal. (He is better known as Mephibosheth because his name has been confused throughout 2 Samuel with the name of Saul's son Mephibosheth. 1 Chron. 8:34 and 9:40 preserve the correct name.[8]) The story depicts David as showing great kindness to Meribbaal because of his pledge of loyalty to Jonathan. Thus, David restored Saul's land to Meribbaal and brought him to his (David's) own house in Jerusalem to live, always "to eat at the king's table" (2 Sam. 9:13).

In reality, David's generosity toward Meribbaal was a kind of "house arrest." Meribbaal had suffered an injury as a child that had damaged his feet and left him unable to walk. Ironically, it was his disability that kept him alive. He posed less of a threat to David as a potential usurper than his brothers and nephews who were whole. Still, because Meribbaal was a descendant of Saul, David was wary of him and brought him to Jerusalem where he could be closely watched. Dtr developed this cautious treatment of Meribbaal into the theme of David's loyalty to his covenant with Jonathan. We witnessed the stress that he placed on this theme in David's dialogues with Jonathan in 1 Samuel.

In addition to destroying Saul's heirs, David ensured that no others would be produced. This is what lies behind the story of Michal's confrontation of David after he had installed the ark in Jerusalem (2 Sam. 6:20–23). The text reports that Michal was disgusted by the spectacle of David dancing nearly naked in celebration (v. 20). She chided him in words dripping with sarcasm for acting so inappropriately for a king: "How the king of Israel honored himself today by exposing himself today in the sight of his servants' female slaves."(v. 20) She thus accused him of shamelessly consorting with the lowest element of Israelite society—his servants' servants. Obviously, she no longer had the same affection for David that was reported earlier in the story. Her remark also implies that David does not belong on the throne. The reason she now "despises him" (v. 16) is that he has destroyed her family. David defends his actions on religious grounds, reminding Michal that Yahweh chose him in place of her father (v. 21). With equal sarcasm he informs Michal that he is more concerned with how his subjects view him than with what she thinks (v. 22).

The key to this passage is the last line (v. 23), which mentions that Michal had no children. The writer does not explain why. David's reference to Yahweh choosing him suggests that God prevented Michal from bearing children because she had denounced his chosen king. But David's political motives point to another explanation. Michal may have had no children because David refused to sleep with her—and not just because of hostility between them. His primary reason was political. Any child she bore would be Saul's descendant and thus a potential rival for the throne. David kept Michal from having children for the same reason he killed off Saul's male heirs—to assure and maintain his position as king.

The First True King of Israel

The Bible (2 Sam. 5:4–5) says that David reigned thirty-three years in Jerusalem and seven more in Hebron before that, for a grand total of forty years. It is hard to know how seriously to take these figures. The number forty is often used as a round number for a generation in the Bible, and it looks suspiciously like one in David's case. Perhaps thirty-three was simply added to his seven and one-half years in Hebron (a more reliable number?) in order to bring the total to forty. Solomon is also credited with a forty-year reign.

The book of 2 Samuel recounts strikingly little of David's thirty-three years in Jerusalem, especially given David's reputation as Israel's greatest king. The bulk of the book concentrates on the revolt of Absalom (chap. 13–19), which is presented as God's punishment for David's sin with Bathsheba (chap. 11–12) as the story now stands. Otherwise, the material about David's reign over Israel is diverse and fragmentary. There are accounts of military victories (8:1–14; 10:1–19; 11:1; 12:26–31); lists of David's sons born in Jerusalem (5:11–12), of his cabinet officials (8:15–18; 20:23–26), and of his military heroes (23:8–39); two psalms attributed to David (22:1–51; 23:1–7); and a brief reference to the builders sent by Hiram for constructing David's palace (5:11–12). Aside from the battle accounts there are only two extended narratives in all of this material: that of Yahweh's promise to David in 7:1–29 and that of David's punishment for his census in 24:1–25. All in all, this is very little to go on for a reign that is supposed to have extended more than three decades.

It is possible to get an idea of the nature of David's reign by piecing together various details that we get in the Bible. Second Samuel characterizes his reign as a time of great transition. David effected a great many changes. By sampling key features of his reign as compared to Saul's, we can get a sense of the evolution of Israel's government, at least as the Bible reconstructs it. In most cases, we can continue to trace the trajectory into the reign of Solomon. Basically, under David Israel took on the characteristics typical of Middle Eastern monarchy. David either introduced these characteristics or cultivated them to a much fuller stage than Saul had done.[9]

Capital

As noted, the Bible describes the taking of Jerusalem as David's first act upon becoming king of Israel. But it does so for religious reasons. His conquest of Jerusalem sets the stage for him to bring up the ark. He is thus a model of piety whose first thought is for God. In addition, Jerusalem was very important to the writer. A principal tenet of Dtr's theology was that Jerusalem was the only legitimate place for worshiping Yahweh. But we have also seen that David's establishment of his capital—the "City of David" —was perfectly in line with ancient Middle Eastern practice. And David's choice of Jerusalem was probably politically motivated, as it helped him preserve the unity of Israel and Judah under his rule.

Saul's "capital," in contrast, remained his hometown of Gibeah. There was no "City of Saul." "Kingship" changed nothing about where he lived. The Bible describes Jerusalem as more than a residence for David. It was the administrative center of his government. Solomon enhanced Jerusalem's central role even more by his building activities in the capital and by reorganizing the administrative network of Israel. It was the centralized government that made all the other changes introduced by David and enlarged upon by Solomon both necessary and possible. There was no such centralization under Saul.

Palace

Second Samuel 5:11 contains a notice about construction on David's "house" in Jerusalem. It is evident from the fact that he contracted with King Hiram of Tyre for skilled Phoenician artisans that this "house" was more than a common dwelling. It was the residence of the king, a palace. This does not necessarily mean that it was large or luxurious by today's standards or even compared to the palaces of the great kings of ancient

Egypt and Mesopotamia. But it was more than what Saul had. The Bible depicts Saul as retaining his residence in Gibeah, and apparently continuing to live on his family's estate there where he had lived before becoming king. Indeed, the story in 1 Samuel 11, as it now stands, locates Saul back on his father's land plowing behind the oxen. David, in contrast, founded a new, specially designated government center.

The reference to Hiram at this point poses a problem of chronology, since other ancient sources indicate that his reign overlapped only with the very end of David's, at least following the traditional dates.[10] It may have been Hiram's father, Abibaal, who sent these supplies to David at the beginning of his reign over Israel. Hiram was well known for supplying Solomon with building material for the temple (see 1 Kings 5), and his name could have replaced his father's as David's supplier as well. But it is just as likely that Hiram's name is genuine in 2 Sam. 5:11 and that the traditional dates are wrong or that it was only toward the end of David's reign that he began to build a palace in Jerusalem. The latter hypothesis would fit with Solomon's statement in 1 Kings 5:3 that David was too busy fighting wars to build the temple. After David's death, Solomon continued what David had begun, embarking on an extensive building program of palace and temple in Jerusalem (1 Kings 5–8).

Nation

The fact that Saul maintained his "capital" at his hometown is one indication of the parochial nature of his rule. As mentioned earlier, Saul controlled little more than Benjamin, his own tribe, and the hill country of Ephraim. His hold on Judah was tenuous at best and non-existent after David emerged as its leader. Saul did not reign over the entire land of Israel as David apparently did; indeed Israel was not a true nation in Saul's day. It was David who first united it into a nation. He combined Saul's domain in Benjamin and Ephraim with his own in Judah and held them together. He annexed the other clans and tribes in Palestine and then went abroad to build an empire. What had been at most a loose confederation of tribes under Saul gained national status under David. In the language of one anthropological model, the chiefdom became a state.

Harem

Unlike David and Solomon, Saul did not collect a harem. The books of Samuel name only two women as Saul's wives: Ahinoam (1 Sam. 14:50) and Rizpah (2 Sam. 3:7). David had at least nineteen wives and concubines.[11] Besides Michal, Abigail, and Ahinoam, who are mentioned in 1 Samuel, Maacah, Haggith, Abital, and Eglah appear as mothers of sons born to David in Hebron (2 Sam. 3:2–5). The list of David's sons born in Jerusalem (2 Sam. 5:13–16) begins by noting that David took more concubines and wives from Jerusalem. How many more, we are not told. But he left ten concubines behind when he fled the city before Absalom (2 Sam. 15:16). Bathsheba is added to the list in 2 Samuel 11 and Abishag in 1 Kings 1.

David's Wives and Concubines

Michal (1 Sam. 18; 25:44; 2 Sam. 6:20–23)
Ahinoam (1 Sam. 25:43; 2 Sam. 2:2; 3:2)
Abigail (1 Sam. 25; 2 Sam. 2:2; 3:3)
Maacah (2 Sam. 3:3)
Haggith (2 Sam. 3:4)
Abital (2 Sam. 3:4)
Eglah (2 Sam. 3:5)
unnamed (2 Sam. 5:13–16)
10 concubines (2 Sam. 15:16; 16:21–22; 20:3)
Bathsheba (2 Sam. 11–12; 1 Kings 1–2)
Abishag (1 Kings 1–2)

All of the marriages that we know anything about (with the possible exception of Bathsheba) were political. Maacah, Absalom's mother, is a good example. She is called a Geshurite princess, indicating that David's marriage to her sealed a treaty between him and her father. Thus, David's harem was a reflection of his international dealings as king. This is even more the case with Solomon, who is reputed to have had seven hundred wives and three hundred concubines! First Kings 11:1–3, which reports this, says that many of his wives were foreign. Even if these numbers are exaggerated, as seems likely, they reflect Solomon's extensive diplomatic contacts.

Cabinet

There are two lists of cabinet members for David's reign in 2 Samuel, and they are nearly identical:

2 Sam. 8:16–18	*2 Sam. 20:23–26*
army commander—Joab	army commander—Joab
"recorder"—Jehoshaphat	"recorder"—Jehoshaphat
priests—Zadok, Abiathar,[12] + David's sons	priests—Zadok, Abiathar, Ira
"secretary"—Shausha	"secretary"—Shausha[13]
commander of the "Cherethites and Pelethites"—Benaiah[14]	commander of the "Cherethites and Pelethites"—Benaiah
	head of "forced labor"—Adoram

These are most likely two variants of a single original list. The duplication occurred when the story of David's execution of Saul's heirs in 21:1–14 (which directly follows the list in 20:23–26) was moved from its original location in front of the story of David's treatment of Meribbaal in chapter 9 (which directly follows the list in 8:15–18). Thus, 20:23–26 is the older version of the list. Its organization is more logical: commanders, court personnel, priests. Adoram's name was omitted from 8:16–18 perhaps "to protect David from the sort of reproach leveled against Solomon for his use of enforced labor."[15] The labor force consisted of people from Israel.[16] Solomon used it to work on his building projects. But Judah was exempt. Naturally, the Israelites resented the unequal treatment, and it was a key factor in the later division of the kingdom (1 Kings 12). In fact, this same Adoram was killed when he was sent to deal with the revolt (1 Kings 12:18).

These two variant lists, then, do not attest any changes or growth in David's bureaucracy in the course of his reign. However, other passages refer to offices not included in these lists. For example, 2 Sam. 15:12 mentions Ahithophel as David's counselor. "Friend of David" may also be an official title for a post held by Hushai (15:37).

The very existence of a cabinet under David represents a great change from Saul's reign. Nothing comparable to these lists or offices occurs anywhere in the account for Saul. The closest thing to it is found in 1 Sam. 14:50–51. The only office mentioned there, however, is commander of the army, and all the people named in the list, including the army commander, are described as Saul's relatives. Compared to Saul's rule, David's was more than a monarchy; it was an entire administration. This is even truer of Solomon's reign, which included not only an expanded cabinet (1 Kings 4:1–6) but also a list of officials for the provinces into which Solomon divided Israel for administrative purposes (1 Kings 4:7–19).

Army

Both Saul and David had armies, of course. But there are important differences in the way they are characterized. At the beginning of his rule Saul had no army. First Samuel 11 presents him as marshaling an ad hoc militia to go to war with the Ammonites. The militia gradually evolved into a standing army. All during his reign Saul was on the lookout for worthy soldiers (14:52). But there is no mention of any official measure, such as conscription, to maintain an army. To judge from Saul's speech in 22:7, his army consisted largely of men from his own tribe, Benjamin.

David's band in the wilderness was also a loose, spontaneous collection. But this changed quickly as David rose to power. There were at least three different components of David's army. Two consisted of permanent, professional soldiers. An "honor guard" of David's "mighty men" (Heb. *gibbōrîm*) is listed in 2 Samuel 23. But there was also a royal guard or body guard, the "Cherethites and Pelethites." We have already seen that this royal guard was made up of Philistines. It is mentioned in 2 Sam. 15:18–22 along with a contingent of Gittites—Philistines from the city of Gath—who were among David's most loyal troops and had apparently been with him since his days as a mercenary. They may have been mercenaries themselves.

A third part of the army under David may have been conscripted. When the people first demanded a king, the old prophet Samuel warned them of the consequences. That warning is quoted at the beginning of this chapter. It has long been recognized that the warning draws on the description of Solomon's reign. But Solomon may have simply furthered policies begun under David. David took a census of young men of military age (2 Sam. 24:9), suggesting at least the initiation of a system of compulsory military service. Solomon employed such a system for his army but limited the conscription to Israel (1 Kings 9:22); Judah was exempted.

Taxation and Forced Labor

The conscription about which Samuel warned was not just military. Solomon used a levy of forced labor from Israel to build the temple (1 Kings 5:13–14). In 1 Kings 12 it becomes clear that "Israel" refers to the northern tribes as opposed to Judah. The Israelites withdraw from Judah to form their own country when Rehoboam refuses to "lighten the yoke" that Solomon had laid upon them. That "yoke" also included a tax burden. Solomon divided Israel into twelve districts and charged each with supplying his court with provisions one month out of the year; 1 Kings 4:7–19 lists the officers presiding over those districts. Again, Judah was exempted.

But in the Bible it is David rather than Solomon who first institutes the labor force and puts in place a system of taxation. As we have seen, Adoram, in charge of forced labor, is listed in David's cabinet in 2 Sam. 20:24. Also, the purpose of a census like the one ordered by David in 2 Samuel 24 "was always to lay the basis for levying taxes and registering men for military service" in the ancient world.[17] Suggestively, the route followed by Joab when he takes the census according to 24:5–7 encompasses the same territory that Solomon would later divide into districts for supplying his provisions. Finally, 24:9 reports two separate census totals, one for Israel and one for Judah. This suggests that the tax exemption that Solomon gave to Judah was implicit in David's census. It makes sense that David would levy taxes upon the Israelites, since they were, for all practical purposes, one of his conquests.

Law

The famous Code of Hammurapi, written in Babylon about seven hundred years before David, says that it is the king's duty to see that justice and fair treatment of the disadvantaged are administered throughout his land. A similar ideology was adopted by David as king of Israel. On two occasions in 2 Samuel David was approached to render judgment in a legal case (12:1–6; 14:4–11). While both cases were fictitious, they presupposed the king's role as a giver of justice. Absalom precipitated his revolt by convincing those who "had a suit to come before the king for judgment" that he could do better than the king at giving them satisfaction. Again, 1 Samuel contains no account of any legal cases reviewed by Saul. The system of local judges, as reflected in portions of the book of Judges, continued under Saul with no central, monarchic legal system. The centralization was begun by David and continued under Solomon, who became famous for the wisdom of his judgments (1 Kings 3).

Land

David instituted a feudal system in Israel in which the king made grants of land to faithful subjects. Saul's speech to his fellow Benjaminites mentions such land grants (1 Sam. 22:7) as part of the platform of promises that David was making to gain supporters. David's dealings with Meribbaal in 2 Samuel indicate that he did indeed make such grants once he had ascended to the throne.[18] He restored Saul's land to Meribbaal (9:7). He then withdrew it and awarded it to Ziba (16:4) when Meribbaal failed to appear as David fled Jerusalem. Finally, he divided the land between Meribbaal and Ziba when Meribbaal defended himself as David returned to Jerusalem.

The stories about Saul presuppose a heritage system under which tracts of land were retained within tribal and clan units. There is no report of Saul awarding or seizing land, no sense that his crown gave him that power. Solomon's control of the land, following David's example, is evinced in 1 Kings 4:7–19. He ignored the old tribal divisions and redivided Israel into twelve provinces or districts for purposes of conscription and taxation.

These features together show that Saul's government was small, localized, and provincial while David's was increasingly national and bureaucratic. Solomon carried the innovations introduced by David much further. He enlarged Jerusalem and erected a palace and temple complex. He increased the size and complexity of the national bureaucracy as it emanated from Jerusalem. He also extended Israel's diplomatic ties, at the same time enlarging his harem with the wives who sealed his treaties. Each of these typical trappings of ancient Middle Eastern monarchy had its beginning in Israel with David.

The Nature and Extent of David's Reign

Kingdom and Capital

The first chapter of this book mentioned several scholars who have argued that David's domain was actually much smaller than indicated in the Bible. Some see it as little more than a city-state that encompassed only the immediate area around Jerusalem. One of the justifications for this theory is that 1–2 Samuel was written several centuries after David. It would not be surprising, therefore, if these books contained anachronisms reflecting the more developed features of later kingship but out of place for David's time. However, the author(s) of these books also had sources—if not written ones, then at least oral traditions.

I want to suggest that the Bible's description of David's reign and kingdom, which we have just surveyed, can still be used to reconstruct a realistic portrait of David's reign. There are, to be sure, anachronisms as well as exaggerations occasioned by the later view of the era of David and Solomon as Israel's "Golden Age." But a critical reading of the story may help us to set aside such overstatements in hopes of uncovering a picture of David's rule that is more in line with what we can surmise from other sources about the development of Israel's society.

To begin with, we have seen that Saul's reign was limited to the highlands of Benjamin and southern Ephraim where most of the Bible's stories about him are set. David expanded his hegemony far beyond Saul's, but it was a gradual process. As king of Judah, David's domain consisted of the territory just south of Saul's—the hill country around Bethlehem and the Calebite region around Hebron, which he acquired in his marriage to Abigail. It did not include the Philistine holdings along the Mediterranean coast to the west. He may have claimed the Negev south of Hebron but probably did not have any real presence there except for the occasional raid, as in 1 Sam. 27:10. That story about David's sojourn with Achish puts him the farthest south that he appears in the Bible. Other than a few small settlements, there was nothing in this area to control.

As the new king of Israel, David combined what had been Saul's domain with his own. He conquered Jerusalem, which lay between Saul's Gibeah and his own Bethlehem, and united the two small highland kingdoms. The Jebusite "city" probably amounted to a fortress on the crest of the hill. David made it his capital and the administrative center of his kingdom. But even with his enlargements Jerusalem's population in David's day was not more than fifteen hundred.[19]

Next, David moved against the Philistines. He probably had to fight them before taking Jerusalem. The Bible claims only that he defeated them in the hill country and part of the adjoining lowland (from Geba to Gezer, v. 25) but not along the Philistine coast (2 Sam. 5:17–25). There is a reference to a later defeat of the Philistines (8:1), but the reading is obscure. The verse says that David took Metheg-ammah from the Philistines. But no one knows where or what this was. The tales about victories over Philistine giants (21:15–22) may have their origin in the battles alluded to in 8:1. But the Bible says nothing more about wars with the Philistines. The Philistines still occupied the southern coastal plain long after David's time. They are mentioned in Assyrian inscriptions from around 700 B.C.E. So while David may have removed the threat the Philistines posed to Israel, he did not destroy them or take them from their land. The Philistines David defeated were not a centralized or unified enemy. The Bible uses the term "Philistines" loosely for an ethnically diverse group known elsewhere as the "Sea Peoples," of whom the Philistines were one. Thus, David's victories were likely over individual city-states or settlements or even raiding parties rather than a nation.[20]

The same is true of the rest of Israel north of Benjamin/Ephraim, the remainder of the traditional twelve tribes of Israel. The Bible says nothing about how or when David annexed them. It seems to assume, anachronistically, that these territories were already part of Saul's kingdom. The situation of these tribes was probably much like that of the Philistines. There was no central organization for David to contend with. It may have been simply a matter of annexing various key city-states in the north, most of which were sparsely populated at the end of the Bronze Age anyway. It was under Solomon, at the earliest, that the cities of Hazor, Megiddo, and Gezer were built. Thus, the extent of David's administrative presence in the region was likely minimal. This may be seen, for example, in 2 Samuel 20. Joab chases the rebel Sheba to Abel Beth-Maacah at the northern extreme of traditional Israel. The city of Abel as described in the story has its own government apart from David and seems unaware of his troubles with Sheba.

Empire

After the Philistines, David turned to the neighboring peoples east of the Jordan. There are accounts of battles with Moab, Aram, and Edom (2 Sam.

8:1–14) and with a coalition of Ammonites and Arameans (chap. 10 + 12:26–31). David's major foe was Hadadezer, king of the Aramean district of Zobah, north of Damascus.[21] His defeat was the capstone to David's empire.

Even the Bible, when read carefully, offers indications that David's empire was limited. It was not comparable to the great empires that dominated the Middle East at other periods: those of Egypt, Assyria, Babylon, Persia, Greece, and Rome. It was basically confined to Palestine. David's encounter with Hadadezer probably took place in northern Palestine.[22] There is no claim that David ever went into Mesopotamia or entered Egypt. Even if we accept the Bible's most extensive claims, his empire consisted of Israel and Judah with hegemony over some of the adjoining regions (Edom, Moab, Ammon, and the Philistine coast) (*Map 3*).

The primary reason David was able to form an empire of any kind was that the Middle East was experiencing a power vacuum at the time (ca. 1000 B.C.E.). Egypt, which had dominated Palestine in the Late Bronze Age (ca. 1500–1200 B.C.E.) had ceased to be a force there more than a century before David appeared on the scene.[23] Assyria, which would rise to dominance in the eighth century, was in its early building stages. The fact that these two great civilizations, which controlled Palestine at most other periods, lay dormant in the tenth century made it possible for David to expand his dominion outside the usual borders of Israel and Judah.

David conquered no real nations, as we have noted with regard to his Philistine conquests. Ironically, the same sociopolitical situation that has led scholars to posit for David a small, isolated kingdom around Jerusalem is what makes the Bible's description of his empire believable on a certain level. The peoples whom David is said to have conquered were even less developed politically than the Philistines and Israel and Judah. David faced clans and independent city-states rather than any real nations with centralized authority. Hadadezer, David's most powerful foe, for example, was not the king of all Aram (Syria) but only of the city-state of Zobah. The outcome of their encounter was probably closer to a draw than to a victory for either side.[24]

It is, moreover, open to question how firmly David controlled those areas that the Bible assigns to his empire. It is always difficult for an imperial power to maintain strict control over all its subjects, particularly those at the outskirts of its realm. Repeated military campaigns are usually required to put down rebellions at the far reaches of the empire. David not only had to deal with uprisings on the fringes of his empire (2 Samuel 10), he also had to put down serious revolts from the Benjaminites (2 Samuel 20) and from the heart of his kingdom, indeed from the heart of his family (2 Samuel 15–19). We have already suggested that he left the Philistines pretty much alone. His control of Aramean city-states like Hadadezer's was nominal at best. For most of his reign, they were free to do pretty much as they chose.

Finally, even the degree of David's centralized control of his own highland kingdom is difficult to gauge. The network of "royal cities" (Hazor, Megiddo, Gezer) with Jerusalem at the center was built not by David but by Solomon at the earliest. Even then Jerusalem was not the focal point for the country that it would later become. The city did not experience a significant population increase until two centuries later. That increase is the first tangible sign of the city's central importance. As we have seen, however, the Bible suggests that David initiated policies of taxation and conscription. Such policies would have required a central government. It may be that David's kingship developed in sophistication over the course of his reign. The plans for taxation and conscription may have come toward the end of his reign. This hypothesis receives support from the career of Adoram, who was the head of both David's and Solomon's labor forces (2 Sam. 20:24). Because he is said to have outlived Solomon (1 Kings 12:18), it is likely that he was appointed near the end of David's reign.

Religion

It was common practice in the ancient Middle East for a king to build a temple for his god. The temple served both as a sign of the king's piety and devotion and as a statement that his kingship and dynasty were divinely supported and therefore sacred. It is remarkable, therefore, that the Bible credits Solomon rather than David with constructing the temple to Yahweh in Jerusalem.

The biblical writers struggled to explain why David did not build the temple. The most famous passage on the topic is 2 Samuel 7. One of the most discussed and controversial texts in the Bible, it illustrates the difficulty we face in this chapter—indeed throughout this book—with trying to recover historical information from the biblical narratives.

Second Samuel 7 is widely recognized by scholars as a Dtr composition. It is full of Dtr language.[25] It was, therefore, written centuries after David.

The centrality and exclusiveness of worship at the Jerusalem temple together with the divinely ordained permanence of the Davidic dynasty were key features of Dtr's theology. The fact that David did not build the temple posed a serious dilemma for him, and he offered an ingenious solution. Dtr reasoned that David, being a pious king (his installation of the ark showed as much), must have offered to build a temple for Yahweh. It was Yahweh who declined the offer. Then, playing on the meanings of the word "house," Dtr turned the focus of the chapter to David's dynasty. As a reward for his offer to build Yahweh a "house" (temple) and for his faithfulness in general, Yahweh promised David a "house"—an eternal or enduring dynasty. Thus, while 2 Samuel 7 concedes that David did not build the temple, it does not fail to take advantage of the propagandistic value of the temple for David and his line.

But is there any genuine historical tradition behind Dtr's explanation? Many scholars believe there is. They interpret Nathan's words in 2 Sam. 7:5–7 as an objection to a permanent temple on the grounds that Yahweh's traditional shrine was a portable tabernacle.[26] Some in David's court, they say, must have objected to the idea of building a temple as too radical a departure from Israel's established religious traditions. Unfortunately, Dtr's explanation remains tantalizingly obscure. He never really explains *why* Yahweh objects to David's proposal.[27] In fact, nowhere in 2 Samuel 7 does Yahweh actually forbid David to build a temple. Yahweh merely says that it is David's son who will do so.

The obscurity of Dtr's explanation led the author of Chronicles to add his own. He concluded that David had shed too much blood to be allowed to build a temple: "The word of Yahweh came to me, saying, 'You have shed much blood and have waged great wars; you shall not build a house to my name, because you have shed so much blood in my sight on the earth'" (1 Chron. 22:8) and "God said to me, 'You shall not build a house for my name, for you are a warrior and have shed blood'" (1 Chron. 28:3). This was probably a ritual judgment rather than a moral one; David's bloodshed was justified but still inappropriate for the founder of the holy temple.[28] This added a theological component to Dtr's explanation that David did not have time to build a temple. Nevertheless, David's connection with the temple was very important to the Chronicler. So, in 1 Chronicles 22–29 he describes David as making detailed preparations for the temple's construction. He drafts the plans for the building, gathers all the materials, and makes arrangements for all the workers. He also establishes the divisions of the Levites for the observance of the temple rituals. In a very real sense, according to Chronicles, it was David's temple. The historical David could have made some preparations for Solomon's construction work. But these chapters spring from the Chronicler's interests and are not history.

We do not know why David did not build a temple. It is possible that he was swayed by traditionalists who perceived the temple as a threat. By all indications, David was conservative where religion was concerned.[29] He did not wish to offend his people or their god. That is why he tried to preserve the traditions of both Israel and Judah. We have seen this tendency in David's bringing of the (northern) ark to Jerusalem. It also surfaced in his appointment of two priests—Abiathar from Israel and Zadok from Judah. Worship continued at local shrines throughout the history of Israel and Judah—even after Solomon's temple had been built. The idea that the temple in Jerusalem was the only legitimate place for worshiping Yahweh was developed first in Deuteronomy and the Deuteronomistic History, nearly four hundred years after David.

Whatever the reason that David did not build the temple, whether it was theological or that he was simply otherwise occupied, it fits well with the Bible's description of his reign as a time of transition. There is no mention of a temple under Saul. David brings up the idea of a temple only after he is settled as king of Israel in his house or palace (2 Sam. 7:1a). It is Solomon, who takes on all the other trappings of ancient Middle Eastern monarchy, who finally builds a temple. David is the transitional figure between the two.

Summary

Our close reading of the Bible in this chapter has sketched a portrait of David's kingdom as much smaller and more parochial than traditionally represented. This agrees with what scholars from a variety of fields (archaeology, anthropology, biblical studies) have concluded. The Bible's account was written long after David's time and contains anachronisms. But its overall portrait of David, when read critically in the light of ancient Middle Eastern culture, is not unreasonable.

David's first steps as king of Israel were directed toward consolidating his rule. He was immediately confronted by Philistines who lived close to the hill country and opposed his efforts to unite Saul's domain with Judah. His initial defeat of this contingent allowed him to turn to internal matters. He established the new capital in Jerusalem and then transferred the ark there as part of the effort to unify Israel (Benjamin and Ephraim) and Judah. In typical Middle Eastern fashion, he had his predecessor's heirs executed—all except Meribbaal, whom he kept under guard.

It is David, rather than Saul, who should be thought of as Israel's first king. The characteristics typical of ancient Middle Eastern monarchy appear first for Israel under David. They are later extended by Solomon. These include a central capital with a royal palace and shrine to the king's deity, a bureaucratic government with a standing professional army, a harem, and a feudal system of social organization in which the king is the "supreme court" of the land. It was David, then, who took the first steps of forging Israel into a nation.

David's efforts to expand his hegemony were, for the most part, localized. His "empire" in Iron Age Palestine (ca. 1000 B.C.) was largely the result of a power vacuum in the Middle East. The great states of Egypt and Assyria were preoccupied with their own problems and too weak to do anything about David even if they took notice of him. David's conquests were mainly independent city-states and regions without central authority, most of which bordered Israel and Judah.

David's success was not without its costs. He is credited with beginning such policies as conscription for military and civic service and taxation. The centralization of Israelite society eventually brought about less tangible changes in people's attitudes and in religion. In the next chapter we will see some of the reactions that David's new policies generated.

8

Like Father, Like Son

The Bathsheba Affair and Absalom's Revolt

Plots, true or false, are necessary things,
To raise up commonwealths, and ruin kings.

. . . .

Desire of pow'r, on earth a vicious weed,
Yet, sprung from high, is of celestial seed:
In God 't is glory; and when men aspire,
'T is but a spark too much of heavenly fire.
Th' ambitious youth, too covetous of fame,
Too full of angels' metal in his frame,
Unwarily was led from virtue's ways,
Made drunk with honor, and debauch'd with praise.
Half loth, and half consenting to the ill,
(For loyal blood within him struggled still)

—John Dryden, "Absalom and Achitophel"

For when I look at a rebel like Absalom, a man who gave his life to overthrow his father's outworn reign, I see him as his father's most determined and reckless enemy, certainly; but I can't help seeing him also as
the very man of all those around David who was most impressed by
what David had accomplished, most in awe of David's position, the one
who could think of nothing more important in his life than to seize that
position for himself. The man, in short, who wanted to be David.

—Dan Jacobson, *The Rape of Tamar*

Part of the appeal of the David story has always been the earthiness of its plot. It reads like a modern soap opera with plenty of sex, violence, and struggles for power. The relationships are intricate. One of David's wives is his best friend's sister and his enemy's daughter. She loves him, marries someone else when he goes away, and finally comes to despise him. Some of his brides were new widows whose husbands had very recently died under suspicious circumstances. In the case of Bathsheba, the Bible admits that David plotted her husband's murder in order to cover up his adulterous affair with her.

Truth be told, these faults of David's attract our attention more than his virtues. We admire the fearless and pious young hero, but we cannot identify with him. The adulterer who gets caught in a cover-up, on the other hand, is one of us. We empathize with the father who is a failure with his own children. The seamier, lustier episodes of the David story are concentrated in the Court History, the source lying behind much of 2 Samuel (see Chapter Two).

The book of 2 Samuel is our primary source of information regarding David's reign. Although his reign is often represented as the Golden Age of Israel, it was not the era of ideal peace and prosperity that such a title conjures up. The longest section of 2 Samuel recounts the revolt led by David's own son Absalom, which succeeded in overthrowing him and forcing him into exile. And immediately following it is the story of a smaller revolt against David's rule.

Outline of 2 Samuel 13–24

11–12	David's affair with Bathsheba
13–19	Absalom's revolt
20:1–22	Sheba's revolt
20:23–26	David's cabinet
21:1–14	execution of the sons of Saul
21:15–22	victories over Philistine giants
22	a psalm of deliverance
23:1–7	the "last words" of David
23:8–39	David's military heroes
24	David's census

The success of Absalom's revolt reflects widespread unhappiness with David's administration. The book of 2 Samuel never specifies the exact causes for this unhappiness. But it is possible to surmise what some of them were, based on our characterization of David and his reign.

The long-standing rivalry between Israel and Judah continued; it was a considerable struggle for David to keep them together. Each also had its own independent reasons for distrusting David. In Judah the people were displeased at his having moved the capital from Hebron to Jerusalem and then bringing the ark, a northern artifact, to Jerusalem.[1] This is why Absalom chose to initiate his revolt in Hebron.

If Judah had grounds for complaint against David, Israel had more. There were Benjaminites who continued to resent David's replacement of Saul and his slaughter of Saul's heirs. Shimei, an important Benjaminite leader, is shown ridiculing David as he fled from Absalom (2 Sam. 16:5–14; 19:17–24). Sheba, who led a less threatening revolt after Absalom, was also from Benjamin (2 Sam. 20:1). The Israelites were a conquered people. The burdens of taxation and conscription that David laid upon them were a constant reminder of their position as inferiors.

David's other wars of conquest were costly in terms both of supplies and of the lives of his men. Even natural disasters such as plague were blamed on David and viewed as punishment for offensive religious and administrative policies (2 Samuel 24). As David's popularity waned, many of his subjects began to seek a change. It was into this setting that Absalom stepped. He played on the general sense of injustice that pervaded the country (2 Sam. 15:1–12). Absalom also emulated David in making promises to gain supporters, even though David's own failure to keep his promises was probably another source of disaffection. As we explore the Bible's account of Absalom's revolt, we will keep an eye out for evidence of these various sources of discontent.

David's Affair with Bathsheba

We have seen that the Bathsheba episode was a later addition to 2 Samuel. It was added in its present place in order to produce a scheme of "sin and punishment" or "cause and effect" with respect to Absalom's revolt. In the battle account in which the Bathsheba story is embedded (2 Sam. 10:1–11:1a + 12:26–31), David mentions the loyalty that had been shown him by the Ammonite king Nahash (2 Sam. 10:2). This act of loyalty apparently consisted of sending provisions to David when he fled from Absalom (2 Sam. 17:27–29). There is no other interaction between Nahash and David in the Bible that would qualify as this act of loyalty. This means that David's affair with Bathsheba probably took place after Absalom's revolt rather than before it. As it now stands, however, the book of 2 Samuel describes Absalom's revolt as punishment for David's affair with Bathsheba and murder of her husband, Uriah.

The negative portrait of David in the Bathsheba narrative differs radically from the apologetic material that surrounds it. Nevertheless, the story accords well with the image of David that our critical analysis has yielded. It is in essence the same story as the Nabal-Abigail episode, only without the cover-up. Moreover, both the Bathsheba affair and the rape of Tamar by her own half-brother (2 Samuel 13), point to corruption and abuse of power within the royal household that must have spread distrust of David among his subjects. Hence, the Bathsheba story, despite being a later addition, merits close reading. It may be based on a historical event. It is also a masterfully told tale that prods its audience to "read between the lines" to discern the motives of the characters. So, it may also prove useful for the characterizations we are building of David and those around him.

The story in 2 Samuel 11–12 is dated a year after the battles in chapter 10. A literal translation of 11:1 is: "At the turn of the year, the time when the kings had gone forth [to battle]." The statement is often mistranslated. For example, the NRSV reads, "In the spring of the year, the time when kings go out to battle." This translation provides a kind of false romantic background to the story. It implies that kings were supposed to go to war in the spring and that by staying in Jerusalem David failed to carry out his royal obligation and therefore got himself into trouble. The writer is making no such claim. The "turn of the year" probably meant the spring and perhaps designated the start of a new year. But the point is that this story took place a year after the battle recounted in chapter 10. There was no requirement that David or any other king had to go to war in the spring.

The story begins with David sending Joab to war against Rabbah. It is not clear why David himself stayed behind. A later passage (2 Sam. 21:15–17) tells of an occasion when David was almost killed in battle and his men urged him to stay back from then on. But 11:1 does not allude to that occasion. The story does seem to be set in the latter part of David's reign. Some have even tried to relate it to a midlife crisis. But this reads too much of a modern perspective into it. The writer certainly makes no attempt to mitigate David's guilt or to make any excuse for his lustful abuse of power. In fact, the story of Joab's siege of Rabbah continues in 12:26, so that 11:1 + 12:26–31 seems to have been an independent narrative into which the Bathsheba episode (11:2–12:25) was inserted. David's remaining in Jerusalem was part of the originally independent story of the conquest of Rabbah, but a later editor made use of it as the setting for the Bathsheba story.

David was consumed by desire for Bathsheba from the moment he saw her. It is a familiar story—the older man infatuated with a much younger woman (apparently the granddaughter of David's leading advisor—see below). He was on the palace roof following a late afternoon nap and spotted her bathing in the courtyard of her house (11:2). He decided to "take" her (a theme of the chapter), despite the fact that she was already married to Uriah the Hittite (11:3), whose name occurs in the list of David's honor guard (2 Sam. 23:39). Uriah's name is last on the list and looks suspiciously like a later addition—perhaps a subtle reminder of David's crime. But if it is genuine, David must have known Uriah, and known him to be among his most capable and loyal servants. The fact that he is called a "Hittite" magnifies David's crime rather than lessens it. Uriah was a resident alien, one of the groups, along with widows and orphans, whose rights the king was especially charged to protect. As if to underline David's obligation to him, Uriah's name is not that of a foreigner but is Hebrew for "Yahweh is my light."

David's deed is described succinctly. He sent for Bathsheba and "lay" with her (11:4). Nothing is said of her feelings. She is presented as the passive victim of his lust. Considering his position as king, she had no choice. A parenthesis in v. 4 that explains the reason for Bathsheba's bath is very important to the story. A woman was ritually unclean during her menstrual period and for seven days thereafter (Lev. 15:19–30). At the end of the seven days, she was supposed to bathe, after which she would be ritually clean (Lev. 15:13, 28). It was this bath that Bathsheba was taking when David saw her. In this subtle way, the writer makes two important points. First, Bathsheba was at the optimal point for conception in her monthly cycle when David "took" her. The ancients would not have known the biological reasons, but they were well aware of such matters relating to fertility. Thus the story reports immediately (11:5) that she became pregnant. Second, the child Bathsheba bore had to be David's, since she had experienced her menstrual period just before he had sex with her.

David tried to cover up his crime by bringing Uriah home (11:6–12). If Uriah slept with his wife, then her pregnancy would raise no questions. But David failed to invent a satisfactory excuse for his summons of Uriah. After singling him out and bringing him all the way to Jerusalem, all David could think to do was ask general questions about the welfare of the army and the war. That information was supplied by the messengers who routinely ran between David and Joab. There was no need to take a soldier, especially one of Uriah's superior quality, away from the battle simply for a routine report.

This made Uriah suspect that his loyalty was being tested. The result was that he became especially conscientious in displaying his faithfulness to David and the army (11:6–13). This in turn made him particularly observant of the vows of celibacy that he had taken in preparation for war. Ironically, therefore, the more insistent David became that Uriah go home and "wash his feet" (a euphemism for sexual intercourse in v. 8), the more Uriah resisted in order to prove his devotion to David and Israel.

David had no doubts about Uriah's loyalty. He sent his letter to Joab by Uriah's own hand (11:14–15). Uriah was carrying his own death warrant. The situation, however, did not develop quite as David had planned (11:16–25). Uriah was killed due to a tactical error on Joab's part rather than because of David's plan. The sequence of events is discernible from the Hebrew text but is clearer in the LXX reading. Joab allowed some of his soldiers to draw too near to the city wall of Rabbah, making them an easy target for the city's defenders. Eighteen men were killed in the assault. When Joab sent the messenger to report the loss to David, he expected that David would be angry. So, he instructed the messenger to watch for David's reaction. If he became angry the messenger was to mention that Uriah was among the casualties. Joab did not know exactly what the king had done, but he assumed that his motive for having Uriah killed involved something underhanded. Just as David used Uriah to cover up his sin with Bathsheba, Joab used him to escape blame for his military blunder.

In the LXX, when David heard the news of Joab's disaster, he did indeed become angry. He began to lecture Joab through the messenger on military tactics. In his speech, he cited the story of Abimelech (Judg. 9:50–57), in which Abimelech and his army were besieging the city of Thebez where the residents had scrambled up a strong tower. When Abimelech approached the tower to set fire to it, a woman inside the tower dropped a heavy grinding stone on his head. As he lay dying, Abimelech asked his servant to finish him off with the sword so that it would not be said, to his shame, that a woman had killed him.

David cited this story as a classic lesson of warfare—don't go too close to the wall of a city you are besieging. The irony of David's citation of this story is that Abimelech's attempt to cover up the way he died clearly failed. It was common knowledge that he had been killed by a woman. And David's effort at covering up his own crime would not work any better.

The time frame for all of these events can only be estimated. It would take at least a month for Bathsheba to determine that she was pregnant. Uriah spent three days in David's palace. We are not told how long it took for David to come up with the plan to send for him or how long it was until Uriah was killed. Bathsheba's mourning period for him (11:26–27) was probably a week, though it could have been as long as a month. All in all, the story seems to envision a two- or three-month period from the time of David's adultery with Bathsheba to the day of their marriage. When she gave birth only six months or so later, the rumors must have run rampant. The palace servants knew that Uriah had not gone home during his visit to Jerusalem. David's adultery was thus widely known and his complicity in Uriah's death widely suspected. In short, David did not succeed in covering up anything. By the time the prophet Nathan came to David, the crime was probably common knowledge.

Nathan pretended that the reason for his visit was to present a legal case before the king (2 Sam. 12:1–4), who was the "supreme court" of ancient Israel. The case was a fictional one; it was actually a parable. Of course, David did not know that, though the absence of concrete details is a hint that the story was invented. Neither the characters nor their city are named. It was designed to teach him a lesson by getting him to pronounce judgment on himself.[2] The text says a poor man had a lamb that was like a daughter to him. A wealthy neighbor stole the lamb and butchered it to serve to a guest. David's judgment was heated: "The man who did this is a scoundrel.[3] He shall repay the lamb sevenfold[4] because he did this and because he had no compassion"[5] (2 Sam. 12:5–6).

Nathan's reply (12:7a) was curt: "You are the man." David had pronounced himself guilty. But he did not realize he was judging his own case
until Nathan elaborated by specifying the nature of David's offense and
relating it to the parable.[6] Verse 8, in particular, points out that David was
like the rich man in that Yahweh had given him his master's (i.e., Saul's)
house and wives along with the house of Israel and Judah. The words
"house" (*bêt*) and "daughter" (*bat*) are very similar in Hebrew and have likely
been confused in the transmission of this verse. The point of Nathan's parable is clearer if one reads "daughter(s)" for "house" in both instances in v. 8:
"I gave you your master's *daughter* and your master's wives into your embrace,
and I gave you the *daughters* of Israel and Judah, and if they had been too few,
I would have added as many more." The daughter of David's master was
Michal, and the mention of his master's wives refers to the harem, perhaps
specifically to Ahinoam. Nathan's parable becomes an allegory. Just as the
rich man had many sheep, so David had many women. But like the rich man,
David was unsatisfied and stole what belonged to his neighbor.

These verses go on to connect David's adultery and murder with Absalom's revolt. Verse 11 continues the theme of taking wives. "I will take your
wives in your sight and will give them to your neighbor who will lie with
your wives in the sight of this very sun." The threat here is not to David's
wives. Nor is it merely a matter of shaming him. It plays once again on the
notion that to sleep with a member of the harem was to lay claim to the
throne itself. David's neighbor could lie with David's wives in full sunlight
only if David were deposed. These words threatened nothing less than
David's removal as king, which occurred in Absalom's revolt. David's
"neighbor" turns out to be his own son!

Other statements in 12:7b–12 allude to events in chapters 13–20: "the
sword will not depart from your house" (12:10), "I will raise up trouble
against you from within your own house" (12:11). While these verses attest
an awareness of the Absalom story on the part of the author of the
Bathsheba story, the converse is not true. That is, there is no allusion to
David's adultery with Bathsheba in the account of Absalom's revolt. This is
another indication that 2 Samuel 11–12 were added later.[7]

David's sin is a double crime involving both adultery and murder. His
punishment is also a double one. It includes not only his loss of the throne
but also the death of his newborn child, the product of the adultery. A
death was necessary because David was guilty of shedding innocent blood;

this could only be atoned for by the life of another. Since Yahweh had decided not to kill David, his guilt was transferred to his newborn son. The baby's life substituted for his father's.

Some scholars believe that Solomon was the real offspring of the adulterous union between David and Bathsheba.[8] To protect him from the stigma attached to such an origin, the story of the death of his older brother was invented. The problem with this scenario is that Solomon's birth is only an afterthought to the story (12:24–25). Its reference to Solomon as Yahweh's beloved (the meaning of the name Jedidiah) hints that he will be David's successor. This is yet another indication that the entire story in chapters 11–12 is secondary. Outside of this passage it is not clear until 1 Kings 1 who will take David's place on the throne. No late editor would take such an interest in protecting Solomon at David's expense. So, it is unlikely that there was an earlier version of this story in which Solomon was the bastard child.

Absalom's Revolt

The narrative in 2 Samuel 13–19 offers its own set of causes behind Absalom's revolt, apart from both the historical factors mentioned at the beginning of the chapter and the Bathsheba affair. The event that sparked the conflict between David and Absalom was the rape of Tamar. But the conflict that the Bible describes was also grounded in the personalities of David and his two sons, Amnon and Absalom. The familial relationships between the main characters can be illustrated as follows:

David

by Ahinoam	by Maacah
Amnon	Absalom
	Tamar

Absalom and Tamar had the same mother; Amnon was their half-brother. Amnon was David's firstborn son and therefore the crown prince. Absalom was David's third son, following Chileab, according to 2 Sam. 3:2–5. Nothing more is said in the Bible about the second son. Even his name is uncertain.[9] He probably died in childhood. This means that Absalom was next in line after Amnon as David's successor.

The Story of Absalom's Revolt

13:1–22	Amnon rapes Tamar
13:23–39	Absalom kills Amnon and flees
14:1–24	Absalom is allowed to return to Jerusalem through the agency of Joab and the "wise woman" of Tekoa
14:25–27	Absalom's beauty and his daughter, Tamar
14:28–33	Absalom readmitted into David's presence
15:1–6	Absalom "steals the hearts" of the people of Israel
15:7–12	Absalom begins the revolt from Hebron
15:13–16:14	David flees Jerusalem
16:15–23	Absalom enters Jerusalem
17:1–14	Absalom rejects Ahithophel's advice for Hushai's
17:15–22	Hushai warns David through the sons of Abiathar and Zadok
17:23	Ahithophel's suicide
17:24–29	David arrives in Mahanaim
18:1–17	Absalom's defeat and death

In 2 Samuel as it now exists, the troubles in David's family are his own fault because of his adultery with Bathsheba and attempted murder of Uriah. But if the Bathsheba story is set aside as a later addition, the account of Absalom's revolt appears in quite a different light. The apologetic intent of the original author comes through. This author sought to evoke sympathy for David by portraying him as a loving father who was victimized by his rebellious son. Throughout the narrative David is portrayed as a gentle man, perhaps too gentle and loving for his own good. He is literally tender to a fault. The blame for the disasters that occur in his reign falls first upon his evil sons, Amnon and Absalom, who take advantage of his gentle nature. It also falls upon Joab and the "sons of Zeruiah," whose harsh and violent nature contrasts with David's gentleness. David's refrain in this section repeatedly distances him from their deeds (16:10; 19:22): "What have I to do with you, you sons of Zeruiah?"

This apologetic portrayal of David begins with Amnon's rape of Tamar (2 Sam. 13:1–19). David does not, as is sometimes alleged, ignore the crime. He is furious at Amnon. It is just that he loves his firstborn son so deeply he cannot bring himself to punish him. "When King David heard of all these things, he became very angry, but he would not punish his son Amnon, because he loved him, for he was his firstborn" (2 Sam. 13:21, NRSV).[10] Later, when David learns of Amnon's murder, his outpouring of grief (13:36) is also meant to show the great affection he had for his son.

Absalom held a grudge against Amnon for two years. Then when everyone else seemed to have forgotten Amnon's crime, Absalom lured him to a party (actually a drinking bout) and had him killed. Absalom had also invited David, but David declined to go. The writer is at pains to show that David was not present at Amnon's murder and that Absalom was acting alone, without David's knowledge or consent. We will consider this in more detail momentarily.

It took David three years to get over Amnon's death—another sign of how much he loved him. Only then did he permit Absalom, who had fled to his grandfather's kingdom of Geshur, to return to Jerusalem (13:38–39). The writer's point here has often been misunderstood because of mistranslation in v. 39. It is usually translated along the lines of the NRSV: "the heart of the king went out, yearning for Absalom." This is taken to show David's continuing affection for his son and longing for his return. But if this was the case, why did Joab have to concoct the ruse in chapter 14 to convince David to permit Absalom to return? And why even then did David refuse to allow Absalom into his presence? The verse is better read "the spirit of the king was spent for going out against Absalom."[11] In other words, the writer claims that David was so angry with Absalom for killing Amnon that he tried for three years to capture him. Only then did his anger abate sufficiently to consider allowing Absalom to return home. David was gentle but not unjust; he did not intend to permit even his own son to get away with murder.

Even after three years it was Joab, not David, who was responsible for bringing Absalom back (2 Samuel 14). Joab thought he was acting in the best interests of king and country. He perceived that David's mind was on Absalom—yet one more sign of the loving father. Joab devised a ruse to be played out by the "wise woman" from Tekoa. She posed as a woman with two sons, one of whom had killed the other. The rest of her clan, she said, wanted to execute her remaining son in retribution for his crime, and she had come to the king to beg for his life. This was a setup, another fictional case like Nathan's, aimed at getting David to judge himself without knowing it. The woman's goal was to induce David to take an oath that her son's life would be protected despite his crime.[12] She could then apply that judgment to David's case with his own sons and compel him to allow Absalom to return.

Oddly, the woman's story is not an exact parallel to David's situation with Absalom, but differs in one crucial respect. The entire basis of her petition is that she would be left childless if her second son were executed for murder. This is certainly not the case with David, who had many more sons after Absalom. This oddity does not detract from the apologetic function of the story. The writer's point, despite the imperfect parallelism of the woman's story, is that the ruse succeeded. David swore, "As Yahweh lives not one of your son's hairs will fall to the ground" (14:11). The two cases were enough alike that David was compelled by his oath to allow Absalom's return. In this way, David's fairness as a judge and his desire for justice remain intact while Absalom comes back. The oath finds an ironic fulfillment in Absalom's death suspended above the ground (14:26; 18:9–15).[13]

Restoration to David's presence followed two years later when Absalom compelled Joab to intercede for him again (14:28–33). Here we have an insight into Absalom's character, at least as David's apologist portrayed him. He was patient and calculating. He had plotted revenge against Amnon for two years. But when his patience ran out, he was also a man of extreme acts. He had now been banned from the king's presence for a total of five years. He needed Joab's help to be restored. Joab had no interest in helping Absalom further and ignored his requests. So finally Absalom burned Joab's fields just to get his attention (2 Sam. 14:30). The deed hints at Absalom's arrogance and spoiled nature. And it provides a personal motive for Joab to dispatch him at the end of his revolt.

Permitting the prince to return was a big mistake in the long run. In the writer's perspective, it let a moral wrong go unpunished and left "innocent" blood unrequited. But again the writer's concern was to show both that David was not primarily responsible for this error and that even if he erred it was on the side of compassion and tenderheartedness, not of the violence of which he was accused.

Absalom exploited David's gentleness to his advantage. His use of a chariot and runners was an overt claim of kingship. It was the same thing Adonijah would later do when he declared himself king: "Adonijah son of Haggith exalted himself saying, 'I will be king.' So he prepared a chariot and horsemen for himself and fifty runners to go before him" (1 Kings 1:5).

Absalom waged a campaign against David, attacking him as uncaring and unjust. He succeeded in "stealing the hearts" of the people of Israel (2 Sam. 15:6). Yet David did not reprimand him. As with Amnon, he loved Absalom too much. The result was that Absalom succeeded in overthrowing him and driving him out of Jerusalem.

David's meekness was apparent as he fled before his son. He was not vengeful or retaliatory but trusted his fate to Yahweh (15:25–26). He went forward in humility with his head and his feet bared, weeping. When he was ridiculed by Shimei, he resisted the impulse of Abishai, one of the harsh sons of Zeruiah, to kill him. Instead, he trusted Yahweh to deal with his suffering (16:5–14). Nevertheless, the ten concubines he left behind (15:16) were a clear sign that David had not abandoned his claim to the throne.[14]

Most important, despite all that Absalom had done against him, David explicitly ordered his army not to harm his son (18:5). It was Joab, another son of Zeruiah, acting independently and against orders, who was responsible for the prince's death (18:9–15). David was heartbroken at the news. His bitter mourning was another illustration of his tender nature (19:1–5). Only Joab's harsh rebuke and review of the situation caused the king to quit his mourning, though certainly not his sorrow (19:6–9). And David was no less gentle in victory than in defeat. Again counter to the wishes of Abishai, he accepted the apology of Shimei (19:19–24). He also took Meribbaal back even though he believed Ziba's accusation enough to let him keep part of Meribbaal's property (19:25–31).

A Historical Assessment

While the outline of the Absalom story may be basically historical, the stress on David's gentleness is apologetic. It was designed to counter charges that he maintained ruthless control over his kingdom even to the point of killing his own sons. Violent deeds are consistently blamed on the "sons of Zeruiah," who are just too rough for gentle David. A modern historian evaluating these stories will doubt that a man with David's political savvy and longevity was quite so gentle with his enemies as the writer describes. Even 1 Samuel portrays him as a man who annihilated entire cities to keep his activities from being reported to the Philistines. The historical David was probably a great deal more like the sons of Zeruiah than he was different from them.

The writer makes a special point of noting that Absalom invited David to the festival where Amnon was killed (2 Sam. 13:24–25). Absalom even pressed David trying to persuade him to come. But in the end David refused. Why should Absalom be so intent on inviting David? Historically, this makes no sense. Security would only be tighter with David present. Some have suggested that Absalom planned to kill David as well. But the story does not indicate that Absalom had begun to think about revolting against his father. He had not yet built the necessary power base for a revolt. The reason is literary or apologetic rather than historical. "It may be that David was later suspected of complicity in the murder of Aminon. The narrator seems to be exerting himself to show that the king was in no way implicated."[15] The writer wants to make it abundantly clear that Amnon's death was Absalom's doing alone.

This defense was similar to the one used in previous cases, such as the death of Saul and the murder of Abner. As in the case of Joab, Absalom's motive is presented as a personal desire for revenge. David was completely unaware of Absalom's actions, as he had been of Joab's. As with Saul, David was not present when Amnon was killed. And as he had done with both Saul and Abner, David exhibited extreme sorrow at the news of Amnon's passing.

Here again, we suspect that the charge the writer defends against was true. That is, David likely was a party to Amnon's assassination. This conclusion is further supported by one of the details of the story. The claim that Absalom took refuge from David for three years in Geshur (2 Sam. 13:37–39) is curious. David had a treaty with Talmai, king of Geshur. The treaty had been sealed by marriage to Maacah, Absalom's mother. Thus, Talmai was Absalom's grandfather. David was presumably the stronger party in the treaty relationship. So why did he not compel Talmai to return Absalom from Geshur? If we are correct that David was involved in the conspiracy against Amnon, we may assume that he sent Absalom to Geshur for safekeeping and for appearances' sake. He had no real intention of punishing Absalom. Again, as with Joab, David cursed and threatened Absalom but never punished him for his crime. After three years, when the furor over Amnon's murder had died down, David could send for Absalom. The story about the wise woman from Tekoa tells us that David was compelled to accept Absalom back. As we have seen, it is an apologetic invention.

David may have sought Amnon's life simply because he had raped Tamar. But the fact that Amnon was David's oldest son (2 Sam. 3:2) suggests another reason. David likely perceived him as a threat to his own rule—all the more so since Amnon's mother was Ahinoam, who may once have been Saul's wife. Thus, "[Amnon's] removal eliminate[d] the last vestiges of Saul's legacy from the succession."[16]

The reality of these fears was borne out in Absalom. Absalom had inherited his father's charm and craftiness, and he wielded them every bit as skillfully. In fact, Absalom followed in his father's footsteps at several stages of his revolt. For two years after his return to Jerusalem, Absalom observed the national discontent with David that we described earlier. Then he began turning it to his advantage. His appeal to those unhappy with the status quo, intimating that things would be better under him, is reminiscent of David's attraction of the discontented under Saul (1 Sam. 22:2) and the promises that he made to them (22:7). Absalom's use of a chariot and runners was a blatant declaration that he was vying for kingship (2 Sam. 15:1; cf. 1 Kings 1:5).

David's inaction in the face of Absalom's activities is difficult to believe. The David we have come to know would never have let Absalom get away with such an obvious conspiracy. This picture is part of the presentation of him as meek and gentle. It is more likely that Absalom's plot was secret and that the announcement that he had "stolen the hearts of the people of Israel" (2 Sam. 15:13) caught David by surprise. It was an illustration of how out of touch with his people David had become.

Absalom announced his kingship in Hebron, where he had gone ostensibly to fulfill a vow to Yahweh. The choice of Hebron was deliberate and highly symbolic. It was in Hebron that David had first been made king. In fact, according to 2 Samuel, he had been crowned there twice—once as king over Judah and again as king over all Israel. So Absalom was once more imitating his father. David's move from Hebron was a sore point with the people of Judah. So Absalom exploited Hebron's standing as a center for the worship of Yahweh for his own political ends. But Absalom's revolt was not limited to the heart of Judah. Second Samuel 15:10 indicates that Absalom had support "throughout all the tribes of Israel." The revolt gathered more and more strength until Absalom was able to depose David and drive him out of Jerusalem (15:12).

Despite the general popularity of Absalom's revolt, most of David's court remained loyal to him. The most important exception was the renowned advisor Ahithophel. The account in 2 Samuel does not explain why Ahithophel turned against David and went over to Absalom's side. He may have borne a personal grudge against David because of the Bathsheba affair. Bathsheba was the daughter of Eliam (2 Sam. 11:5), and Ahithophel had a son named Eliam, who was among David's best warriors (2 Sam. 15:12; 23:34). If these two Eliams were the same person, which is likely since both passages refer to Ahithophel as "the Gilonite," then Bathsheba was Ahithophel's granddaughter. Assuming the order of events in 2 Samuel, Ahithophel may have acted against David as revenge for Uriah's death and the humiliation of Bathsheba. Moreover, Ahithophel's hometown, Giloh, was close to Hebron. He may have believed that David had betrayed his native tribe and the traditions of the Calebites when he moved the political and religious capital from Hebron to Jerusalem. He may have hoped that Absalom would restore Hebron's prominence.

Whatever Ahithophel's motive, the story makes it clear that Absalom would have done well to follow his advice. Ahithophel wanted to lead an immediate attack against David. When Absalom rejected this counsel and chose instead to follow Hushai's recommendation to wait until Absalom himself could lead a larger force, it was the turning point of the revolt. Hushai was a plant from David (17:1–23). His very words to Absalom, as the writer reports them, reflect his duplicity: "Long live the king! Long live the king! . . . the one whom Yahweh and this people and every person in Israel have chosen, his I will be and with him I will stay" (2 Sam. 16:18). It is David whom Hushai still regards as the king chosen by Yahweh and the people. Absalom is so egocentric that he does not perceive Hushai's true meaning. Hushai continues in v. 19: "Again, whom should I serve if not his son? As I served your father, so I will serve you." These words are also ambiguous. What Hushai is really saying is: "Whom should I serve?—not his son. I will continue to serve your father by (pretending that I am) serving you."

Ahithophel recognized the need to pursue David immediately while he was at his weakest. But Hushai was trying to buy time for David. He succeeded, though perhaps at the cost of his life. Hushai is never mentioned again; it is likely that Absalom eventually uncovered his duplicity and had him executed.

The delay that Hushai secured for David allowed him time to prepare for Absalom's attack. It also afforded him the chance to choose the battle site. The direction in which he fled is significant.[17] He did not go north into Israel or south into Judah, because Absalom had taken advantage of the discontent with David in both. He could have fled west to the Philistines as he had from Saul. But the Philistines were weaker than in Saul's day and might not have been able to protect him. Besides, this revolt was largely David's own doing. He would not likely have received the refuge and help he needed among the Philistines. Like Ishbaal before him, David fled east, across the Jordan to Mahanaim. There, he received aid from several loyal subjects and treaty partners, including Saul's old enemy Nahash, king of the Ammonites (18:27–29; compare 1 Sam. 10:27b–11:15). Once in Mahanaim, David waited for Absalom to come to him, and he used the rugged terrain and thick forest around Mahanaim to neutralize Absalom's larger numbers (2 Samuel 18).

Absalom himself was killed in the battle. The story of his death has a familiar ring to it. The narrative strives to distance David from Absalom's end and even to evoke sympathy for David at the loss of his son. It makes Joab responsible—in direct violation of David's explicit order not to harm Absalom (18:5). David became distraught when he learned of his son's fate and mourned profusely (19:1–5). The device of pinning violent deeds on Joab and illustrating David's innocence by his lamentation is one we have seen before in 2 Samuel. The account of Abner's death is again the most similar. But there are also parallels in the death reports of Saul and Ishbaal. Son or not, Absalom posed a serious threat to David's sovereignty and the unity of the kingdom. If David had a hand in Amnon's assassination because he suspected him of treason, he surely had Absalom killed for rebellion. Support for this conclusion is again found in the fact that the narrative reports no effort by David to punish Joab for dispatching Absalom. Joab was probably following orders, not disobeying them.

Sheba's Revolt

David succeeded in putting down Absalom's revolt, but he did not deal with the root causes that had led to it. This is evident from his parade back to Jerusalem after Absalom's defeat (2 Samuel 19). His return revisited the encounters with Shimei and Ziba that had taken place when he fled. The writer has used David's leniency with Shimei to highlight again the king's gentleness. Citing the joyfulness of occasion, David refused Abishai's second offer to execute Shimei. But the real reason for the pardon probably had more to do with the one thousand Benjaminites accompanying Shimei (19:18) than with any spirit of clemency on David's part. The resentment toward David on the part of Saul's family and tribe continued.

Even the lame Meribbaal, Saul's one remaining grandson, had not given up hope of ruling. His servant, Ziba, had come to David as he fled Jerusalem (16:1–4) claiming that Meribbaal had stayed behind in hopes of recovering Saul's kingdom for himself. In response, David awarded all of the land belonging to Saul's family to Ziba. Now, as David returned victorious, Meribbaal met him denying Ziba's allegation and lodging the counterclaim that Ziba had refused to help him ride out with David (19:24–30). David spared Meribbaal but restored only half of his property, leaving the rest to Ziba. His handling of this matter exemplified the autocracy that many of his subjects apparently found offensive. The land in question was the heritage of the household of Saul that was never supposed to leave his line. David had no right to confiscate it or parcel it out to someone else. This was a flagrant breach of one of the oldest and most revered traditions in Israel. Such acts of tyranny had brought success to Absalom's revolt and were another source of continuing resentment against David and his dynasty.

The sectional division that persisted in David's kingdom is evident in the dispute in 19:41–43 between Israel and Judah over which of them would be the first to welcome David back. The speed with which the dispute became acrimonious indicates the kind of nepotism and favoritism that David's subjects had come to expect from him. David's own bias in favor of his tribe is clear not only from his message to the elders of Judah (19:11–13) but also in the fact that Sheba tried to pit Benjamin and Israel against Judah.

> We have no portion in David,
> no share in the son of Jesse!
> Every man to his tents O Israel (2 Sam. 20:1)

This cry is echoed in 1 Kings 12:16 in the account of the secession of the northern tribes away from Rehoboam. Thus, after Absalom's revolt David was still faced with the continuing problem of appeasing both Israel and Judah and trying to hold them together in a single nation.

Sheba's revolt (2 Samuel 20) was smaller and less serious than Absalom's. Sheba appears to have been more or less a renegade rebel in search of an army. Still, David took no chances. He took Sheba's appeal to the Israelites as a threat to the fabric of the kingdom he had built. So he quickly ordered his forces to pursue Sheba and put down his rebellion.

According to 2 Sam. 20:4, Amasa was now David's army commander. We are not told when the appointment was made or why. Indeed the appointment itself is historically dubious. The last time we saw Amasa he was commanding Absalom's army (17:25). Why would David appoint the enemy he had just defeated as commander of his troops? The account of Amasa's murder (20:1–13) bears a striking resemblance to that of Abner's death (2 Samuel 3). In fact, the Amasa story may have been patterned after the one about Abner. In each case, David made an undisclosed arrangement with the opposing commander. Then Joab assassinated the commander without David's knowledge. Even Joab's technique was similar in both cases. He greeted his enemy with one hand and stabbed him in the belly with the other. The pattern is quite familiar by now. One of the "sons of Zeruiah," usually Joab, murders someone who is a political threat to David. The text deflects blame from David, explaining that he knew nothing of the plot and showing that he was not present when the killing took place. But as before, we ask who stood to benefit, and the answer is David. David had Amasa executed as he had done before to Nabal, Saul, Abner, Ishbaal, Amnon, and Absalom.

David had plenty of reasons for wanting to get rid of Amasa. The most obvious one was to punish him for rebelling. Amasa would have been a future danger to David because of his influence in the army. But another reason suggests itself in 2 Sam. 17:25. There we learn that Amasa was Abigail's son by Ithra or Jether (1 Chron. 2:17), the man we have tentatively identified as "Nabal" in 1 Samuel 25. This would explain both Amasa's joining the revolt in the first place and his continuing threat to David. He no doubt saw David as the man responsible for his father's death, the man who had usurped his father's place as Calebite chieftain before he had usurped Saul's kingship. If this was so, David had to kill Amasa before Amasa killed him.

Sheba's small rebellion did not last long. It was quickly and brutally quashed, and he was beheaded at Abel Beth-Maacah. The name of this city could mean "the mourning of the house of Maacah," which is very apropos following the death of Absalom, whose mother was Maacah. This sort of literary note coupled with the apology for Amasa's assassination makes the critical reader wonder how much history really lies behind the story of Sheba's revolt. But there is no reason to doubt that, following the removal of his enemies, Amnon, Absalom, Amasa, and Sheba, the kingdom was once again firmly in David's hands.

Summary

The account of Absalom's and Sheba's revolts in 2 Samuel 13–20 is also apologetic for David. It casts David as unaware of and uninvolved in the deaths of Amnon, Absalom, and Amasa. The deaths of these men, as recounted in 2 Samuel, are strikingly similar to those of David's earlier political foes. Each represented a threat to David. Amnon and Absalom were David's oldest surviving sons. Each had his eye on his father's throne. Absalom even seized it for a time. Amasa was the heir to the Calebite chieftaincy that David had usurped years before. He sought to avenge his father's death and to recover his own heritage.

The text claims innocence for David in these deaths. Amnon was assassinated by Absalom in a personal vendetta. Absalom and Amasa were both killed by Joab. David greatly lamented the deaths of his sons, as he had the deaths of Saul, Jonathan, and Abner. But he did not punish either Absalom or Joab. In all three cases, the writer is at pains to assert that David was elsewhere when the slayings occurred. Throughout the narrative he is consistently presented as a gentle man who could not bear to discipline his sons, much less have them killed. The blame for these deaths is laid at the feet of David's own sons and of the sons of Zeruiah, especially Joab. Amnon and Absalom are spoiled and rebellious; the sons of Zeruiah, violent, coarse, and willful. If anything, the writer says, David was too soft, and others took advantage of him.

The pervasively apologetic flavor of this material leads us to doubt its portrait of David. There are also peculiarities in the narrative—things that seem unrealistic or do not quite make sense in the story: Absalom's insistence that David attend the party at which Amnon was killed, the unsuitability of the woman's story about her two sons in chapter 14, and the sudden appearance of Amasa at the head of David's army. These peculiarities serve as clues to the apologetic nature of the account and sometimes about what may have really happened.

The apologetic gloss on Absalom's revolt has been significantly compromised by the insertion of the Bathsheba story in 2 Samuel 11–12. It is not apologetic and could be based in history. It is like a straightforward version of the Abigail and Nabal story. Because of its addition David's problems with his sons now appear as punishments from Yahweh, and his gentleness like weakness brought on by guilt.

The long and short of David's reign historically is that he retained power the same way he got it in the first place—by getting rid of any and all rivals—including his own sons. In the next and final chapter we will explore the ironic end of David's reign, in which he plays a role in someone else's apology.

9

Poetic Justice

The Last Days of King David

But it is one thing to walk naked before the Lord; another to strip oneself in the sight of men. . . . Almost all men would rather confess to wrongdoing than to weakness, and in this respect at least, I am no different from the common run. There may be grandeur in wrongdoing; it is at least an act, an expression of the will, and often, the will to power, that food which restores vitality, and quickens the appetite it feeds on. But weakness is an abnegation of the will; weakness is always to be despised. And that is what I must confess to.

—Allan Massie, *King David*

Of all the novels written about David, the most entertaining is Joseph Heller's 1984 *God Knows*. It is certainly the most raucous and irreverent. Heller has David write a retrospective on his life that is also aware of developments in art, politics, and fashion in the three thousand years since. The book is full of insights into both the life and story of David and modern Jewish life. It is at once hilarious and touching. Though impotent and on his deathbed, David still desires Bathsheba. He is a man of few scruples and no regrets for anything he has done. In fact, he is angry with God over the loss of the child produced in his adultery with Bathsheba.

In the opening chapter, David compares his story to the stories of other biblical characters, showing why his is the best. The following quotation sets the theme for the book.

I've got all those wars and conquests and rebellions and chases to talk about. I built an empire the size of Maine, and I led the people of Israel out of the Bronze Age and into the Iron Age. I've got a love story and a sex story, with the same woman no less, and both are great, and I've got this ongoing, open-ended Mexican standoff with God, even though He might now be dead. Whether God is dead or not hardly matters, for we would use Him no differently anyway. He owes me an apology, but God won't budge so I won't budge. I have my faults, God knows, and I may even be among the first to admit them, but to this very day I know in my bones that I'm a much better person than He is.[1]

In this chapter, we will examine the biblical account of David's last days, which Heller used as the premise for his novel. Our particular interest is in what we can learn from 1 Kings 1–2 about the end of David's life and the transition from his reign to Solomon's.

The Irony of Apology

After the account of Sheba's revolt in 2 Samuel 20 comes a collection of miscellaneous materials connected with David. These are not in chronological order. Our next real glimpse of David is as an old man on his deathbed in 1 Kings 1–2. The book of Kings is a continuation of the same large work as the book of Samuel. But the narrative obviously skips over a sizable portion of David's reign. There is no explanation as to what happened during that time, why it was skipped over, or even how long it was. If we take literally the biblical report that David's reign lasted forty years, that would indicate that he died at seventy (2 Sam. 5:4). But as we said before, this looks suspiciously like the round number for a generation. David's reign and life could have been significantly shorter.

The first two chapters of 1 Kings are once more apologetic, but the subject of the apology has changed. It is no longer David but Solomon who is defended. These two chapters rather transparently attempt to justify the succession of Solomon to David's throne and the bloodbath that ensued. David plays a very significant role in this story. Thus, in analyzing this narrative for historical information, we may use the same techniques as we did for the apology of David. We will try to determine what the true motives behind Solomon's actions are likely to have been. We will also look at the part David plays in the apology for Solomon and suggest what his actual role was.

The tale set forth in these two chapters is remarkably candid. It is filled with palace intrigue and blatant deceit. The apology is paper thin and obvious.[2] The scene begins with a description of David in his last days. He is feeble of body and of mind. He cannot keep warm though his servants cover him with clothing (1 Kings 1:1). The remedy his servants come up with is unique. They find a beautiful young virgin, Abishag, to "attend" him by lying (naked) next to him in order to warm him. The technique is unusual, and indeed, there is more going on here than meets the reader's eye. The intent of the servants was not really to keep the old king warm but to test his virility. Verse 4 notes that "the king did not know her." This is an idiom for sexual intercourse. As the NRSV translates it, "the king did not know her sexually."

The test proved that the king was impotent. This was intolerable. The king was the symbol of his nation, its strength and fertility. Israel simply could not have an impotent king. In short, it was time to choose a replacement for David. The irony of this episode is inescapable. The king who had fathered so many children and once allowed his lust to control him now found himself impotent. The powerful sovereign who had built and directed a nation now was being tested and manipulated by his servants. And this was just the beginning of the manipulation of David.

Abishag's true function as a test of David's potency is made clear in v. 5. At the news that David had failed the test, Adonijah declared himself king. He may even have been the one who engineered the Abishag test in the first place. As the next in line behind Absalom, he was David's oldest surviving son (2 Sam. 3:3), the crown prince and by all rights the heir to the throne. Most of David's subjects made this assumption. Indeed, in his speech to Bathsheba, Adonijah says, "You know that the kingdom was mine, and that all Israel expected me to reign" (1 Kings 2:15). She does not challenge this statement. The apology is necessary because that is not what happened. Solomon's accession needs explaining.

Adonijah had the support of some important members of David's court, including Joab and Abiathar (1:7). But there was also a powerful element at court who favored Solomon over Adonijah: Zadok, Benaiah, and Nathan, among others (1:8). The Solomon supporters were better organized and caught Adonijah off-guard by staging what amounted to a coup d'etat.

First Kings 1:11–48 reports how Nathan the prophet, in league with Bathsheba, manipulated David into designating Solomon as his successor. The alliance of Nathan and Bathsheba is surprising in light of their roles in the affair of 2 Samuel 11–12 and suggests that the two stories have different origins. Bathsheba and Nathan "remind" David of a promise to Bathsheba that Solomon would sit on his throne. Such a promise would have been extraordinary since Solomon was not David's oldest son. It should have been widely known and remembered. But there is no other record of this promise in Samuel or Kings. It is clear that the promise was made after the fact. Perhaps Nathan and Bathsheba really did meet with David. If so, they took advantage of his senility to manufacture a promise that he would not remember. More likely, though, the entire story is a fiction. The individuals whom David supposedly summoned and commanded to anoint Solomon (1:32) were all listed earlier as Solomon's supporters. The conspirators simply took over the government. David had nothing to do with it and probably no idea what was going on.

It is important to the apology that David is depicted as still mentally sound though physically frail. Otherwise, his designation of Solomon would be invalid. Thus, he is still in charge (1:32–37). Bathsheba and Nathan address him as "my lord, the king." David is still lucid. However, it is not hard to see below the surface of this apologetic story a David who has lost his mental powers as well as his physical ones. This is likely the true picture of David at the end—senile and flaccid, a pawn in the struggle among his sons and courtiers for power. It seems poetically just that the tyrant who ruled with an iron fist should have completely lost control. The king whose apologetic propaganda remains the primary source of information about him found himself impotent except as the tool for his successor's apology.

David's usefulness for Solomon's apology did not end with the latter's accession. David's final charge to Solomon in 2:1–9 is the clearest instance of apology for Solomon in 1 Kings 1–2. Included in this charge are David's orders to execute Joab (2:5–6) and Shimei (2:8–9). Even in this attempt to portray David positively, his last thought is for vengeance.

There are many reasons to doubt that David really gave these orders. It makes no sense for him to have waited over thirty years to punish Joab for

killing Abner and another several years to punish his assassination of
Amasa. Punishment of this nature would be appropriate only shortly after
the offense. The real reason for Joab's execution was that he had supported
Solomon's rival, Adonijah, for king. Joab was much too wily and powerful an
adversary for Solomon to leave alive. The story in 1 Kings 2 goes on to relate
the banishment of Abiathar and the execution of Adonijah. Eventually,
Adonijah and all his prominent supporters except Abiathar are killed. Abiathar alone is banished because he is a priest. David's order regarding Joab is
an apologetic invention. It justifies Solomon's execution of Joab on other
than political grounds: he was only carrying out his father's dying wishes.

The situation for Shimei is only slightly different. Shimei was not a supporter of Adonijah but a supporter of Saul. He had cursed and ridiculed
David as he fled from Jerusalem before Absalom (2 Sam. 16:5–14). He
made it clear that he regarded David as a usurper and thought that one of
Saul's descendants, or at least someone from Benjamin, his own tribe,
should reign. He then showed up with a thousand Benjaminites to apolo-
gize as David returned from Absalom's defeat (19:18–23). Abishai wanted
to kill him both times, but David refused.

As with Joab, it makes no sense for David to have waited such a long
time to punish Shimei. Solomon was not concerned about Shimei's insult
to David as much as the following he commanded among the people of
Benjamin. Solomon wanted no rivals and no rebellions. According to the
story, he perceived enough of a threat in Shimei to have him confined to
Jerusalem, away from his native tribe where he might foment trouble. After
two years, Shimei violated Solomon's orders not to leave the city and was
summarily executed.

It is possible that this story is basically historical. That is, Solomon may
have placed Shimei in some sort of confinement, which he violated after a
couple of years. Another possibility is that the story of Shimei's confinement
is fictional and that Solomon simply had him executed for political reasons
shortly after assuming power. The political reason for Solomon's acts is mani-
fest in the statement in 1 Kings 2:46 (cf. 2:12) that with the slaughter of his
rivals, "the kingdom was firmly established in the grasp of Solomon." Again,
therefore, David's order to kill Shimei in 1 Kings 2:8–9 has no basis in history.

Of David's final days, then, we can surmise only that he lived a long life
for his time and that he died of old age. At the end, he was probably both
physically and mentally weak. He became incompetent to rule and had to

be replaced as king before his actual passing. At the end, he had no control over his family or his court and no voice in deciding who would succeed him.

The Greatest Irony

Throughout this book we have seen how apologetic concerns for David have shaped the characterizations of the people who surrounded him. Saul is described as paranoid and inept in a deliberate contrast to David. Jonathan and Michal are portrayed as infatuated with David as a way of explaining his rise to prominence in Saul's house and the irrational nature of Saul's jealousy. Later, Michal's affection turns to disgust, which in turn accounts for why she has no children. Abigail's intelligence and charm match David's and suggest that her first husband, who is her opposite, does not deserve her. The "sons of Zeruiah" are depicted as violent and impulsive because they must bear the blame for the deaths of prominent people whose removal ensured David's acquisition and retention of power.

The one major character who is involved with David but not featured in apologetic material for him is Bathsheba. She appears in three stories: David's adultery (2 Samuel 11–12), the accession of Solomon (1 Kings 1:11–31), and her intercession before Solomon on behalf of Adonijah (1 Kings 2:13–25). The first of these is not apology; the other two are apology for Solomon rather than for David. This situation affords us a unique opportunity for a glimpse at the character of Bathsheba and her importance for the historical David.

If all we knew about Bathsheba was the story of her adultery, she would be virtually a cipher to us. Other than reporting her pregnancy to David (11:5) and naming Solomon (12:24),[3] she says nothing in the story and plays no active part. She is simply the object of David's lust and power. She may even be the victim of rape. However, the two later stories involving Bathsheba force one to read 2 Samuel 11–12 in a different way. And the three stories together yield quite a different impression of her.[4]

In 1 Kings 1 Bathsheba is characterized as the opposite of a victim. Here she is a co-conspirator with Nathan and perhaps others in a plan to place Solomon on the throne. She deceives her husband, the king, invoking both his (fictitious) promise (1:17) and his pity (1:20–21). Her fear is that she will be regarded as an offender if Adonijah succeeds (v. 21). Adonijah's own career demonstrates that to be counted as an offender meant death. Bathsheba's statement is an implicit confession that she has been active in conspiracy for some time and that this is well known. This Bathsheba is far from passive. She is actively, if deceptively, engaged in promoting her son as king. She shows herself to be very shrewd and capable at getting David to do what she wants.

I suggested earlier that this story is a fiction by Solomon's apologist. It seeks to attribute Solomon's succession of David to David's own order rather than to a palace coup. It is not, therefore, historical. It is still remarkable, however, that Bathsheba is given such a crucial role in the conspiracy for Solomon. It was certainly in her own best interests. But we do not expect to find a woman, even the queen mother, credited with such prominence in the transition. Historically, therefore, perhaps Bathsheba did have an active role in promoting her son to follow David as king.

It is this same Bathsheba whom we expect to encounter in the third story about her (1 Kings 2:13–25). This is a strange story. Adonijah wants to marry Abishag and asks Bathsheba to intercede for him in the matter before King Solomon. Bathsheba makes the request, but Solomon perceives it as a ploy by Adonijah to lay claim to the crown and has him executed.

The political implications of Adonijah's request are inescapable and would have been as obvious both to him and to Bathsheba as they were to Solomon. Abishag was a member of the harem. Marrying her would have constituted a claim to the throne. It is hard to believe that Adonijah can have been so stupid as to make such a request. The entire story is again an apologetic invention to justify Solomon's execution of his half-brother.

But why is Bathsheba mentioned? Her involvement is completely unnecessary for the apology. If the writer had described Adonijah making the request himself, in person, it would have had the same effect. Besides, Adonijah could not have chosen a worse mediator. Not only was Bathsheba a fervent advocate of Solomon, but she may also have been jealous of the beautiful young Abishag. This text functions partly as an apology for Bathsheba. She was trying to help Adonijah, though Solomon would have none of it. One suspects that, historically, Bathsheba was really the catalyst for Adonijah's destruction.[5] Her counsel to Solomon was that he rid himself of his rival on the grounds of the pretended charge of conspiracy to revolt (1 Kings 1:23).

The accounts in 2 Samuel 11–12 and 1 Kings 1–2 probably come from different writers. The difference between them is apparent in their portrayals of Nathan. In 2 Samuel 11–12, he is the courageous prophet who forcefully denounces the king for wrongdoing. In 1 Kings 1–2, he is subservient to the king's wishes and is part of the behind-the-scenes plot. We would expect the Nathan of 2 Samuel 11–12 to *tell* David who his successor will be. Instead, in 1 Kings 1–2 he prefers manipulation to direct confrontation. Of the two, 1 Kings 1–2 is more realistic. Its apologetic veneer is thin and allows us to get a fairly good view of the characters. Second Samuel 11–12 is a text written by prophets. The prophet is the hero, the king the villain. Bathsheba is in the role of victim. Since the story is written in favor of prophets and against kings, any involvement Bathsheba may have had was insignificant to the author.

Our characterization of Bathsheba, however, must take account of all the stories about her. If we reread the story of her adultery with her character in 1 Kings 1–2 as background, we see her in an entirely different light. It is not difficult to see in the supposed victim a woman who is just as shrewd and just as much an advocate of her son as in the later episodes. There is, first of all, the fact that she was bathing where the king could see her. He had a couch or bed on his roof and often took naps there. Bathsheba knew when and where he slept. The fact that he saw her bathing was no mere coincidence. It was also no accident that she conceived. The text makes clear that she slept with David at her optimal time for conception. This suggests the possibility that her seduction of David and the conception of his child were planned.[6] They were steps by which she might secure her future and advance herself. It is worth recalling here that marriages at the time were arranged and not made for love. The fact that she was married to Uriah did not mean she had any affection for him.

Bathsheba's scheme worked better than she could have imagined. It landed her in the royal household. Then she started working on her son's future. Consider the name she gave him: Solomon. It means "his replacement."[7] Solomon is no doubt seen to be the replacement for the first son of David and Bathsheba who died as punishment for their sin (2 Sam. 12:24–25). But the name is also pregnant with meaning in other directions. It could be taken as "Uriah's replacement" in a continuation of the attempt to cover up the sin.[8] Then of course, it could also be "David's replacement." In this light it is striking that verse 25 reports that David called the boy Jedidiah ("beloved of Yahweh"), which is itself another hint that this child would replace David. Nevertheless, it was the name Solomon that stuck and is used everywhere else.

The recognition of Bathsheba's role in the story in 2 Samuel 11–12 does not in any way excuse David's actions or minimize his culpability. He abused his power to satisfy his lust. He was the one in charge; the entire event hinged on his actions. What this does do is to enhance Bathsheba's character, to add dimension to her. Bathsheba was a much fuller character than she appears to be on first glance at the narrative. She was very much like Abigail in some respects. More than victims, perhaps not victims at all, they were both intelligent women who used the resources at their disposal to advance themselves. Like David, Bathsheba did what she had to do to get ahead. Her accomplishments were remarkable considering the subordinate role of women in ancient Israelite society.

In the Introduction to this book, I mentioned the recent novel by Torgny Lindgren (*Bathsheba*, 1989). With this glimpse of Bathsheba's character we come full circle in our biography of David. Lindgren attributes the major events of David's reign to Bathsheba's manipulative hand. There may be more to this hypothesis than even he realized. Historically, Bathsheba may have been involved in the conspiracy to seat her son Solomon on the throne after David in place of the rightful heir, Adonijah. David's one-time "victim" took advantage of him at the end of his life for her political purposes. The possibility that David's supposed victim used him and his reign more than he used her provides a highly ironic ending to the life of David.

Conclusion

David's final appearance in the Deuteronomistic History (1 Kings 1–2) is in a piece of apology for Solomon. He is depicted as very old and physically weak, though still mentally acute. He orders that Solomon be designated as his successor. He also charges Solomon to execute Joab for his assassinations of Abner and Amasa and to take vengeance on Shimei.

The historical David was likely senile at the end of his life. The account in 1 Kings 1–2 hints that this was the case. He was manipulated by his courtiers and probably had no idea that Solomon reigned in his place. He certainly did not order the executions of Joab or Shimei. These were undertaken independently by Solomon for his own political reasons.

The great irony at the end of David's life is the discovery of the fuller character of Bathsheba. She does not play a role in the apologetic accounts of David's reign, as do characters like Michal, Jonathan, and Joab, and this gives us a better chance at recovering something of her historical nature. She is credited with having a leading role in the plot to unseat Adonijah in favor of Solomon (1 Kings 1–2). To judge from this text, she was intelligent, industrious, and devoted to her son. It is possible to find the same cleverness operating in 2 Samuel 11–12. So it may be that she was able to maneuver her way into David's court and then to exercise a far greater impact on the course of events during his reign than she is usually given credit for.

IO

Finished Portrait

A Synopsis

David was a brave and aggressive ruler. He combined Judah and Israel under his sway and he made the surrounding peoples largely tributary to Israel. But the spread of Israel's power was almost wholly due to his military power and cruelty. He was loyal to his friends, but ruthless to his foes. He was a liar, deceiver, and traitor. That later tradition should have glorified and magnified him so much notwithstanding his many limitations passes all understanding. These later writers deliberately ignored most of his crimes and faults and focused attention upon his virtues. From that point of view he is presented as a great figure. But his place in the minds of modern men who take into account all the known facts is relatively small.

—J. M. P. Smith, "The Character of David," 1933

An investigation into the David character . . . based upon an analysis of the textual organisation of the story and a close reading of the text shows that, apart from a few positive traits . . . David is pictured as an inefficient, knavish, nepotist, unjust, and rather foolish man.

—F. E. Deist, "David: A Man after God's Own Heart?" 1986

Materials and Tools

I have likened this biography throughout to the task of painting a portrait. The artist begins with pigments. Ours have been the sources of information about David's life, especially the Bible. But the paints are useless without the tools to apply them; brushes and canvas are needed. So for us the question is how to use the Bible to extract biographical information about David.

The story of David, or at least the Court History, was once considered objective history and the first example of history writing in Israel.[1] No serious scholar today takes this view. More recent scholarship, as we have seen, has recognized that political and religious interests have influenced the Bible's account of David. Also, recent literary treatments have revealed the artistry and creativity of the biblical story. Nevertheless, the assumption that David really lived and that the Bible preserves historical information about him is still viable. Recent archaeological discoveries, especially inscriptions containing the name David, add weight to this assumption, even if they are not conclusive.

The strongest argument for the historical basis of the biblical account of David is its apologetic nature, which is widely acknowledged by scholars. The fact that the author felt the need to try to explain the motives behind David's deeds indicates that those deeds were widely believed to have occurred. An author would not invent accusations against David—such as that he once served as a mercenary to the Philistines—just to try to explain them away. The key to historical reconstruction for the life of David, therefore, lies in understanding that the Bible's story is apology.

Apology by definition is not objective but seeks to give a distorted idea of the events of the past and especially of the causes behind them. The fact is we can never know for certain what actually happened in David's lifetime. We can only make an educated guess. Our guess, though, is informed by the recognition that the biblical story is designed to idealize David by justifying his actions. We can replace the authors' explanations of David's motives with others that are more in line with what we know of ancient Middle Eastern rulers and of human nature in general. Our biography of David, therefore, is not an exact recounting of history but is rather, to borrow another scholar's title, a plausible tale.[2]

"A Plausible Tale"

David came from the area of Bethlehem in the central highlands of Judah. His family was an old and prominent one in Judah. He was the youngest son of Jesse, a respected elder of Bethlehem and a wealthy man with significant holdings of land and livestock. Rather than follow in his father's footsteps, however, David struck out on his own—perhaps forced by economic circumstances brought on by a population increase and diminished arable land.

David cultivated a variety of skills for survival. He seems to have been a person of considerable intelligence and charm but was also extremely ambitious and ruthless. He may have come to Saul initially as a musician, charged with driving away evil spirits and bringing good fortune. But he quickly gained renown for his military skill. He may even have joined Saul as a mercenary. He distinguished himself in battle against the Philistines and soon rose to become a commander in Saul's army. His success and personal charm gained him popularity and a loyal following among those he commanded. He may even have cultivated close personal relationships with Saul and his family.

David's success and popularity in the army gave him the power to be a threat to Saul. And he had the ambition to try to usurp the kingship. Saul perceived the threat and moved against him. But this may have been a reaction rather than a first strike. The vigor with which the apology asserts David's innocence against Saul strongly suggests that he was in fact involved in a plot against him. But before Saul could capture him, David escaped, perhaps with inside help.

David fled from Saul to the rugged Judean wilderness, which had long given refuge to outlaws and fugitives. There he became the chief of such a group. Through force of arms he gained control over an expanding area in the Negev and in Judah. His assassination of the Calebite chief "Nabal" and his assumption of the man's wealth and status brought him to the threshold of the kingship of Judah. When the elders of Judah anointed David king, they were merely giving official recognition to the *de facto* control he and his outlaw band were exercising over most of Judah. David combined the tribe or clan of Judah with that of Caleb and perhaps others so as to form the larger domain (later the nation) of Judah.

During the time that he ruled in Hebron, David was a rival chieftain to Saul. David joined forces with the Philistines and eventually succeeded in effecting Saul's downfall. There is reason to suspect that he engineered Saul's death. He then provoked war with Saul's figurehead successor, Ishbaal. The war ended when David made a treaty with Abner that brought the army of Israel over to his side. David then arranged for the assassinations of both Abner and Ishbaal, leaving the elders of Israel no choice but to capitulate to him as their new king.

As king, David sought to consolidate his power by defeating his onetime allies the Philistines, and by destroying Saul's heirs. He kept Meribbaal alive, perhaps out of affection for Jonathan, and because his lameness removed any real threat he may have otherwise posed. Still, David kept even Meribbaal under palace arrest and made sure that neither he nor Michal produced grandchildren to Saul. David also took steps to enhance the unity between Israel and Judah. These included establishing a neutral capital in Jerusalem and giving the ark, Israel's principal religious artifact, a new home there. David gradually adopted the trappings of Middle Eastern monarchy and at the same time expanded his own hegemony to create a small empire in Palestine.

David maintained power in the same way he had attained it in the first place—by removing anyone who was in his way. This included his two oldest sons, Amnon and Absalom, both of whom came to violent ends when they stood to replace their father. And David's power came at a price for his people as well. There was conscription and taxation to support the king's projects, military and domestic. David probably confiscated other lands, as he did those of Meribbaal, in order to reward his supporters. This was a king who *took* what he wanted, as in the story of Bathsheba. The story of Absalom's revolt indicates that there was widespread discontent with David and sectionalism fostered by his unequal treatment of Israel and Judah. As usual, David regained control by military means.

Ironically, at the end of his life David himself became the victim of others' political maneuvering. His own son Solomon used contrived orders from David to launch a coup against the presumed successor, Adonijah, and to get rid of the members of the old regime (Joab, Abiathar) who supported Adonijah. Bathsheba herself may have orchestrated the coup.

A Man After Our Own Hearts

The quotation from Smith at the beginning of this synopsis raises an intriguing question. How is it that a character like David—a Middle Eastern tyrant—came to be such a popular religious hero? As we saw in the

Introduction, the history of interpretation of David is long and complicated. But the simple answer to Smith's question is that the apology
worked. It altered David's historical image by legitimating his deeds. Dtr
enhanced the apologetic material and used it to convey his own theological
principles. (One scholar appropriately warns, "The danger of making
David a hero is the danger of accepting the principle that success proves
the approval of God."[3] But this principle and its converse [that failure or
ruin are signs of divine punishment] are integral to Dtr's theology, though
not shared by all biblical writers [e.g., the writer of Job].) Dtr even made
David the standard of faithfulness by which the kings of Israel and Judah
were judged. Other biblical writers further elaborated this image such that
David became nearly perfect. His major offenses were omitted, as the
Chronicler did with the Bathsheba and Absalom episodes. Alternatively,
David became the model of penitence, as in Psalm 51.

As we noted in our survey of literary images of David, the biblical
authors are not the only ones to find in David the traits that they most
admire. Readers today still exhibit this same tendency. This is a further
answer to Smith's puzzlement about the traditional depiction of David. It
is common for people to recast David in their own image of perfection.

In a sense, this biography is truer to the Bible than the more traditional
images of David that have been formed along the trajectory begun by the
apology. The Bible never denies or downplays David's humanity. Critical
scholars have simply explored what a human being of David's social rank in
the Middle East three thousand years ago would have been like. The image
that I have constructed in this biography is a composite of the results of
those scholarly explorations. We can probably never know the *real* David.
This image is at least a *realistic* likeness of David.

Notes

Introduction

1. Two standard works for overviews of the subjects in Western art are James Hall, *Dictionary of Subjects and Symbols in Art* (New York: Harper & Row, 1974) and Louis Réau, *Iconographie de l'art chrétien* (Paris: Presses Universitaires de France, 1956). For a more detailed survey of David as a subject see Martin O'Kane, "The Biblical King David and His Artistic and Literary Afterlives," *Biblical Interpretation* 6 (1998), pp. 311–47, esp. 325–34.

2. On David in Western literature see Charles A. Huttar and Raymond-Jean Frontain, "David," in *A Dictionary of Biblical Tradition in English Literature*, ed. David Lyle Jeffrey (Grand Rapids, MI: Eerdmans, 1992), pp. 180–85, and Raymond-Jean Frontain and Jan Wojcik (eds.), *The David Myth in Western Literature* (West Lafayette, IN: Purdue University Press, 1980). The latter is a collection of papers from a special session devoted to David at the 1976 meeting of the Modern Language Association.

3. Gene Edward Veith, Jr., "'Wait upon the Lord': David, Hamlet, and the Problem of Revenge," in *The David Myth in Western Literature*, ed. Frontain and Wojcik, pp. 70–83, esp. p. 71. Veith goes on to acknowledge that any influence would have been indirect, since these were all common motifs in Renaissance literature.

4. Abraham Cowley, *The Complete Works in Verse and Prose*, ed. Alexander Grosart, vol. 2 (Hildesheim: Georg Olms, 1969), pp. 45–103.

5. Marcus Walsh and Karina Williamson (eds.), *The Poetical Works of Christopher Smart*, vol. 2, *Religious Poetry 1763–1771* (Oxford: Clarendon Press, 1983), pp. 129–47.

6. Charlotte Porter and Helen A. Clarke (eds.), *Poems of Robert Browning* (New York: Thomas Y. Crowell), pp. 198–207.

7. William Hebel (ed.), *The Works of Michael Drayton*, vol. 3 (Oxford: Basil Blackwell, 1932), pp. 418–39.

8. John C. Shields (ed.), *The Collected Works of Phillis Wheatley* (New York/ Oxford: Oxford University Press, 1988), pp. 31–42.

9. Ann Fairbairn, *Five Smooth Stones* (New York: Crown, 1966).

10. George R. Noyes, *The Poetical Works of Dryden* (Boston: Houghton Mifflin, 1950), pp. 109–22.

11. D. H. Lawrence, *David: A Play* (New York: Alfred A. Knopf, 1926).

12. Allan Massie, *King David* (London: Sceptre, 1995).

13. William Faulkner, *Absalom, Absalom!* (New York: Random House, 1936).

14. Grete Weil, *The Bride Price*, trans. J. Barrett (Boston: David R. Godine, 1991), p. 17.

15. Torgny Lindgren, *Bathsheba*, trans. Tom Geddes (New York: Harper & Row, 1989), p. 19.

16. Unique in this genre is the new book by Richard Phillips, *The Heart of an Executive: Lessons on Leadership from the Life of King David* (New York: Bantam Double-day Dell, 1999), which finds lessons in David for Christian business executives.

17. Some useful older works that are in need of updating are: Juan Bosch, *David: The Biography of a King*, trans. John Marks (New York: Hawthorne, 1966); Jerry M. Landay, *The House of David* (New York: Saturday Review/E. P. Dutton, 1973); and Eugene Maly, *The World of David and Solomon* (Englewood Cliffs, NJ: Prentice Hall, 1966). New from Landay is *David: Power, Lust and Betrayal in Biblical Times* (Berkeley, CA: Seastone, 1998), which is a fictionalized dramatic retelling of the biblical story. Two recent German books come close to this biography: Hans-Martin Gauger, *Davids Aufstieg: Erzählung (David's Rise: A Tale)* (Munich: C. H. Beck, 1993) and Stefan Ark Nitsche, *König David: Gestalt im Umbruch (King David: Figure in Radical Change)* (Zürich: Artemis, 1994). However, neither one fully appreciates the insights biblical scholarship can offer into David's character, and neither is available in English. Finally, the most recent book on David by Marti Steussy, *David* (Columbia: University of South Carolina Press, 1999) is a useful survey of the ways David is portrayed in different parts of the Bible. It does not claim to be biographical or historical.

18. James W. Flanagan, *David's Social Drama. A Hologram of Israel's Early Iron Age*, JSOTSup 73 (Sheffield: Almond, 1988).

Chapter One

1. Christopher Shea, "Debunking Ancient Israel: Erasing History or Facing the Truth?" *The Chronicle of Higher Education* 44, 13 (Nov. 21, 1997), pp. A12–14.

2. P. Kyle McCarter, "The Historical David," *Int* 40 (1986), p. 117.

3. See E. A. Knauf, A. de Pury, and T. Römer, "*BaytDavid ou *BaytDod: Une relecture de la nouvelle inscription de Tel Dan," *BN* 72 (1993), pp. 60–69. Most scholars have now rejected this proposal because of the lack of evidence for a deity named Dod and in light of the fuller context of the inscription, especially as supplied by the additional fragments, as explained below. See Hans M. Barstad, "Dod," in *DDD*, ed. K. van der Toorn, B. Becking, and P. W. van der Horst (Leiden: E. J. Brill, 1995), pp. 493–98, and Hans M. Barstad and Bob Becking, "Does the Stele from Tel–Dan Refer to a Deity Dod?" *BN* 77 (1995), pp. 5–12.

4. Though not everyone believes the three pieces to be from the same inscription, that is the consensus that has emerged, and the flood of discussion about the "house of David" in this inscription ended, for the most part, shortly after the discovery of the second and third fragments. Numerous articles dealing with the inscription may be found in the bibliography.

5. Avraham Biran and Joseph Naveh, "The Tel Dan Inscription: A New Fragment," *IEJ* 45 (1995), p. 13.

6. For general orientation to the Mesha stele, see the article in J. Andrew Dearman (ed.), *Studies in the Mesha Inscription and Moab* (Atlanta: Scholars Press, 1989). On the history of its discovery, see also Neil Asher Silberman, *Digging for God and Country: Exploration in the Holy Land, 1799–1917* (New York: Doubleday, 1982), pp. 100–112.

7. André Lemaire, "'House of David' Restored in Moabite Inscription," *BAR* 20, 3 (May/June 1994), p. 33.

8. Kenneth A. Kitchen, "A Possible Mention of David in the Late Tenth Century B.C.E., and Deity *Dod as Dead as the Dodo?" *JSOT* 76 (1997), pp. 29–44. Cf. Herschel Shanks, "Has David Been Found in Egypt?" *BAR* 25, 1 (January/February 1999), pp. 34–35.

9. Kenneth A. Kitchen, *The Third Intermediate Period in Egypt (1100–650 B.C.)* (Warminster: Aris & Phillips, 1973), p. 440. See also James E. Hoch, *Semitic Words in Egyptian Texts of the New Kingdom and Third Intermediate Period* (Princeton: Princeton University Press, 1994), p. 224.

10. In some passages (e.g., Ezek. 34:24; 37:24–25) a new King David is envisioned for the future. Similarly, the coming king may be described as a "righteous branch" or the like *for David* (Jer. 23:5; 33:15, 17). The broader context (cf. Jer. 33:19–26) makes clear that it is the individual, not the dynasty, that is meant by the name David.

11. Amihai Mazar, *Archaeology of the Land of the Bible 10,000–586 B.C.E.*, ABRL (New York: Doubleday, 1990).

12. Yigal Shiloh, *Excavations at the City of David I 1978–1982, Qedem* 19 (Jerusalem: Institute of Archaeology, Hebrew University, 1984), pp. 17, 27. The

structure has subsequently been dated both earlier and later by other archaeologists. David Tarler and Jane M. Cahill ("David, City of," *ABD* 2, pp. 52–67) date it earlier, to the Jebusite era in the thirteenth and twelfth centuries. Margreet Steiner ("It's Not There: Archaeology Proves a Negative," *BAR* 24, 4 [July/August 1998], pp. 26–33, 62–63) dates it to the end of the tenth century, arguing that this date makes it too late to have been built by David and ultimately supports the position that he never existed. But Dan Bahat ("Jerusalem," *OEANE*, 3:226), the leading archaeologist of Jerusalem today, retains the early tenth-century date.

13. P. Kyle McCarter, *II Samuel*, AB 9 (Garden City, NY: Doubleday, 1984), p. 135.

14. Dan Gill, "How They Met: Geology Solves Mystery of Hezekiah's Tunnelers," *BAR* 20, 4 (July/August 1994), pp. 20–33, 64. Ronny Reich and Eli Shukron, "Light at the End of the Tunnel," *BAR* 25, 1 (January/February 1999), pp. 22–33, 72, now claim to have discovered that Warren's shaft is unrelated to Jerusalem's water system.

15. Mazar, *Archaeology of the Land of the Bible*, pp. 390–96.

16. Mazar, *Archaeology of the Land of the Bible*, p. 362.

17. See Nadav Na'aman, "It Is There: Ancient Texts Prove It," *BAR* 24, 2 (March/April 1998), pp. 42–44.

18. See John S. Holladay, Jr. "The Kingdoms of Israel and Judah: Political and Economic Centralization in the Iron IIA–B (ca. 1000–750 B.C.E.)," in *The Archaeology of Society in the Holy Land*, ed. Thomas E. Levy (London: Leicester University Press), pp. 368–98. Holladay says that he set out to write a social history of the early Israelite monarchy without using the Bible. The existence of two figures like the biblical David and Solomon—one a military conqueror and the other an administrator, he says, is preserved in the archaeological record when, suddenly in the tenth century, "the burnt-out ruin heaps of Hazor, Megiddo, and Gezer . . . were radically transformed into roughly comparable complex fortified governmental centers" (p. 371). He adds that the continuity with later inhabitants and the strategic location of these sites make clear that these activities were carried out by Israelites and were politically motivated.

19. See Israel Finkelstein, "The Archaeology of the United Monarchy: An Alternative View," *Levant* 28 (1996), pp. 177–87, and the replies by Amihai Mazar, "Iron Age Chronology: A Reply to I. Finkelstein," *Levant* 29 (1997), pp. 157–67, and Amnon Ben-Tor and Doron Ben-Ami, "Hazor and the Archaeology of the Tenth Century B.C.E.," *IEJ* 48 (1998), pp. 1–37. The arguments about this matter are summarized in readable form by Herschel Shanks, "Where Is the Tenth Century?" *BAR* 24, 2 (March/April 1998), pp. 56–60.

20. Mazar, "Iron Age Chronology: A Reply to I. Finkelstein," p. 164.

21. As this relates to the Bible see William G. Dever, "Archaeology, Syro-Palestinian and Biblical," *ABD* 1 (1992), pp. 354–67, and William G. Dever, "Biblical Archaeology," in *OEANE* 1, pp. 315–19.

22. Lawrence E. Stager, "The Archaeology of the Family in Ancient Israel," *BASOR* 260 (1985), pp. 1–29.

23. Norman K. Gottwald, "Sociology (Ancient Israel)," *ABD* 6, pp. 79–89, and J. W. Rogerson, "Anthropology and the Old Testament," *ABD* 1, pp. 258–62.

24. James W. Flanagan, "Chiefs in Israel," *JSOT* 20 (1981), pp. 47–73, and Frank S. Frick, *The Formation of the State in Ancient Israel: A Survey of Models and Theories* (Sheffield: Almond, 1985).

25. James W. Flanagan, "Models for the Origin of Iron Age Monarchy: A Modern Case Study," in *Society of Biblical Literature 1982 Seminar Papers* (Chico, CA: Scholars Press, 1982), pp. 135–56, and Flanagan, *David's Social Drama*.

26. Cf. Shlomo Bunimovitz, "How Mute Stones Speak: Interpreting What We Dig Up," *BAR* 21, 2 (March/April 1995), pp. 58–67, 96–100.

Chapter Two

1. Stefan Heym, *The King David Report* (New York: G. P. Putnam's Sons, 1973).

2. Heym, *The King David Report*, p. 9.

3. Heym, *The King David Report*, p. 82.

4. William G. Dever, "Archaeology, Syro-Palestinian and Biblical," *ABD* 1, p. 354.

5. A German scholar named Martin Noth first identified these books as a unit in 1943. His work is now available in English as *The Deuteronomistic History*, JSOTSup 15, 2nd ed. (Sheffield: Sheffield Academic Press. 1991). On scholarship since Noth see A. Graeme Auld, "The Former Prophets: Joshua, Judges, 1–2 Samuel, 1–2 Kings," in *The Hebrew Bible Today: An Introduction to Critical Issues*, ed. S. L. McKenzie and M. P. Graham (Louisville, KY: Westminster John Knox, 1998), pp. 53–68; Steven L. McKenzie, "Deuteronomistic History," *ABD* 2, pp. 160–68; Mark A. O'Brien, *The Deuteronomistic History Hypothesis: A Reassessment*, OBO 92 (Freiburg/Göttingen: Universitätsverlag/Vandenhoeck & Ruprecht, 1989); and Thomas Römer and Albert de Pury, "L'historiographie deutéronomiste (HD): Histoire de la recherche et enjeux du débat," in *Israël construit son histoire: L'historiographie deutéronomiste à la lumière des recherches récentes*, Le monde de la Bible 34, ed. A. de Pury, T. Römer, and J.-D. Macchi (Geneva: Labor et Fides, 1996), pp. 9–120.

6. One of the Dead Sea Scroll fragments for Samuel includes a paragraph of the story in chapter 11 that was accidentally left out of the Hebrew text of the Bible. It is the original beginning of that story and explains the circumstances that led to Nahash's attack on Jabesh-Gilead in chapter 11. It therefore confirms the original independence of chapter 11 from the preceding story in 10:17–27. Most English Bibles do not yet include this additional paragraph, but it is found in the NRSV as verse 10:27b. See Frank Moore Cross, "The Ammonite Oppression of the Tribes of Gad and Reuben: Missing Verses from 1 Samuel 11 Found in 4QSamuelᵃ," in *History, Historiography and Interpretation: Studies in Biblical and Cuneiform Literatures,* ed. H. Tadmor and M. Weinfeld (Jerusalem: Magnes, 1984), pp. 148–58.

7. The intervening material in 15:1–16:13 is a later addition. It lies outside of Dtr's notices in 14:47–52 and interrupts the transition to David as the focal character. Chapter 15 is another story about Saul being rejected as king. Since he was already rejected in 13:8–15a, this second story is unnecessary. Also, the statement in 15:35 that Samuel did not see Saul again before he died is contradicted by a later episode (19:18–24). Finally, according to chapter 15 Saul wiped out all the Amalekites except for their king, whom Samuel subsequently "hewed to pieces" (15:33). Yet the Amalekites appear several times more in 1–2 Samuel. All of these tensions with the surrounding material confirm that 15:1–16:13 is secondary. Cf. John Van Seters, *In Search of History: Historiography in the Ancient World and the Origins of Biblical History* (New Haven: Yale University Press, 1983), pp. 26–64.

8. Again, it was a German scholar who first observed these sources. His work is now available in translation as Leonhard Rost, *The Succession to the Throne of David,* trans. David Gunn (Sheffield: Almond, 1982).

9. Van Seters, *In Search of History,* pp. 264–71, questions the existence of the History of David's Rise as an independent document. He makes a compelling case that this section was composed by Dtr using traditional material.

10. See James W. Flanagan, "Court History or Succession Document?: A Study of 2 Samuel 9–20 and 1 Kings 1–2," *JBL* 91 (1972), pp. 172–81.

11. Van Seters, *In Search of History,* pp. 277–91, sees the entire Court History as a late addition to the Deuteronomistic History. He thinks its author was strongly anti-monarchical and depicted the reigns of David and Solomon in a negative light. I agree with Van Seters's literary judgments regarding the contents of the Court History. But I think he is incorrect in seeing the Court History as against David and Solomon. He fails to account for the same pro-Davidic apologetic tone in the Court History as in the History of David's Rise.

12. For examples see Harry A. Hoffner, Jr., "Propaganda and Political Justification in Hittite Historiography," in *Unity and Diversity: Essays in the History, Lit-*

erature, and Religion of the Ancient Near East, ed. H. Goedicke and J. J. M. Roberts (Baltimore: Johns Hopkins University Press, 1975), pp. 49–62; Leo G. Perdue, "The Testament of David and Egyptian Royal Instructions," in *Scripture in Context II: More Essays on the Comparative Method*, ed. W. W. Hallo, J. C. Moyer, and L. G. Perdue (Winona Lake, IN: Eisenbrauns, 1983), pp. 79–96; Hayim Tadmor, "Autobiographical Apology in the Royal Assyrian Literature," in *History, Historiography and Interpretation*, ed. Tadmor and Weinfeld, pp. 36–57; R. N. Whybray, *The Succession Narrative. A Study of II Samuel 9–20; I Kings 1 and 2*, SBT 2, 9 (London: SCM, 1968), pp. 96–116; Herbert M. Wolf, "The Apology of Hattusilis Compared with Other Ancient Near Eastern Political Self-Justifications" (unpublished Ph.D. diss., Brandeis University, 1967).

13. This list of charges is inspired by a similar list in P. Kyle McCarter, "The Apology of David," *JBL* 99 (1980), pp. 489–504.

14. Cf. P. Kyle McCarter, "Plots, True or False": The Succession Narrative as Court Apologetic," *Int* 35 (1981), pp. 355–67; D. G. Schley, "Joab and David: Ties of Blood and Power," in *History and Interpretation: Essays in Honour of John H. Hayes*, JSOTSup 173, ed. M. P. Graham, W. P. Brown, and J. K. Kwan (Sheffield: Sheffield Academic Press, 1993), pp. 90–105.

15. Cf. Gary N. Knoppers, *Two Nations Under God. The Deuteronomistic History of Solomon and the Dual Monarchies*, vol. 1, *The Reign of Solomon and the Rise of Jeroboam*, HSM 52 (Atlanta: Scholars Press, 1993), pp. 60–77.

16. Van Seters, *In Search of History*, p. 290.

17. For example, McCarter, "The Apology of David," and P. Kyle McCarter, *I Samuel*, AB 8 (Garden City, NY: Doubleday, 1980).

18. Cf. David W. Jamieson-Drake, *Scribes and Schools in Monarchic Judah: A Socio–Archaeological Approach* (Sheffield: Almond, 1991); Nadav Na'aman, "The 'Conquest of Canaan' in the Book of Joshua and in History," in *From Nomadism to Monarchy: Archaeological and Historical Aspects of Early Israel*, ed. I. Finkelstein and N. Na'aman (Jerusalem: Yad Izhak Ben-Zvi/IES/BAS, 1994), pp. 218–81; Donald B. Redford, *Egypt, Canaan, and Israel in Ancient Times* (Princeton: Princeton University Press, 1992), pp. 301–302; and Van Seters, *In Search of History*. Na'aman (p. 221) agrees, though, that the apology in these documents presupposes an audience well acquainted with the accusations they attempt to counter.

19. For a helpful overview of 1–2 Chronicles and their theological interests see Ralph W. Klein, "Chronicles, Book of 1–2," *ABD* 1, pp. 992–1002.

20. The LXX numbers for most of the psalms are one less than those in the Hebrew Bible. For convenience, I follow the numbers in most English Bibles.

21. The *shiggaion*, *maskil*, and *miktam* were all types of psalms. Exactly what distinguished one type from another is unknown.

22. Compare Diana V. Edelman, "Saul ben Kish in History and Tradition," in *The Origins of the Ancient Israelite States*, JSOTSup 228, ed. V. Fritz and P. R. Davies (Sheffield: Sheffield Academic Press, 1996), pp. 144–49. Edelman lists the following steps in this process for her work on Saul: (1) textual criticism, which tries to determine the original reading of the biblical text by comparing the various manuscripts; (2) a close reading of the text from the perspective of the ancient audience, with attention to the author's intent as revealed through structuring patterns and devices; (3) a consideration of the author's sources; and (4) the use of "creative imagination" to reconstruct the past. Edelman's treatment of Saul is very similar to my treatment of David in many respects. I will cover each of these steps in my reconstruction of David's life. If I try to work more on what Edelman calls "the level of event" it is because there is much more to work with for David than for Saul.

23. As shown by David M. Gunn's books *The Story of King David. Genre and Interpretation,* JSOTSup 6 (Sheffield: JSOT, 1978) and *The Fate of King Saul* JSOT-Sup 14 (Sheffield: JSOT, 1980).

24. Cf. Joseph Blenkinsopp, "The Quest of the Historical Saul," in *No Famine in the Land: Studies in Honor of John L. McKenzie,* ed. J. W. Flanagan and A. W. Robinson (Missoula, MT: Scholars Press, 1975), pp. 75–99, and W. Lee Humphreys, "From Tragic Hero to Villain: A Study of the Figure of Saul and the Development of 1 Samuel," *JSOT* 22 (1982), pp. 95–117.

25. J. Maxwell Miller, "Reading the Bible Historically: The Historian's Approach," in *To Each Its Own Meaning: An Introduction to Biblical Criticisms and Their Applications,* ed. S. L. McKenzie and S. R. Haynes (Louisville, KY: Westminster/John Knox, 1993), pp. 11–28.

26. J. W. Wesselius, "Joab's Death and the Central Theme of the Succession Narrative (2 Samuel IX–1 Kings II)," *VT* 40 (1990), pp. 339–40.

27. For example, Adele Berlin, "Characterization in Biblical Narrative: David's Wives," *JSOT* 23 (1982), pp. 69–85, and *Poetics and Interpretation of Biblical Narrative* (Sheffield: Almond, 1983), esp. pp. 23–42.

Chapter Three

1. Nahman Avigad, "The King's Daughter and the Lyre," *IEJ* 28 (1978), pp. 146–51; Ivor H. Jones, "Music and Musical Instruments," *ABD* 4, pp. 930–39; E. Werner, "Musical Instruments," *IDB* 3, pp. 469–76.

2. B. D. Napier, "Sheep," *IDB* 4, pp. 315–16; Jack W. Vancil, "Sheep, Shepherd," *ABD* 5, pp. 1187–90.

3. Cf. Cyrus H. Gordon's review of *The Goddess Anath* by U. Cassuto in *JAOS* 72 (1952), pp. 180–81.

4. Walter Brueggemann, *David's Truth in Israel's Imagination and Memory* (Philadelphia: Fortress, 1985), p. 27.

5. As deduced by Lawrence E. Stager, "The Archaeology of the Family in Ancient Israel," *BASOR* 260 (1985), pp. 1–29.

6. As suggested by John Van Seters, "Problems in the Literary Analysis of the Court History of David," *JSOT* 1 (1976), p. 25.

7. Jon D. Levenson, "1 Samuel 25 as Literature and History," *CBQ* 40 (1978), pp. 11–28, and Jon D. Levenson and Baruch Halpern, "The Political Import of David's Marriages," *JBL* 99 (1980), pp. 507–18.

8. See Alan M. Cooper, "The Life and Times of King David According to the Book of Psalms," in *The Poet and the Historian. Essays in Literary and Historical Biblical Criticism*, Harvard Semitic Studies 26, ed. R. E. Friedman (Chico, CA: Scholars Press, 1983), pp. 117–31.

9. Stager, "The Archaeology of the Family."

10. Peter Riede, "David und der Floh. Tiere und Tiervergleiche in den Samuelbüchern," *BN* 77 (1995), pp. 86–114.

11. Riede, "David und der Floh."

12. The Hebrew text here is ungrammatical. This translation is P. Kyle McCarter's, *I Samuel*, AB 8 (Garden City, NY: Doubleday, 1980), pp. 274–75.

Chapter Four

1. The LXX actually lacks vv. 41 and 48b, which were accidentally omitted in the process of copying. See Ralph W. Klein, *1 Samuel*, Word Biblical Commentary 10 (Waco, TX: Word, 1983), p. 172. See Klein, *1 Samuel*, pp. 168–83; P. Kyle McCarter's, *I Samuel*, AB 8 (Garden City, NY: Doubleday, 1980), 284–309; Julio Trebolle, "The Story of David and Goliath (1 Sam 17–18): Textual Variants and Literary Composition," *BIOSCS* 23 (1990), pp. 16–30. Some scholars disagree, seeing the Hebrew (Masoretic) version as older and the LXX as an abbreviation of it. So Walter Dietrich, "Die Erzählung von David und Goliat in I Sam 17," *ZAW* 108 (1996), pp. 172–91; Alexander Rofé, "The Battle of David and Goliath: Folklore, Theology, Eschatology," in *Judaic Perspectives on Ancient Israel*, ed. J. Neusner, B. Levine, and E. Frerichs (Philadelphia: Fortress, 1987), pp. 117–51. For a dialogue between the different views see Dominique Barthélemy, David W. Gooding, Johan Lust, and Emanuel Tov, *The Story of David and Goliath. Textual and Literary Criticism*, OBO 73 (Göttingen: Vandenhoeck

& Ruprecht, 1986), and the response by Arie van der Kooij, "The Story of David and Goliath: The Early History of Its Text," *ETL* 68 (1992), pp. 118–31.

2. Yigael Yadin, *The Art of Warfare in Biblical Lands* (London: Weidenfeld and Nicolson, 1963), pp. 265–67, 354–55.

3. On the origins of the Philistines, see Neal Bierling, *Giving Goliath His Due: New Archaeological Light on the Philistines* (Grand Rapids, MI: Baker, 1992); Trude Dothan, "What We Know about the Philistines," *BAR* 8:4 (July/August, 1982), pp. 20–44, and "Philistines," *ABD* 5, pp. 326–33; and Lawrence E. Stager, "The Impact of the Sea Peoples (1185–1050 B.C.E.)," in *The Archaeology of Society in the Holy Land*, ed. T. E. Levy (London: Leicester University Press, 1995), pp. 332–48.

4. Roland de Vaux, "Single Combat in the Old Testament," in *The Bible in the Ancient Near East*, trans. D. McHugh (Garden City, NY: Doubleday, 1971), pp. 123–35.

5. Kurt Galling, "Goliat und seine Rüstung," in *Volume du Congrès: Genève 1965*, VTSup 15 (Leiden: E. J. Brill, 1966), pp. 150–69.

6. See the discussion of Yadin (*The Art of Warfare*, p. 355) and the response by Galling ("Goliat und seine Rüstung").

7. Ariella Deem, " '. . . And the Stone Sank into His Forehead': A Short Note on 1 Samuel XVII 49," *VT* 28 (1978), pp. 349–51.

8. Moshe Dayan, "The Spirit of the Fighters," in *Tales of Heroism: Twenty Years of Independence* 11 (Jerusalem: Israel Ministry of Defense, 1968). (Hebrew)

9. Saul's question in v. 8b, "What more can he have than the kingdom?" is part of the series of additions to the Masoretic text that are lacking in the LXX. In the original version of the story, Saul did not immediately jump to the conclusion that David was out to overthrow him. But he did begin to be suspicious.

10. Compare McCarter, *I Samuel*, p. 298.

11. See Ora Horn Prouser, "Suited to the Throne: The Symbolic Use of Clothing in the David and Saul Narratives," *JSOT* 71 (1996), pp. 27–37, and "Clothes Maketh the Man: Keys to Meaning in the Stories of Saul and David," *BR* 14, 1 (February 1998), pp. 22–27.

12. According to the story, Samuel conducted David to "Naioth." This word means "camps." It is not clear whether it is used here as a proper name for a small settlement near Ramah or whether it simply refers to the "camps" where the prophets lived. In either case, the idea is that they lived near their mentor, Samuel.

13. This story is in tension with two previous episodes in 1 Samuel. It contradicts the statement in 15:35 that Samuel did not see Saul again "until the day of his death." It also provides a different explanation from the one in 10:12 for

the saying, "Is Saul also among the prophets?" We have already seen that 15:1–16:13 was a later addition to Dtr's History. The story of David's flight to Ramah in 19:18–24 presupposes the knowledge that Samuel anointed David (16:1–13) and is therefore also a post-Dtr addition. Its relationship to the story of Saul's prophesying in 10:10–13 is harder to determine. The latter may be Dtr's addition to the old story about Saul's search for his father's donkeys in 9:1–10:16. Cf. John Sturdy, "The Original Meaning of 'Is Saul Also Among the Prophets?' (1 Samuel X 11, 12; XIX 24)," *VT* 20 (1970), pp. 206–13.

14. The farewell of Jonathan and David at the end of this chapter (20:41–42) is confusing. If the two of them could meet personally, then there was no need for the signal that Jonathan used in vv. 34–39 to warn David. The last two verses are an addition to the older story. Their point is to stress the covenant between David and Jonathan with David's promise to care for Jonathan's descendants. He fulfills this promise by taking care of Jonathan's surviving son in 2 Samuel 9.

15. For literary critical treatments see Robert Alter, *The Art of Biblical Narrative* (New York: Basic Books, 1981), pp. 114–30; David J. A. Clines and Tamara Eskenazi (eds.), *Telling Queen Michal's Story: An Experiment in Comparative Interpretation*, JSOTSup 119 (Sheffield: Sheffield Academic Press, 1991); and David Jobling, "Saul's Fall and Jonathan's Rise: Tradition and Redaction in 1 Sam 14:1–46," *JBL* 95 (1976), pp. 367–76, and *The Sense of Biblical Narrative: Three Structural Analyses in the Old Testament*, JSOTSup 7 (Sheffield: JSOT, 1978), pp. 6–23.

16. See Peter R. Ackroyd, "The Verb Love—'*aheb* in the David-Jonathan Narratives—A Footnote," *VT* 25 (1975), pp. 213–14; William L. Moran, "The Ancient Near Eastern Background of the Love of God in Deuteronomy," *CBQ* 25 (1963), pp. 77–87; and J. A. Thompson, "The Significance of the Verb Love in the David-Jonathan Narratives in 1 Samuel," *VT* 24 (1974), pp. 334–38.

17. Cf. Marcus Zehnder, "Exegetische Beobachtungen zu den David-Jonathan Geschichten," *Bib* 79 (1998), pp. 153–79.

18. J. W. Wesselius, "Joab's Death and the Central Theme of the Succession Narrative (2 Samuel IX–Kings 11)," *VT* 40 (1990), pp. 339–40.

Chapter Five

1. The verse numbers of English translations in this chapter differ from those of the Hebrew. For the reader's convenience I follow the English numbers.

2. Reading "commander" with the versions. The Hebrew text has a verb, "who turns aside," which the NRSV tries to make sense of.

3. Cf. P. Kyle McCarter's, *I Samuel*, AB 8 (Garden City, NY: Doubleday, 1980), pp. 366–67.

4. The report of Abiathar's arrival to David in 23:6 is probably out of place. It belongs before 23:1–5 in which David also inquires of Yahweh, presumably through Abiathar's ephod.

5. Reading with the LXX and Dead Sea Scroll fragment for Samuel. See McCarter, *I Samuel*, pp. 86–89.

6. Nitsche, *König David*, n. 89.

7. The verse numbers of English translations differ in chapter 24 from those of the Hebrew, and 24:1–23 in Hebrew is 23:29–24:22 in English. For convenience I follow the English numbers.

8. McCarter (*I Samuel*, pp. 385–87) argues that chapter 24 was written on the basis of chapter 26. Cf. also Cynthia Edenburg, "How (Not) to Murder a King: Variations on a Theme in 1 Sam 24; 26," *SJOT* 12 (1998), pp. 64–85. But Klaus Koch, *The Growth of the Biblical Tradition. The Form-Critical Method*, trans. S. M. Cupitt (New York: Scribner's, 1969), pp. 132–48, believes both chapters to be independent variants of the same original tradition.

9. See the excellent article by Levenson "1 Samuel 25 as Literature and History." See also Levenson and Halpern, "The Political Import of David's Marriages." Much of the discussion that follows is based on these two articles.

10. I owe this observation to my colleague Dr. Carey Walsh.

11. An alternative proposed by Dr. Carey Walsh.

12. So both Klein, *1 Samuel*, p. 247, and McCarter, *I Samuel*, p. 394.

13. As shown by Van Seters, *In Search of History*, pp. 261–64.

14. The origin of the word "Hebrew" is difficult. There is a similar term, *Ḥabiru* or *ʿAabiru*, found in Egyptian and Akkadian, that designates a mercenary class. But it does not correspond philologically to "Hebrew" (*ʿibrî*) in the Hebrew language. In the Bible the term "Hebrews" is used mainly by foreigners to designate Israelites rather than by Israelites for themselves. McCarter's explanation (*I Samuel*, pp. 240–41) that in 1 Samuel the name refers to Israelites who were politically allied with the Philistines is not entirely satisfying, but it does accord with the idea that David and his men were mercenaries.

15. See Meir Malul, "Was David Involved in the Death of Saul on the Gilboa Mountain?" *RB* 103 (1996), pp. 517–45.

Chapter Six

1. Bosch, *David: The Biography of a King*, p. 122.

2. Levenson, "1 Samuel 25 as Literature and History," p. 27.

3. Compare Baruch Halpern's article "Text and Artifact: Two Monologues?" in *The Archaeology of Israel: Constructing the Past, Interpreting the Present,* JSOTSup 237, ed. N. A. Silberman and D. Small (Sheffield: Sheffield Academic Press, 1997), pp. 311–41, and James C. Vanderkam, "Davidic Complicity in the Deaths of Abner and Eshbaal: A Historical and Redactional Study," *JBL* 99 (1980), pp. 521–39.

4. See Zafrira Ben-Barak, "The Legal Background to the Restoration of Michal to David, in *Studies in the Historical Books of the Old Testament,* VTSup 30, ed. J. A. Emerton (Leiden: E. J. Brill, 1979), pp. 15–29.

5. Some scholars believe that the *bōsheth* element is an original and genuine part of the name based on parallels in other languages where a similar element appears in proper names with the meaning "protective spirit." See most recently Gordon J. Hamilton, "New Evidence for the Authenticity of *bšt* in Hebrew Personal Names and for Its Use as a Divine Epithet in Biblical Texts," *CBQ* 60 (1998), pp. 228–50, and previous works cited by him.

6. The *-vi* in Ishvi could be a mistaken writing (transposition of consonants) for *-yw*, which in turn is an abbreviation for the name Yahweh. Since the *-baal* element may refer to Yahweh, Ishbaal and Ishvi would be the same name.

7. Edelman ("Saul ben Kish in History and Tradition," p. 154n) suggests that the age of forty for Ishbaal reflects an attempt by the writer to make the adolescent into a more worthy opponent for David.

8. Or possibly "the Asherites," that is, people from the tribe of Asher. The Hebrew text has "Assyrians" (i.e., of northern Mesopotamia), which is certainly an error. Some versions have "Geshur," which makes sense geographically.

Chapter Seven

1. See Flanagan, "Chiefs in Israel"; Frick, *The Formation of the State in Ancient Israel;* and Gottwald, "Sociology (Ancient Israel)," all of which are cited in full in notes 23 and 24 for Chapter One.

2. See the critique by William G. Dever, "From Tribe to Nation: A Critique of State Formation Processes in Ancient Israel," in *Nouve fondazioni nel Vicino Oriente: realtà e ideologia,* ed. S. Mazzoni (Pisa: University of Pisa, 1995), pp. 213–38.

3. As described by Christa Schäfer-Lichtenberger, "Sociological and Biblical Views of the Early State," in *The Origins of the Ancient Israelite States,* ed. Fritz and Davies, pp. 78–105.

4. An observation made by Baruch Halpern, "The Construction of the Davidic State: An Exercise in Historiography," in *The Origins of the Ancient Israelite States,* ed. Fritz and Davies, pp. 55–58.

5. A great deal has been written on this troublesome passage. For bibliography see the recent article by Saul Olyan, "Anyone Blind or Lame Shall Not Enter the House": On the Interpretation of Second Samuel 5:8b," *CBQ* 60 (1998), pp. 218–27.

6. On these matters see the following articles: James W. Flanagan, "Social Transformation and Ritual in 2 Samuel 6," in *The Word of the Lord Shall Go Forth: Essays in Honor of David Noel Freedman in Celebration of His Sixtieth Birthday*, ed. C. Meyers and M. P. O'Connor (Winona Lake, IN: Eisenbrauns, 1983), pp. 361–72; P. Kyle McCarter, "The Ritual Dedication of the City of David in 2 Samuel 6," in the same volume, pp. 273–78; and Wolfgang Zwickel, "David als Vorbild für den Glauben: Die Veränderung des Davidbildes im Verlauf der alttestamentlichen Geschichte, dargestellt an 2 Sam 6," *BN* 79 (1995), pp. 88–101.

7. The destruction of Shiloh is almost too convenient. Could the story have been contrived to justify the transferal of the ark and the rise of the Zadokite priesthood in Jerusalem?

8. Cf. McCarter, *II Samuel*, pp. 124–25.

9. Cf. the discussion by Niels Peter Lemche, *Ancient Israel: A New History of Israelite Society*, The Biblical Seminar, trans. F. Cryer (Sheffield: Sheffield Academic Press, 1988), pp. 137–41.

10. On the dates for Hiram's reign see Alberto Green, "David's Relations with Hiram: Biblical and Josephan Evidence for Tyrian Chronology," in *The Word of the Lord Shall Go Forth*, ed. Meyers and O'Connor, pp. 373–97.

11. The difference between a wife and a concubine was one of status. A concubine was a female slave brought to the king for sexual purposes. She had no royal status, and her children were only secondary heirs. A wife, on the other hand, did have royal status and bore heirs to the king. Rizpah is actually called Saul's concubine.

12. The Hebrew (Masoretic) text has "Ahimelech son of Abiathar" instead of "Abiathar son of Ahimelech" as one would expect based on 1 Samuel 21–22. It is possible that Abiathar had a son who was named after his grandfather. But it seems more likely in light of the later list that a mistake occurred in the transmission of this verse resulting in the accidental inversion of Abiathar's name with his father's.

13. The textual evidence favors reading "Shausha" in both lists, though the Hebrew text has "Seraiah" in 8:17 and "Sheva" in 20:25. Cf. McCarter, *II Samuel*, p. 254.

14. Reading with 20:23. The Hebrew text in 8:18 has "Benaiah son of Jehoiada and the Cherethites and Pelethites."

15. McCarter, *II Samuel*, p. 435.

16. 1 Kings 9:15–22 claims that no Israelites were used in the labor force, which is a blatant contradiction of 5:13–14. However, the complaint of the Israelites against Solomon's heavy yoke in 1 Kings 12 makes it clear that the labor force, which included Israelites, was a permanent institution and not just for building the temple.

17. John Bright, "The Organization and Administration of the Israelite Empire," in *Magnalia Dei. The Mighty Acts of God. Essays on the Bible and Archaeology in Memory of G. Ernest Wright*, ed. F. M. Cross, W. Lemke, and P. D. Miller (Garden City, NY: Doubleday, 1976), p. 198.

18. Cf. Zafrira Ben-Barak, "Meribaal and the System of Land Grants in Ancient Israel," *Bib* 62 (1981), pp. 73–91.

19. See Graeme Auld and Margreet Steiner, *Jerusalem I: From the Bronze Age to the Maccabees*, Cities of the Biblical World (Macon, GA: Mercer University Press, 1996), pp. 33–38, who estimate that about two thousand people lived in Jerusalem during Solomon's reign, when the city included the Temple Mount. The population was significantly smaller in David's reign. The average population density of ancient Middle Eastern cities was about two hundred fifty per 2.5 acres (Magen Broshi, "Demography," *OEANE*, 2:142). The area covered by the city of David is about 12 acres, 15 if the eastern slope is included—room for twelve hundred to fifteen hundred people. But since, as Auld and Steiner observe, David's city was largely administrative, there may have been far fewer people actually living there.

20. On the Philistines in general see Bierling, *Giving Goliath His Due*; Dothan, "What We Know about the Philistines" and "Philistines"; and Stager, "The Impact of the Sea Peoples," all of which are cited in full in note 3 of Chapter Four. On David's victories in 2 Samuel 21 see N. L. Tidwell, "The Philistine Incursions into the Valley of Rephaim," in *Studies in the Historical Books of the Old Testament*, VTSup 30, ed. J. A. Emerton (Leiden: E. J. Brill, 1979), pp. 190–212.

21. See Wayne T. Pitard, *Ancient Damascus: A Historical Study of the Syrian City-State from Earliest Times until Its Fall to the Assyrians in 732 B.C.E.* (Winona Lake, IN: Eisenbrauns, 1987), pp. 88–95.

22. The Hebrew of 2 Sam. 8:3 says that David attacked Hadadezer "when he went to restore his monument at the river." "The river" usually refers to the Euphrates but in this case may mean the Jordan, since Hadadezer would hardly have run into David going from Zobah to the Euphrates. In neither case does the Bible claim that David waged a northern campaign against Aram (Syria), much less that he actually controlled the Aramaean territory. See Halpern, "The Construction of the Davidic State."

23. See Redford, *Egypt, Canaan, and Israel in Ancient Times*, esp. pp. 283–311.

24. The fact that both sides of such battles typically claim victory in their official reports accounts for 2 Sam. 8:1–8. Cf. Halpern, "The Construction of

the Davidic State." This passage does contain details that reflect historical veracity. David's hamstringing of most of the horses captured from the Aramaeans makes sense only if the Israelite army was not yet heavily dependent on chariotry or cavalry but still fought primarily on foot.

25. As shown by Frank Moore Cross, *Canaanite Myth and Hebrew Epic: Essays in the History and the Religion of Israel* (Cambridge, MA: Harvard University Press, 1973), pp. 252–54.

26. Cf. esp. Cross, *Canaanite Myth*, pp. 219–73, esp. p. 231 and n. 51, where he argues that the difference between a temple and a tabernacle was a very significant one in David's day. In Canaanite mythology, the residence of the god El was a tent, while Baal built a house. This difference was reflected in the respective shrines for these gods. El was worshiped in a portable tent or tabernacle and Baal in a temple. Since Israel grew out of and retained many features of Canaanite society, this difference would have been felt in a proposal to build a temple for Yahweh (7:2). If the two kinds of shrines could represent two distinct deities in Canaan, then the building of a temple in Jerusalem to replace the tabernacle would have been a revolutionary, even threatening, innovation.

27. A textual problem in 2 Sam. 7:1 has evidently obscured Dtr's explanation of why Yahweh refused David's offer. The explanation relates to one of the key themes of the Deuteronomistic History—the theme of "rest." The book of Deuteronomy (esp. chapter 12) looked forward to a time when Yahweh would give Israel rest from its enemies. Then, Yahweh would choose a "place for his name to dwell"—a central shrine (Deut. 12:5, 9–11). The statement in 2 Sam. 7:1 that Yahweh had given David rest from his enemies would indicate that this chapter is the climax of that theme. But that cannot be, since the wars of David in 2 Samuel 8 and 10 show that he did not have rest. Solomon says as much in his letter to Hiram in 1 Kings 5:3–4: "You know that my father David could not build a house for the name of Yahweh his God because of the warfare with which his enemies surrounded him, until Yahweh put them under the soles of his feet." The statement about rest in 2 Sam. 7:1 does not belong there. It is a copyist's error. The explanation in Samuel and Kings for why David did not build the temple is simply that it was not yet time according to the divine plan. David's role was to fight wars. He was Yahweh's instrument to bring "rest" to Israel by conquering its enemies. The real climax to the theme of rest came with Solomon. It was he who would have rest and who would be charged with building the temple, as 2 Samuel 7 itself says (vv. 11–13). See my article, "Why Didn't God Let David Build the Temple? The History of a Biblical Tradition," in *Worship in the Old Testament: Essays in Honor of John T. Willis*, ed. M. P. Graham, R. R. Marrs, and S. L. McKenzie, JSOTSup 284 (Sheffield: Sheffield Academic Press, 1999), pp. 204–24.

28. So Sara Japhet, *I & II Chronicles: A Commentary*, Old Testament Library (Louisville, KY: Westminster/John Knox, 1993), p. 397.

29. David has sometimes been depicted as a religious revolutionary who radically changed the worship of Yahweh by adapting it to the institutions of Jebusite religion. The classic statement of this so-called "Jebusite Hypothesis" was articulated by H. H. Rowley in 1939 in "Zadok and Nehushtan," *JBL* 58, pp. 113–41. It was effectively countered by Cross, *Canaanite Myth*, pp. 209–15. Still, the view that David took over the Jebusite religion wholesale persists in the literature. There were revolutionary changes in Israelite religion taking place in the days of David and Solomon. But these were part of broader changes in Israelite society. The elevation of Jerusalem as the center of Israel's government and society would gradually have a profound effect on its religion. But its revolutionary nature is evident only in hindsight.

Chapter Eight

1. On this see James W. Flanagan, "The Relocation of the Davidic Capital," *JAAR* 47 (1979), pp. 223–44.

2. Uriel Simon, "The Poor Man's Ewe Lamb: An Example of a Juridical Parable," *Bib* 48 (1967), pp. 207–42.

3. Literally, "son of death." For this translation instead of the more common "deserves to die," see McCarter, *II Samuel*, p. 299.

4. Reading with the LXX. The Hebrew text has "fourfold," probably in an effort to conform to the specified punishment for theft of a lamb in Exod. 22:1 (Heb. 21:37). The word "sevenfold" in Hebrew (*šib'atāyim*), by the way, resembles the name "Bathsheba."

5. With a slight textual change the last sentence might be translated, ". . . because he did this and spared what was his own." Some scholars prefer this latter reading. Both readings would be pronounced the same in Hebrew, and the ambiguity may be deliberate.

6. Some scholars regard Nathan's elaboration in verses 7b–12 as a later addition. However, this is unlikely since without these verses Nathan's message is too terse and lacks the explanation of judgment that is essential to such oracles.

7. Uriah is referred to only twice more in the books of Samuel and Kings. One is the reference at the end of the honor guard list in 2 Sam. 23:39. Even if his name is not secondary here, its mere mention does not presuppose familiarity with the story in 2 Samuel 11–12. The other reference to Uriah is in 1 Kings 15:5. This verse describes David's righteousness and devotion to Yahweh: "David did what was right in the sight of the LORD, and did not turn aside from any-

thing that he commanded him all the days of his life, except in the matter of Uriah the Hittite" (NRSV). This reference to Uriah clearly presupposes the story in 2 Samuel 11–12, but it is also suspect as an addition. David's adultery and murder are serious crimes, and it is hard to believe that Dtr could dismiss them in such an off-handed fashion and still refer to David as a model of obedience. It is more likely that this was a gloss by a pious scribe made after the insertion of the story in chapters 11–12 (Van Seters, *In Search of History*, p. 290).

8. Cf. Timo Veijola, "Salomo—der erstgeborgene Bathsebas," in *Studies in the Historical Books of the Old Testament*, ed. Emerton, pp. 230–50, who also raises the possibility that Solomon was Uriah's son, not David's.

9. The Hebrew (Masoretic) text calls him Chileab, but a better reading may be Daluiah. Cf. McCarter, *II Samuel*, p. 101.

10. The NRSV translation is based on the LXX. The Masoretic text lacks everything after "became very angry."

11. McCarter, *II Samuel*, p. 344.

12. See J. Hoftijzer, "David and the Tekoite Woman," *VT* 20 (1970), pp. 419–44.

13. As pointed out by Joseph Blenkinsopp, "Theme and Motif in the Succession Narrative (2 Sam. XI 2ff) and the Yahwist Corpus," in *Volume du Congrès: Genève 1965*, VTSup 15 (Leiden: E. J. Brill, 1966), p. 51n, and Larry L. Lyke, *King David with the Wise Woman of Tekoa: The Resonance of Tradition in Parabolic Narrative*, JSOTSup 255 (Sheffield: Sheffield Academic Press, 1997), pp. 172–73.

14. A point made by Nitsche, *König David: Gestalt im Umbruch*, p. 246.

15. McCarter, *II Samuel*, p. 334.

16. Baruch Halpern, "Text and Artifact: Two Monologues?" p. 322.

17. Pointed out by Nitsche, *König David: Gestalt im Umbruch*, p. 246.

Chapter Nine

1. Joseph Heller, *God Knows* (New York: Alfred A. Knopf), p. 16.

2. It is so obvious that some scholars argue that the original document behind these chapters was anti-monarchical and anti-Solomonic. So Lienhard Delekat, "Tendenz und Theologie der David-Salomo-Erzählung," in *Das ferne und nahe Wort*, ed. F. Maass (BZAW 105; Berlin: Töpelmann, 1967), pp. 26–36; F. Langlemet, "Pour ou contre Salomon? La rédaction prosalomonienne de 1 Rois, I–II," *RB* 83 (1976), pp. 321–79, 481–529; F. Langlemet, "David et la maison de Saül," *RB* 86 (1979), pp. 194–213, 385–436, 481–513; 87 (1980), pp. 161–210; 88 (1981), pp. 321–32; Van Seters, *In Search of History*, pp. 277–91; Timo Veijola, *Die ewige Dynastie: David und die Entstehung seiner Dynastie nach der deuterono-*

mistischen Darstellung, AASF B 193 (Helsinki: Suomalainen Tiedeakatemia, 1975); and Ernst Würthwein, *Die Erzählung von der Thronnachfolge Davids—theologische oder politische Geschichtsschreibung,* Theologische Studien (B) 115 (Zürich: Theologischer Verlag, 1974). Repr. in *Studien zum Deuteronomistischen Geschichtswerk,* BZAW 227 (Berlin: W. de Gruyter, 1994). Most of these scholars argue that a later editor, perhaps Dtr, added the apologetic flavor. Van Seters is unique in this regard as he sees the entire Court History as a post-Dtr addition. He is forced, therefore, to see the positive statements about David and Solomon as sarcasm.

3. The preferred reading in 2 Sam. 12:24 is "she [Bathsheba] named him Solomon" instead of "he [David] named him Solomon," as the NRSV has it. The feminine verb appears in the Masoretic text as the form that is to be read (*Qere'*) in place of the one that is written (*Ketib*). The significance of this reading will be discussed below.

4. See the studies by George C. Nicol, "Bathsheba, A Clever Woman?" *ET* 99 (1988), pp. 360–63, and "The Alleged Rape of Bathsheba: Some Observations on Ambiguity in Biblical Narrative," *JSOT* 73 (1997), pp. 43–54, but also the intermediate response by J. Cheryl Exum, *Fragmented Women: Feminist (Sub)versions of Biblical Narratives,* JSOTSup 163 (Sheffield: Sheffield Academic Press, 1993), pp. 172–201.

5. Wesselius, "Joab's Death and the Central Theme of the Succession Narrative," pp. 345–48.

6. Following the law in Deut. 22:23–27, Bathsheba's failure to cry out would indicate her complicity in the liaison, as Lyke, *King David with the Wise Woman of Tekoa,* p. 86n, points out.

7. As shown by G. Gerleman ("Die Wurzel *šlm,*" *ZAW* 85 [1973], pp. 1–14) and J. J. Stamm ("Der Name des Königs Salomo," *TZ* 16 [1960], pp. 285–97).

8. See Veijola, "Salomo—der erstgeborgene Bathsebas."

Chapter Ten

1. See the famous essay by Gerhard von Rad, "The Beginnings of Historical Writing in Ancient Israel," in von Rad, *The Problem of the Hexateuch and Other Essays,* trans. E. W. Trueman Dicken (New York: McGraw-Hill, 1966), pp. 176–204.

2. James A. Wharton, "A Plausible Tale: Story and Theology in II Samuel 9–20, I Kings 1–2," *Int* 35 (1981), pp. 341–54.

3. John L. McKenzie, *The Old Testament without Illusion* (Garden City, NY: Image, 1980), pp. 226–27.

Bibliography

Abbreviations

AASF	Annales Academiae Scientiarum Fennicae
AB	Analecta Biblica
ABD	*Anchor Bible Dictionary*. Edited by D. N. Freedman. 6 vols. New York: Doubleday, 1992
ABRL	Anchor Bible Reference Library
BA	*Biblical Archaeologist*
BAR	*Biblical Archaeology Review*
BASOR	*Bulletin of the American Schools of Oriental Research*
BE	*Biblische Enzyklopädie*
Bib	*Biblica*
BIOSCS	*Bulletin of the International Organization for Septuagint and Cognate Studies*
BN	*Biblische Notizen*
BR	*Bible Review*
BZAW	Beihefte zur *ZAW*
CBQ	*Catholic Biblical Quarterly*
CQR	*Church Quarterly Review*
DDD	*Dictionary of Deities and Demons in the Bible*. Edited by K. van der Toorn, B. Becking, and P. W. van der Horst. Leiden: E. J. Brill, 1995.
EF	Erträge der Forschung
ET	*Expository Times*
ETL	*Ephemerides Theologicae Lovanienses*
HSM	Harvard Semitic Monographs

IDB	*Interpreter's Dictionary of the Bible.* Edited by G. A. Buttrick. 4 vols. Nashville: Abingdon, 1962.
IEJ	*Israel Exploration Journal*
Int	*Interpretation*
JAAR	*Journal of the American Academy of Religion*
JANES	*Journal of the Ancient Near Eastern Society*
JAOS	*Journal of the American Oriental Society*
JBL	*Journal of Biblical Literature*
JSOT	*Journal for the Study of the Old Testament*
JSOTSup	*JSOT Supplemental Series*
JSS	*Journal of Semitic Studies*
NRSV	New Revised Standard Version of the Bible
OBO	Orbis Biblicus et Orientalis
OEANE	*The Oxford Encyclopedia of Archaeology in the Near East.* Edited by Eric M. Meyers. 5 vols. New York: Oxford University Press, 1997.
OTG	Old Testament Guides
OTWSA	Die ou-Testamentiese Werkgemeenskap in Suid-Afrika
RB	*Revue Biblique*
RQ	*Restoration Quarterly*
SBLDS	Society of Biblical Literature Dissertation Series
SBT	Studies in Biblical Theology
SJOT	*Scandinavian Journal of the Old Testament*
TZ	*Theologische Zeitschrift*
UF	*Ugarit Forschungen*
VT	*Vetus Testamentum*
WBC	Word Biblical Commentary
VTSup	Supplements to *VT*
ZAW	*Zeitschrift für die alttestamentliche Wissenschaft*

Ackroyd, Peter R. 1975. The Verb Love—*'aheb* in the David-Jonathan Narratives—A Footnote. *VT* 25:213–14.

———— 1981. The Succession Narrative (so-called). *Int* 35:383–96.

Alter, Robert. 1981. *The Art of Biblical Narrative.* New York: Basic Books.

Auld, A. Graeme. 1994. *Kings without Privilege: David and Moses in the Story of the Bible's Kings.* Edinburgh: T & T Clark.

———— 1998. The Former Prophets: Joshua, Judges, 1–2 Samuel, 1–2 Kings. Pp. 53–68 in *The Hebrew Bible Today: An Introduction to Critical Issues,* ed. Steven L. McKenzie and M. Patrick Graham. Louisville, KY: Westminster John Knox.

Auld, Graeme and Margreet Steiner. 1996. *Jerusalem I: From the Bronze Age to the Maccabees.* Cities of the Biblical World. Macon, GA: Mercer University Press.

Avigad, Nahman. 1978. The King's Daughter and the Lyre. *IEJ* 28:146–51.

Bahat, Dan. 1997. Jerusalem, *OEANE.* 3:224–38.

Bailey, Randall C. 1990. *David in Love and War: The Pursuit of Power in 2 Samuel 10–12.* JSOTSup 75. Sheffield: JSOT.

Ballhorn, Egbert. 1995. "Um deines Knechtes David willen" (Ps 132,10): Die Gestalt Davids im Psalter. *BN* 76:16–31.

Barstad, Hans M. 1995. Dod. *DDD.* 493–98.

Barstad, Hans M., and Bob Becking. 1995. Does the Stele from Tel–Dan Refer to a Deity Dod? *BN* 77:5–12.

Barthélemy, Dominique, David W. Gooding, Johan Lust, and Emanuel Tov. 1986. *The Story of David and Goliath. Textual and Literary Criticism.* OBO 73. Göttingen: Vandenhoeck & Ruprecht.

Becking, Bob. 1996. The Second Danite Inscription: Some Remarks. *BN* 91:21–30.

Ben-Barak, Zafrira. 1979. The Legal Background to the Restoration of Michal to David. Pp. 15–29 in *Studies in the Historical Books of the Old Testament,* ed. J. A. Emerton. VTSup 30. Leiden: E. J. Brill.

———— 1981. Meribaal and the System of Land Grants in Ancient Israel. *Bib* 62:73–91.

Ben-Tor, Amnon, and Doron Ben-Ami. 1998. Hazor and the Archaeology of the Tenth Century B.C.E. *IEJ* 48:1–37.

Ben–Zvi, Ehud. 1994. On the Reading "bytdwd" in the Aramaic Stele from Tel Dan. *JSOT* 64:25–32.

Berlin, Adele. 1982. Characterization in Biblical Narrative: David's Wives. *JSOT* 23:69–85.

———— 1983. *Poetics and Interpretation of Biblical Narrative.* BLS 9. Sheffield: Almond.

Bierling, Neal. 1992. *Giving Goliath His Due: New Archaeological Light on the Philistines.* Grand Rapids: Baker.

Biran, Avraham, and Joseph Naveh. 1993. An Aramaic Stele Fragment from Tel Dan. *IEJ* 43:81–98.

———— 1995. The Tel Dan Inscription: A New Fragment. *IEJ* 45:1–21.

Birch, Bruce C. 1976. *The Rise of the Israelite Monarchy: The Growth and Development of I Samuel 7–15.* SBLDS 27. Missoula, MT: Scholars Press.

Blenkinsopp, Joseph. 1966. Theme and Motif in the Succession Narrative (2 Sam. XI 2ff) and the Yahwist Corpus. Pp. 44–57 in *Volume du Congrès:Genève 1965.* VTSup 15. Leiden: E. J. Brill.

————— 1975. The Quest of the Historical Saul. Pp. 75–99 in *No Famine in the Land: Studies in Honor of John L. McKenzie*, ed. James W. Flanagan and Anita Weisbrod Robinson. Missoula, MT: Scholars Press.

Bosch, Juan. 1966. *David: The Biography of a King*. Translated by John Marks. New York: Hawthorne.

Brettler, Marc Zvi. 1995. *The Creation of History in Ancient Israel*. New York: Routledge.

Bright, John. 1976. The Organization and Administration of the Israelite Empire. Pp. 193–208 in *Magnalia Dei. The Mighty Acts of God. Essays on the Bible and Archaeology in Memory of G. Ernest Wright*, ed. F. M. Cross, W. Lemke, and P. D. Miller. Garden City, NY: Doubleday.

Broshi, Magen. 1997. Demography. *OEANE*. 2:142–44.

Brueggemann, Walter. 1985. *David's Truth in Israel's Imagination and Memory*. Philadelphia: Fortress.

Bunimovitz, Shlomo. 1995. How Mute Stones Speak: Interpreting What We Dig Up. *BAR* 21,2 (March/April): 58–67, 96–100.

Cahill, Jane. 1988. It Is There: The Archaeological Evidence Proves It. *BAR* 24,4 (July/August): 34–41, 63.

Camp, Claudia. 1981. The Wise Women of 2 Samuel: A Role Model for Women in Early Israel? *CBQ* 43:14–29.

Cargill, Jack. 1986. David in History: A Secular Approach. *Judaism* 35:211–22.

Carlson, R. A. 1964. *David the Chosen King: A Traditio-Historical Approach to the Second Book of Samuel*. Uppsala: Almqvist & Wiksell.

Ceresko, Anthony R. 1985. A Rhetorical Analysis of David's "Boast" (1 Samuel 17:34–37): Some Reflections on Method. *CBQ* 47:58–74.

Clines, David J. A., and Tamara Eskenazi, eds. 1991. *Telling Queen Michal's Story: An Experiment in Comparative Interpretation*. JSOTSup 119. Sheffield: Sheffield Academic Press.

Coats, George W. 1981. Parable, Fable, and Anecdote: Storytelling in the Succession Narrative. *Int* 35:368–82.

Conroy, Charles. 1978. *Absalom Absalom! Narrative and Language in 2 Sam 13–20*. AB 81. Rome: Biblical Institute.

Cooper, Alan M. 1983. The Life and Times of King David According to the Book of Psalms. Pp. 117–31 in *The Poet and the Historian. Essays in Literary and Historical Biblical Criticism*, ed. Richard E. Friedman. Harvard Semitic Studies 26. Chico, CA: Scholars Press.

Cooper, Duff. 1943. *David*. New York: Harper & Row.

Coxon, Peter W. 1981. A Note on "Bathsheba" in 2 Samuel 12, 1–6. *Bib* 62:247–50.

Cross, Frank Moore. 1973. *Canaanite Myth and Hebrew Epic: Essays in the History and the Religion of Israel*. Cambridge, MA: Harvard University Press.

———— 1984. The Ammonite Oppression of the Tribes of Gad and Reuben: Missing Verses from 1 Samuel 11 Found in 4QSamuel[a]. Pp. 148–58 in *History, Historiography and Interpretation: Studies in Biblical and Cuneiform Literatures*, ed. H. Tadmor and M. Weinfeld. Jerusalem: Magnes.

Cryer, F. H. 1985. David's Rise to Power and the Death of Abner: An Analysis of 1 Samuel xxvi 14–16 and its Redaction-Critical Implications. *VT* 35:385–94.

———— 1994. On the Recently Discovered "House of David" Inscription. *SJOT* 8:3–19.

———— 1995a. A "BETDAWD" Miscellany: DWD, DWD' or DWDH? *SJOT* 9:52–74.

———— 1995b. King Hadad. *SJOT* 9:223–35.

———— 1996. Of Epistemology, Northwest–Semitic Epigraphy and Irony: The "BYTDWD/House of David" Inscription Revisited. *JSOT* 69:3–17.

Damrosch, David. 1987. *The Narrative Covenant: Transformations of Genre in the Growth of Biblical Literature*. San Francisco: Harper & Row.

Davies, Philip R. 1992. *In Search of "Ancient Israel."* JSOTSup 148. Sheffield: Sheffield Academic Press.

———— 1994a. BYTDWD and SWKT DWYD: A Comparison. *JSOT* 64:23–24.

———— 1994b. "House of David" Built on Sand: The Sins of the Biblical Maximizers. *BAR* 20,4 (July/August): 54–55.

Dayan, Moshe. 1968. The Spirit of the Fighters. Pp. 50–63 in *Tales of Heroism: Twenty Years of Independence* 11. Jerusalem: Israel Ministry of Defense. (Hebrew)

Dearman, J. Andrew. 1989. Historical Reconstruction and the Mesha' Inscription. Pp. 155–210 in *Studies in the Mesha Inscription and Moab*, ed. J. Andrew Dearman. ASOR/SBL Archaeology and Biblical Studies 2. Atlanta: Scholars Press.

Dearman, J. Andrew, ed. 1989. *Studies in the Mesha Inscription and Moab*. ASOR/SBL Archaeology and Biblical Studies 2. Atlanta: Scholars Press.

Deem, Ariella. 1978. ". . . And the Stone Sank into His Forehead" A Short Note on 1 Samuel XVII 49. *VT* 28:349–51.

Deist, F. E. 1986. David: A Man After God's Own Heart? An Investigation into the David Character in the So-Called Succession Narrative. Pp. 99–129 in *Studies in the Succession Narrative*, ed. W. C. van Wyk. OTWSA Proceedings 1984–85.

Delekat, Lienhard. 1967. Tendenz und Theologie der David-Salomo-Erzählung. Pp. 26–36 in *Das ferne und nahe Wort*, ed. F. Maass. BZAW 105. Berlin: Töpelmann.

Demsky, Aaron. 1995. On Reading Ancient Inscriptions. *JANES* 23:29–35.

Dever, William G. 1980. Archaeological Method in Israel: A Continuing Revolution. *BA* 43:40–48.

———— 1981. The Impact of the "New Archaeology" on Syro-Palestinian Archaeology. *BASOR* 242:14–29.

———— 1982. Retrospects and Prospects in Biblical and Syro–Palestinian Archaeology. *BA* 45:103–107.

———— 1985. Syro–Palestinian Archaeology. Pp. 31–74 in *The Hebrew Bible and Its Modern Interpreters*, ed. Douglas A. Knight and Gene M. Tucker. Chico, CA: Scholars Press.

———— 1988. Impact of the "New Archaeology." Pp. 337–52 in *Benchmarks in Time and Culture: An Introduction to Palestinian Archaeology*, ed. Joel F. Drinkard, Jr., Gerald L. Mattingly, and J. Maxwell Miller. Atlanta: Scholars Press.

———— 1990. *Recent Archaeological Discoveries and Biblical Research*. Seattle: University of Washington.

———— 1992. Archaeology, Syro-Palestinian and Biblical. *ABD*. 1:354–67.

———— 1995. From Tribe to Nation: A Critique of State Formation Processes in Ancient Israel. Pp. 213–38 in *Nouve fondazioni nel Vicino Oriente: realtà e ideologia*, ed. S. Mazzoni. Pisa: University of Pisa.

———— 1997. Biblical Archaeology. *OEANE* 1:315–19.

De Vries, Simon J. 1973. David's Victory over the Philistine as Saga and as Legend. *JBL* 92:23–36.

Dietrich, Walter. 1996. Die Erzählung von David und Goliat in I Sam 17. *ZAW* 108:172–91.

———— 1997. *Die frühe Königszeit in Israel: 10. Jahrhundert v. Chr.* BE 3. Stuttgart: W. Kohlhammer.

Dietrich, Walter, and Thomas Naumann. 1995. *Die Samuelbücher*. EF 287. Darmstadt: Wissenschaftliche Buchgesellschaft.

Dijkstra, Meindert. 1994. An Epigraphic and Historical Note on the Stela of Tel Dan. *BN* 74:10–12.

Dirksen, Piet B. 1996. Why was David Disqualified as Temple Builder? The Meaning of 1 Chronicles 22.8. *JSOT* 70:51–56.

Dothan, Trude. 1982. What We Know about the Philistines. *BAR* 8:4 (July/August): 20–44.

———— 1992. Philistines. *ABD*. 5:326–33.

Drinkard, Joel. 1989. The Literary Genre of the Mesha' Inscription. Pp. 131–54 in *Studies in the Mesha Inscription and Moab*, ed. J. Andrew Dearman. ASOR/SBL Archaeology and Biblical Studies 2. Atlanta: Scholars Press.

Edelman, Diana V. 1991. *King Saul in the Historiography of Judah*. JSOTSup 121. Sheffield: JSOT.

—————— 1996. Saul ben Kish in History and Tradition. Pp. 142–59 in *The Origins of the Ancient Israelite States,* ed. by Volkmar Fritz and Philip R. Davies. JSOTSup 228. Sheffield: Sheffield Academic Press.

Edenburg, Cynthia. 1998. How (Not) to Murder a King: Variations on a Theme in 1 Sam 24; 26. *SJOT* 12:64–85.

J. A Emerton, ed. 1979. *Studies in the Historical Books of the Old Testament.* VTSup 30. Leiden: E. J. Brill.

Exum, J. Cheryl. 1993. *Fragmented Women: Feminist (Sub)versions of Biblical Narratives.* JSOTSup 163. Sheffield: Sheffield Academic Press.

Fairbairn, Ann. 1966. *Five Smooth Stones.* New York: Crown.

Faulkner, William. 1936. *Absalom, Absalom!* New York: Random House.

Finkelstein, Israel. 1996. The Archaeology of the United Monarchy: An Alternative View. *Levant* 28:177–87.

Finkelstein, Israel, and Nadav Na'aman, eds. 1994. *From Nomadism to Monarchy: Archaeological and Historical Aspects of Early Israel.* Jerusalem: Yad Izhak Ben-Zvi/IES/BAS.

Flanagan, James W. 1972. Court History or Succession Document?: A Study of 2 Samuel 9–20 and 1 Kings 1–2. *JBL* 91:172–81.

—————— 1975. Judah in All Israel. Pp. 101–16 in *No Famine in the Land: Studies in Honor of John L. McKenzie,* ed. James W. Flanagan and Anita Weisbrod Robinson. Missoula, MT: Scholars Press.

—————— 1979. The Relocation of the Davidic Capital. *JAAR* 47:223–44.

—————— 1981. Chiefs in Israel. *JSOT* 20:47–73.

—————— 1982. Models for the Origin of Iron Age Monarchy: A Modern Case Study. Pp. 135–56 in *Society of Biblical Literature 1982 Seminar Papers.* Chico, CA: Scholars Press.

—————— 1983. Social Transformation and Ritual in 2 Samuel 6. Pp. 361–72 in *The Word of the Lord Shall Go Forth: Essays in Honor of David Noel Freedman in Celebration of His Sixtieth Birthday,* ed. Carol Meyers and Michael Patrick O'Connor. Winona Lake, IN: Eisenbrauns.

—————— 1988. *David's Social Drama. A Hologram of Israel's Early Iron Age.* JSOTSup 73. Sheffield: Almond.

Flanagan, James W., and Anita Weisbrod Robinson, eds. 1975. *No Famine in the Land: Studies in Honor of John L. McKenzie.* Missoula, MT: Scholars Press.

Fokkelmann, J. P. 1981–1993. *Narrative Art and Poetry in the Books of Samuel.* 4 vols. Assen: Van Gorcum.

Freedman, David Noel, and Jeffrey C. Geoghegan. 1995. "House of David" Is There! *BAR* 21,2 (March/April):78–79.

Frick, Frank S. 1985. *The Formation of the State in Ancient Israel: A Survey of Models and Theories.* Social World of Biblical Antiquity, Series 4. Sheffield: Almond.

Friedman, Richard Elliott. 1998. *The Hidden Book in the Bible: The Discovery of the First Prose Masterpiece.* San Francisco: Harper.

Fritz, Volkmar. 1996. Monarchy and Re-urbanization: A New Look at Solomon's Kingdom. Pp. 187–95 in *The Origins of the Ancient Israelite States,* ed. Volkmar Fritz and Philip R. Davies. JSOTSup 228. Sheffield: Sheffield Academic Press.

Fritz, Volkmar, and Philip R. Davies, eds. 1996. *The Origins of the Ancient Israelite States.* JSOTSup 228. Sheffield: Sheffield Academic Press.

Frontain, Raymond-Jean, and Jan Wojcik, eds. 1980. *The David Myth in Western Literature.* West Lafayette, IN: Purdue University Press.

Galling, Kurt. 1966. Goliat und seine Rüstung. Pp. 150–69 in *Volume du Congrès: Genève 1965.* VTSup 15. Leiden: E. J. Brill.

Garsiel, Moshe. 1985. *The First Book of Samuel: A Literary Study of Comparative Structures, Analogies and Parallels.* Ramat Gan: Revivim.

Gauger, Hans-Martin. 1993. *Davids Aufstieg: Erzählung.* Munich: C. H. Beck.

Gerleman, G. 1973. Die Wurzel *šlm. ZAW* 85:1–14

Gill, Dan. 1994. How They Met: Geology Solves Mystery of Hezekiah's Tunnelers. *BAR* 20,4 (July/August): 20–33, 64.

Gordon, Cyrus H. 1952. Review of *The Goddess Anath* by U. Cassuto. *JAOS* 72:180–81.

Gordon, Robert P. 1980. David's Rise and Saul's Demise: Narrative Analogy in 1 Samuel 24–26. *Tyndale Bulletin* 31:37–64.

———— 1984. *1 & 2 Samuel.* OTG. Sheffield: JSOT.

———— 1994. In Search of David: The David Tradition in Recent Study. Pp. 285–98 in *Faith, Tradition and History: Old Testament Historiography in Its Near Eastern Context,* ed. A. R. Millard, James K. Hoffmeier, and David W. Baker. Winona Lake, IN: Eisenbrauns.

Gottwald, Norman K. 1992. Sociology (Ancient Israel). *ABD.* 6:79–89.

Graham, M. Patrick. 1989. The Discovery and Reconstruction of the Mesha' Inscription. Pp. 41–92 in *Studies in the Mesha Inscription and Moab,* ed. J. Andrew Dearman. ASOR/SBL Archaeology and Biblical Studies 2. Atlanta: Scholars Press.

Green, Alberto. 1983. David's Relations with Hiram: Biblical and Josephan Evidence for Tyrian Chronology. Pp. 373–97 in *The Word of the Lord Shall Go Forth: Essays in Honor of David Noel Freedman in Celebration of His Sixtieth Birthday,* ed. Carol Meyers and Michael Patrick O'Connor. Winona Lake, IN: Eisenbrauns.

Grosart, Alexander B., ed. [1881] 1969. *Abraham Cowley: The Complete Works in Verse and Prose.* Reprinted in Anglistica and Americana. Vol. 2. Hildesheim: Georg Olms.

Gunn, David M. 1978. *The Story of King David. Genre and Interpretation.* JSOTSup 6. Sheffield: JSOT.

———— 1980. *The Fate of King Saul*. JSOTSup 14. Sheffield: JSOT.

Gunn, David M., ed. 1991. *Narrative and Novella in Samuel: Studies by Hugo Gressmann and Other Scholars 1906–1923*. JSOTSup 116. Translated by David E. Orton. Sheffield: Almond.

Hall, James. 1974. *Dictionary of Subjects and Symbols in Art*. New York: Harper & Row.

Halpern, Baruch. 1988. *The First Historians: The Hebrew Bible and History*. San Francisco: Harper & Row.

———— 1994. The Stela from Dan: Epigraphic and Historical Considerations. *BASOR* 296:63–80.

———— 1996. The Construction of the Davidic State: An Exercise in Historiography. Pp. 44–75 in *The Origins of the Ancient Israelite States*, ed. Volkmar Fritz and Philip R. Davies. JSOTSup 228. Sheffield: Sheffield Academic Press.

———— 1997. Text and Artifact: Two Monologues? Pp. 311–41 in *The Archaeology of Israel: Constructing the Past, Interpreting the Present*, ed. Neil Asher Silberman and David Small. JSOTSup 237. Sheffield: Sheffield Academic Press.

Hamilton, Gordon J. 1998. New Evidence for the Authenticity of *bšt* in Hebrew Personal Names and for Its Use as a Divine Epithet in Biblical Texts. *CBQ* 60:228–50.

Hauer, Christian E., Jr. 1969. The Shape of Saulide Strategy. *CBQ* 31:153–67.

———— 1982. David and the Levites. *JSOT* 23:33–54.

Hebel, J. William, ed. 1932. *The Works of Michael Drayton*. Vol. 2. Oxford: Basil Blackwell.

Heller, Joseph. 1984. *God Knows*. New York: Alfred A. Knopf.

Hercus, John. 1968. *David*. Chicago: Inter-Varsity.

Heym, Stefan. 1973. *The King David Report*. New York: G. P. Putnam's Sons.

Hoch, James E. 1994. *Semitic Words in Egyptian Texts of the New Kingdom and Third Intermediate Period*. Princeton: Princeton University Press.

Hodder, Ian. 1991. *Reading the Past: Current Approaches to Interpretation in Archaeology*. 2d ed. Cambridge: Cambridge University Press.

Hoffner, Harry A., Jr. 1975. Propaganda and Political Justification in Hittite Historiography. Pp. 49–62 in *Unity and Diversity: Essays in the History, Literature, and Religion of the Ancient Near East*, ed. Hans Goedicke and J. J. M. Roberts. Baltimore: Johns Hopkins University Press.

Hoftijzer, J. 1970. David and the Tekoite Woman. *VT* 20:419–44.

Holladay, John S., Jr. 1995. The Kingdoms of Israel and Judah: Political and Economic Centralization in the Iron IIA–B (ca. 1000–750 B.C.E.). Pp. 368–98 in *The Archaeology of Society in the Holy Land*, ed. Thomas E. Levy. London: Leicester University Press.

Humphreys, W. Lee. 1972. From Tragic Hero to Villain: A Study of the Figure of Saul and the Development of 1 Samuel. *JSOT* 22:95–117.

Huttar, Charles A., and Raymond-Jean Frontain. 1992. Pp. 180–85 in *A Dictionary of Biblical Tradition in English Literature*, ed. David Lyle Jeffrey. Grand Rapids: Eerdmans.

Ishida, Tomoo. 1977. *The Royal Dynasties in Ancient Israel: A Study in the Formation and Development of Royal-Dynastic Ideology*. BZAW 142. Berlin: Walter de Gruyter.

Jackson, Kent P. 1989. The Language of the Mesha Inscription. Pp. 96–130 in *Studies in the Mesha Inscription and Moab*, ed. J. Andrew Dearman. ASOR/SBL Archaeology and Biblical Studies 2. Atlanta: Scholars Press.

Jacobson, Dan. 1970. *The Rape of Tamar*. New York: Macmillan.

Jamieson-Drake, David W. 1991. *Scribes and Schools in Monarchic Judah: A Socio-Archaeological Approach*. The Social World of Biblical Antiquity 9. Sheffield: Almond, 1991.

Japhet, Sara. 1993. *I & II Chronicles: A Commentary*. Old Testament Library. Louisville, KY: Westminster/John Knox.

Jason, Heda. 1979. The Story of David and Goliath: A Folk Epic? *Bib* 60:36–70.

Jobling, David. 1976. Saul's Fall and Jonathan's Rise: Tradition and Redaction in 1 Sam 14:1–46. *JBL* 95:367–76.

———— 1978. *The Sense of Biblical Narrative: Three Structural Analyses in the Old Testament*. JSOTSup 7. Sheffield: JSOT.

Jones, Gwilym H. 1990. *The Nathan Narratives*. JSOTSup 80. Sheffield: JSOT.

Jones, Ivor H. 1992. Music and Musical Instruments. *ABD*. 4:930–39.

Kaiser, Otto. 1986. Some Observations on the Succession Narrative. Pp. 130–47 in *Studies in the Succession Narrative*, ed. W. C. van Wyk. OTWSA Proceedings 1984–85.

———— 1990. David und Jonathan: Tradition, Redaktion und Geschichte in I Sam 16–20: Ein Versuch. *ETL* 66:281–96.

Kelly, Brian E. 1998. David's Disqualification in 1 Chronicles 22.8: A Response to Piet B. Dirksen. *JSOT* 80:53–61.

Kessler, Martin. 1970. Narrative Technique in 1 Sm 16, 1–13. *CBQ* 32:543–54.

Kitchen, Kenneth A. 1973. *The Third Intermediate Period in Egypt (1100–650 B.C.)*. Warminster: Aris & Phillips.

———— 1997. A Possible Mention of David in the Late Tenth Century B.C.E., and Deity *Dod as Dead as the Dodo? *JSOT* 76:29–44.

Klein, Ralph W. 1983. *1 Samuel*. Word Biblical Commentary 10. Waco, TX: Word.

———— 1992. Chronicles, Book of 1–2. *ABD*. 1:992–1002.

Kleven, Terence. 1994. The Use of *ṣnr* in Ugaritic and 2 Samuel V 8: Hebrew Usage and Comparative Philology. *VT* 44:195–204.

Knauf, E. A., A. de Pury, and T. Römer. 1993. *BaytDavid ou *BaytDod: Une relecture de la nouvelle inscription de Tel Dan. *BN* 72:60–69.

Knoppers, Gary N. 1993. *The Reign of Solomon and the Rise of Jeroboam.* Vol. 1 of *Two Nations Under God. The Deuteronomistic History of Solomon and the Dual Monarchies.* HSM 52. Atlanta: Scholars Press.

——— 1994. *The Reign of Jeroboam, the Fall of Israel, and the Reign of Josiah.* Vol. 2 of *Two Nations Under God. The Deuteronomistic History of Solomon and the Dual Monarchies.* HSM 52. Atlanta: Scholars Press.

Koch, Klaus. 1969. *The Growth of the Biblical Tradition. The Form-Critical Method.* Trans. S. M. Cupitt. New York: Scribner's.

van der Kooij, Arie. 1992. The Story of David and Goliath: The Early History of Its Text. *ETL* 68:118–31.

Kokoschka, Oskar. 1970. *David und Saul: Einundvierzig Lithographien von Oskar Kokoschka. Biblische Texte übersetzt von Martin Buber.* Lucern and Frankfurt/M: C. J. Bucher.

Landay, Jerry M. 1973. *The House of David.* New York: Saturday Review/E. P. Dutton.

———1998. *David: Power, Lust and Betrayal in Biblical Times.* Berkeley, CA: Seastone.

Langlemet, F. 1976. Pour ou contre Salomon? La rédaction prosalomonienne de 1 Rois, I–II. *RB* 83:321–79, 481–529.

———1979–81. David et la maison de Saül. *RB* 86:194–213, 385–436, 481–513; 87:161–210; 88:321–32.

Lawrence, D. H. 1926. *David: A Play.* New York: Alfred A. Knopf.

Lawton, Robert B. 1993. Saul, Jonathan and the "Son of Jesse." *JSOT* 58:35–46.

Lemaire, André. 1994. "House of David" Restored in Moabite Inscription. *BAR* 20,3 (May/June): 30–37.

Lemche, Niels Peter. 1978. David's Rise. *JSOT* 10:2–25.

——— 1988. *Ancient Israel: A New History of Israelite Society.* The Biblical Seminar. Translated by Fred Cryer. Sheffield: Sheffield Academic Press.

Lemche, Niels Peter, and Thomas L. Thompson. 1994. Did Biran Kill David?: The Bible in the Light of Archaeology. *JSOT* 64:3–22.

Levenson, Jon D. 1978. 1 Samuel 25 as Literature and History. *CBQ* 40:11–28.

Levenson, Jon D., and Baruch Halpern. 1980. The Political Import of David's Marriages. *JBL* 99:507–18.

Levy, Thomas E., ed. 1995. *The Archaeology of Society in the Holy Land.* London: Leicester University Press.

Lindgren, Torgny. 1989. *Bathsheba.* Trans. Tom Geddes. New York: Harper & Row.

Lyke, Larry L. 1997. *King David with the Wise Woman of Tekoa: The Resonance of Tradition in Parabolic Narrative.* JSOTSup 255. Sheffield: Sheffield Academic Press.

Malul, Meir. 1996. Was David Involved in the Death of Saul on the Gilboa Mountain? *RB* 103:517–45.

Maly, Eugene. 1966. *The World of David and Solomon.* Englewood Cliffs, NJ: Prentice Hall.

Mason, Julian D., Jr. 1989. *The Poems of Phillis Wheatley.* Rev. ed. Chapel Hill, NC: University of North Carolina.

Massie, Allan. 1995. *King David.* London: Sceptre.

Mayes, A. D. H. 1978. The Rise of the Israelite Monarchy. *ZAW* 90:1–19.

Mays, James Luther. 1986. The David of the Psalms. *Int* 40:143–55.

Mazar, Amihai. 1990. *Archaeology of the Land of the Bible 10,000–586 B.C.E.* Anchor Bible Reference Library. New York: Doubleday.

———— 1994. Jerusalem and Its Vicinity in Iron Age I. Pp. 70–91 in *From Nomadism to Monarchy: Archaeological and Historical Aspects of Early Israel,* ed. Israel Finkelstein and Nadav Na'aman. Jerusalem: Yad Izhak Ben-Zvi/IES/BAS.

———— 1997. Iron Age Chronology: A Reply to I. Finkelstein. *Levant* 29: 157–67.

Mazar, Benjamin. 1963a. David's Reign in Hebron and the Conquest of Jerusalem. Pp. 235–44 in *In the Time of Harvest. Essays in Honor of Abba Hillel Silver,* ed. Daniel Jeremy Silver. New York: Macmillan.

————1963b. The Military Elite of King David. *VT* 13:310–20.

McCarter, P. Kyle. 1980a. The Apology of David. *JBL* 99:489–504.

———— 1980b. *I Samuel.* Anchor Bible 8. Garden City, NY: Doubleday.

———— 1981. "Plots, True or False": The Succession Narrative as Court Apologetic. *Int* 35:355–67.

———— 1983. The Ritual Dedication of the City of David in 2 Samuel 6. Pp. 273–78 in *The Word of the Lord Shall Go Forth: Essays in Honor of David Noel Freedman in Celebration of His Sixtieth Birthday,* ed. Carol Meyers and Michael Patrick O'Connor. Winona Lake, IN: Eisenbrauns.

———— 1984. *II Samuel.* Anchor Bible 9. Garden City, NY: Doubleday.

———— 1986. The Historical David. *Int* 40:117–29.

———— 1994. The Books of Samuel. Pp. 260–80 in *The History of Israel's Traditions: The Heritage of Martin Noth,* ed. Steven L. McKenzie and M. Patrick Graham. JSOTSup 182. Sheffield: Sheffield Academic Press.

McKenzie, John L. 1980. *The Old Testament without Illusion.* Garden City, NY: Image.

McKenzie, Steven L. 1992. Deuteronomistic History. *ABD.* 2:160–68.

———— 1996. Cette royauté qui fait problème. Trans. J.-D. Macchi. Pp. 267–95 in *Israël construit son histoire: L'historiographie deutéronomiste à la lumière des recherches récentes,* ed. Albert de Pury, Thomas Römer, and Jean-Daniel Macchi. Le monde de la Bible 34. Geneva: Labor et Fides.

————— 1997. *All God's Children: A Biblical Critique of Racism.* Louisville, KY: Westminster/John Knox.

————— 1999. Why Didn't God Let David Build the Temple? The History of a Biblical Tradition. Pp. 204–24 in *Worship in the Old Testament: Essays in Honor of John T. Willis,* ed. M. Patrick Graham, Rick Marrs, and Steven L. McKenzie. JSOTSup 284. Sheffield: Sheffield Academic Press.

Mettinger, Tryggve N. D. 1976. *King and Messiah: The Civil and Sacral Legitimation of the Israelite Kings.* Lund: Gleerup.

Meyers, Carol, and Michael Patrick O'Connor, eds. 1983. *The Word of the Lord Shall Go Forth: Essays in Honor of David Noel Freedman in Celebration of His Sixtieth Birthday.* Winona Lake, IN: Eisenbrauns.

Miller, J. Maxwell. 1974. Saul's Rise to Power: Some Observations Concerning 1 Sam 9:1–10:16, 10:26–11:15 and 13:2–14:46. *CBQ* 36:157–74.

————— 1993. Reading the Bible Historically: The Historian's Approach. Pp. 11–28 in *To Each Its Own Meaning: An Introduction to Biblical Criticisms and Their Applications,* ed. Steven L. McKenzie and Stephen R. Haynes. Louisville, KY: Westminster/John Knox.

Miller, J. Maxwell, and John H. Hayes. 1986. *A History of Ancient Israel and Judah.* Philadelphia: Westminster.

Miscall, Peter D. 1983. *The Workings of Old Testament Narrative.* Philadelphia: Fortress.

————— 1986. *1 Samuel: A Literary Reading.* Bloomington: Indiana University Press.

Moran, William L. 1963. The Ancient Near Eastern Background of the Love of God in Deuteronomy. *CBQ* 25:77–87.

Muraoka, Takamitsu. 1995. Linguistic Notes on the Aramaic Inscription from Tel Dan. *IEJ* 45:19–21.

Na'aman, Nadav. 1988. The List of David's Officers *(šališ im). VT* 38:71–79.

————— 1990. The Kingdom of Ishbaal. *BN* 54:33–37.

————— 1994. The "Conquest of Canaan" in the Book of Joshua and in History. Pp. 218–81 in *From Nomadism to Monarchy: Archaeological and Historical Aspects of Early Israel,* ed. Israel Finkelstein and Nadav Na'aman. Jerusalem: Yad Izhak Ben-Zvi/IES/BAS.

————— 1995. Beth-David in the Aramaic Stela from Tel Dan. *BN.* 79:17–24.

————— 1996. Sources and Composition in the History of David. Pp. 170–86 in *The Origins of the Ancient Israelite States,* ed. Volkmar Fritz and Philip R. Davies. JSOTSup 228. Sheffield: Sheffield Academic Press.

————— 1997. Cow Town or Royal Capital? Evidence for Iron Age Jerusalem. *BAR* 23,4 (July/August): 43–47, 67.

————— 1998. It Is There: Ancient Texts Prove It. *BAR* 24,2 (March/April): 42–44.

Napier, B. D. 1962. Sheep. *IDB.* 4:315–16.

Nelson, Richard D. 1981. *The Double Redaction of the Deuteronomistic History.* JSOT-Sup 18. Sheffield: JSOT.

Nicol, George C. 1988. Bathsheba, A Clever Woman? *ET* 99:360–63.

———— 1997. The Alleged Rape of Bathsheba: Some Observations on Ambiguity in Biblical Narrative. *JSOT* 73:43–54.

———— 1998. David, Abigail and Bathsheba, Nabal and Uriah: Transformations within a Triangle. *SJOT* 12:130–45.

Nitsche, Stefan Ark. 1994. *König David: Gestalt im Umbruch.* Zürich: Artemis.

Noll, K. L. 1997. *The Faces of David.* JSOTSup 242. Sheffield: Sheffield Academic Press.

Noth, Martin. 1991. *The Deuteronomistic History.* 2nd ed. JSOTSup 15. Sheffield: Sheffield Academic Press.

Noyes, George R., ed. 1950. *The Poetical Works of Dryden.* The Cambridge Edition of the Poets. Boston: Houghton Mifflin.

O'Brien, Mark A. 1989. *The Deuteronomistic History Hypothesis: A Reassessment.* OBO 92. Freiburg/Göttingen: Universitätsverlag/Vandenhoeck & Ruprecht.

Ofer, Avi. 1994. "All the Hill Country of Judah": From a Settlement Fringe to a Prosperous Monarchy. Pp. 92–121 in *From Nomadism to Monarchy: Archaeological and Historical Aspects of Early Israel,* ed. Israel Finkelstein and Nadav Na'aman. Jerusalem: Yad Izhak Ben-Zvi/IES/BAS.

O'Kane, Martin. 1998. The Biblical King David and His Artistic and Literary Afterlives. *Biblical Interpretation* 6:311–47.

Olyan, Saul. 1998. "Anyone Blind or Lame Shall Not Enter the House": On the Interpretation of Second Samuel 5:8b. *CBQ* 60:218–27.

Pebworth, Ted-Larry. 1980. Cowley's Davideis and the Exaltation of Friendship. Pp. 96–104 in *The David Myth in Western Literature,* ed. Raymond-Jean Frontain and Jan Wojcik. West Lafayette, IN: Purdue University Press.

Perdue, Leo G. 1983. The Testament of David and Egyptian Royal Instructions. Pp. 79–96 in *Scripture in Context II: More Essays on the Comparative Method,* ed. William W. Hallo, James C. Moyer, and Leo G. Perdue. Winona Lake, IN: Eisenbrauns.

———— 1984. "Is There Anyone Left of the House of Saul . . . ?" Ambiguity and the Characterization of David in the Succession Narrative. *JSOT* 30:67–84.

Petersen, David L. 1986. Portraits of David Canonical and Otherwise. *Int* 40:130–42.

Phillips, Richard. 1999. *The Heart of an Executive: Lessons on Leadership from the Life of King David.* New York: Bantam Doubleday Dell.

Pitard, Wayne T. 1987. *Ancient Damascus: A Historical Study of the Syrian City-State from Earliest Times until Its Fall to the Assyrians in 732 B.C.E.* Winona Lake, IN: Eisenbrauns.

Polzin, Robert. 1989. *Samuel and the Deuteronomist.* Part 2 of *A Literary Study of the Deuteronomic History.* San Francisco: Harper & Row.

———— 1993. *David and the Deuteronomist.* Part 3 of *A Literary Study of the Deuteronomic History.* Bloomington/Indianapolis: Indiana University Press.

Porter, Charlotte, and Helen A. Clarke, eds. n.d. *Poems of Robert Browning.* New York: Thomas Y. Crowell.

Portugali, Juval. 1994. Theoretical Speculations on the Transition from Nomadism to Monarchy. Pp. 203–17 in *From Nomadism to Monarchy: Archaeological and Historical Aspects of Early Israel,* ed. Israel Finkelstein and Nadav Na'aman. Jerusalem: Yad Izhak Ben-Zvi/IES/BAS.

Prouser, Ora Horn. 1996. Suited to the Throne: The Symbolic Use of Clothing in the David and Saul Narratives. *JSOT* 71:27–37.

———— 1998. Clothes Maketh the Man: Keys to Meaning in the Stories of Saul and David. *BR* 14,1 (February): 22–27.

Puech, Émile. 1994. La stèle araméenne de Dan: Bar Hadad II et la coalition des Omrides et de la maison de David. *RB* 101:215–41.

de Pury, Albert, Thomas Römer, and Jean-Daniel Macchi, eds. 1996. *Israël construit son histoire: L'historiographie deutéronomiste à la lumière des recherches récentes.* Le monde de la Bible 34. Geneva: Labor et Fides.

Pyper, Hugh S. 1996. *David as Reader: 2 Samuel 12:1–15 and the Poetics of Fatherhood.* Biblical Interpretation Series 23. Leiden: E. J. Brill.

Rad, Gerhard von. 1966. *The Problem of the Hexateuch and Other Essays.* Trans. E. W. Trueman Dicken. New York: McGraw-Hill.

Rainey, Anson F. 1994. The "House of David" and the House of the Deconstructionists. *BAR* 20,6 (November/December): 47.

Réau, Louis. 1956. *Iconographie de l'art chrétien.* Paris: Presses Universitaires de France.

Redford, Donald B. 1992. *Egypt, Canaan, and Israel in Ancient Times.* Princeton: Princeton University Press.

Reich, Ronny, and Eli Shukron. Light at the End of the Tunnel. *BAR* 25,1 (January/February 1999): 22–33, 72.

Rendsberg, Gary A. 1995. On the Writing bytdwd in the Aramaic Inscription from Tel Dan. *IEJ* 45:22–25.

Ridout, George. 1971. Prose Compositional Techniques in the Succession Narrative (2 Sam. 7, 9–20; 1 Kings 1–2). Unpublished Ph.D. diss. Berkeley, CA: Graduate Theological Union.

Riede, Peter. 1995. David und der Floh. Tiere und Tiervergleiche in den Samuelbüchern. *BN* 77:86–114.

Riley, William. 1993. *King and Cultus in Chronicles: Worship and the Reinterpretation of History.* JSOTSup 160. Sheffield: Sheffield Academic Press.

Roberts, J. J. M. 1973. The Davidic Origin of the Zion Tradition. *JBL* 92:3 29–44.

Rofé, Alexander. 1987. The Battle of David and Goliath: Folklore, Theology, Eschatology. Pp. 117–51 in *Judaic Perspectives on Ancient Israel,* ed. Jacob Neusner, Baruch A. Levine, and Ernest S. Frerichs. Philadelphia: Fortress.

Rogerson, J. W. 1992. Anthropology and the Old Testament. *ABD.* 1:258–262.

Römer, Thomas, and Albert de Pury. 1996. L'historiographie deutéronomiste (HD): Histoire de la recherche et enjeux du débat. Pp. 9–120 in *Israël construit son histoire: L'historiographie deutéronomiste à la lumière des recherches récentes,* ed. Albert de Pury, Thomas Römer, and Jean-Daniel Macchi. Le monde de la Bible 34. Geneva: Labor et Fides.

Rose, Ashley S. 1974. The "Principles" of Divine Election: Wisdom in 1 Samuel 16. Pp. 43–67 in *Rhetorical Criticism: Essays in Honor of James Muilenburg,* ed. Jared J. Jackson and Martin Kessler. Pittsburgh: Pickwick.

Rost, Leonhard. 1982. *The Succession to the Throne of David.* Historic Texts and Interpreters in Biblical Scholarship. Trans. David Gunn. Sheffield: Almond.

Rowley, H. H. 1939. Zadok and Nehushtan. *JBL* 58:113–41

Sasson, Victor. 1995. Tell Dan: Philological, Literary, and Historical Aspects. *JSS* 40:11–30.

Schäfer-Lichtenberger, Christa. 1996. Sociological and Biblical Views of the Early State. Pp. 78–105 in *The Origins of the Ancient Israelite States,* ed. Volkmar Fritz and Philip R. Davies. JSOTSup 228. Sheffield: Sheffield Academic Press.

Schley, D. G. 1993. Joab and David: Ties of Blood and Power. Pp. 90–105 in *History and Interpretation: Essays in Honour of John H. Hayes,* ed. M. Patrick Graham, William P. Brown, and Jeffrey K. Kwan. JSOTSup 173. Sheffield: Sheffield Academic Press.

Schmitt, Gladys. 1946. *David the King.* New York: Dial.

Schniedewind, William M. 1996. Tel Dan Stela: New Light on Aramaic and Jehu's Revolt. *BASOR* 302:75–90.

Scudder, Horace E., ed. 1895. *The Complete Poetic and Dramatic Works of Robert Browning.* The Cambridge Edition of the Poets. Boston: Houghton Mifflin.

Shanks, Herschel. 1994. "David" Found at Dan. *BAR* 20,2 (March/April): 40–45, 94.

———— 1998. Where Is the Tenth Century? *BAR* 24,2 (March/April): 56–60.

———— 1999. Has David Been Found in Egypt? *BAR* 25,1 (January/February): 34–35.

Shea, Christopher. 1997. Debunking Ancient Israel: Erasing History or Facing the Truth? *The Chronicle of Higher Education* 44,13 (Nov. 21): A12–14.

Shiloh, Yigal. 1984. *Excavations at the City of David I 1978–1982. Qedem* 19. Jerusalem: Institute of Archaeology, Hebrew University.

———— 1993. Jerusalem, Topography. Pp. 701–12 in *The New Encyclopedia of Archaeological Excavations in the Holy Land,* ed. E. Stern. Vol. 3. Israel Exploration Society & Carta.

Silberman, Neil Asher. 1982. *Digging for God and Country: Exploration in the Holy Land, 1799–1917.* New York: Anchor Books.

Simon, Uriel. 1967. The Poor Man's Ewe Lamb: An Example of a Juridical Parable. *Bib* 48:207–42.

Singer, Itamar. 1994. Egyptians, Canaanites, and Philistines in the Period of the Emergence of Israel. Pp. 282–338 in *From Nomadism to Monarchy: Archaeological and Historical Aspects of Early Israel,* ed. Israel Finkelstein and Nadav Na'aman. Jerusalem: Yad Izhak Ben-Zvi/IES/BAS.

Smith, J. M. P. 1933. The Character of King David. *JBL* 52:1–11.

Stager, Lawrence E. 1985. The Archaeology of the Family in Ancient Israel. *BASOR* 260:1–29.

———— 1995. The Impact of the Sea Peoples (1185–1050 B.C.E.). Pp. 332–48 in *The Archaeology of Society in the Holy Land,* ed. Thomas E. Levy. London: Leicester University Press.

Stamm, J. J. 1960. Der Name des Königs Salomo. *TZ* 16:285–97

Steiner, Margreet. 1998. It's Not There: Archaeology Proves a Negative. *BAR* 24,4 (July/August): 26–33, 62–63.

Steussy, Marti J. 1999. *David.* Columbia: University of South Carolina Press.

Stone, Ken. 1994. Sexual Power and Political Prestige. *BR* 10,4 (August): 28–31, 52–53.

Sturdy, John. 1970. The Original Meaning of "Is Saul Also Among the Prophets?" (1 Samuel X 11, 12; XIX 24). *VT* 20:206–13.

Tadmor, Hayim. 1984. Autobiographical Apology in the Royal Assyrian Literature. Pp. 36–57 in *History, Historiography and Interpretation: Studies in Biblical and Cuneiform Literatures,* ed. H. Tadmor and M. Weinfeld. Jerusalem: Magnes.

Tadmor, H., and M. Weinfeld, eds. 1984. *History, Historiography and Interpretation: Studies in Biblical and Cuneiform Literatures.* Jerusalem: Magnes.

Tarler, David, and Jane M. Cahill. 1992. David, City of. *ABD.* 2:52–67.

Thornton, T. C. G. 1968. Solomonic Apologetic in Samuel and Kings. *CQR* 169:159–66.

Thompson, J. A. 1974. The Significance of the Verb Love in the David-Jonathan Narratives in 1 Samuel. *VT* 24:334–38.

Thompson, Thomas L. 1992. *Early History of the Israelite People: From the Written and Archaeological Sources.* Leiden: E. J. Brill.

———— 1995a. Dissonance and Disconnections: Notes on the BYTDWD and HMLK.HDD Fragments from Tel Dan. *SJOT* 9:236–40.

———— 1995b. "House of David": An Eponymic Referent to Yahweh as God-father. *SJOT* 9:59–74.

———— 1996. Historiography of Ancient Palestine and Early Jewish Historiography: W. G. Dever and the Not So New Biblical Archaeology. Pp. 26–43 in *The Origins of the Ancient Israelite States,* ed. Volkmar Fritz and Philip R. Davies. JSOTSup 228. Sheffield: Sheffield Academic Press.

Tidwell, N. L. 1979. The Philistine Incursions into the Valley of Rephaim. Pp. 190–212 in *Studies in the Historical Books of the Old Testament,* ed. J. A Emerton. VTSup 30. Leiden: E. J. Brill.

Trebolle, Julio. 1990. The Story of David and Goliath (1 Sam 17–18): Textual Variants and Literary Composition. *BIOSCS* 23:16–30.

Trible, Phyllis. 1984. *Texts of Terror.* Philadelphia: Fortress.

Tropper, Josef. 1993. Eine altaramäische Steleninschrift aus Dan. *UF* 25:395–406.

Vancil, Jack W. 1992. Sheep, Shepherd. *ABD.* 5:1187–90.

Vanderkam, James C. 1980. Davidic Complicity in the Deaths of Abner and Eshbaal: A Historical and Redactional Study. *JBL* 99:521–39.

Van Seters, John. 1976. Problems in the Literary Analysis of the Court History of David. *JSOT* 1:22–29.

———— 1983. *In Search of History. Historiography in the Ancient World and the Origins of Biblical History.* New Haven: Yale University Press.

———— 1994. *The Life of Moses: The Yahwist as Historian in Exodus-Numbers.* Louisville, KY: Westminster/John Knox.

Vaux, Roland de. 1971. Single Combat in the Old Testament. Pp. 123–35 in *The Bible in the Ancient Near East.* Trans. Damian McHugh. Garden City, NY: Doubleday, 1971.

Veijola, Timo. 1975. *Die ewige Dynastie: David und die Entstehung seiner Dynastie nach der deuteronomistischen Darstellung.* AASF B 193. Helsinki: Suomalainen Tiedeakatemia.

———— 1979. Salomo—der erstgeborgene Bathsebas. Pp. 230–50 in *Studies in the Historical Books of the Old Testament,* ed. J. A Emerton. VTSup 30. Leiden: E. J. Brill.

Veith, Gene Edward, Jr. 1980. "Wait upon the Lord": David, Hamlet, and the Problem of Revenge. Pp. 70–83 in *The David Myth in Western Literature,* ed. Raymond-Jean Frontain and Jan Wojcik. West Lafayette, IN: Purdue University Press.

Walsh, Marcus, and Karina Williamson, eds. 1983. *The Poetical Works of Christopher Smart*. Vol. 2, *Religious Poetry 1763–1771*. Oxford: Clarendon Press.

Weil, Grete. 1991. *The Bride Price*. Trans. J. Barrett. Boston: David R. Godine.

Weiser, Artur. 1966. Die Legitimation des Königs David: Zur Eigenart und Entstehung der sogen. Geschichte von Davids Aufstieg. *VT* 16:325–54.

Werner, E. 1962. Musical Instruments. *IDB*. 3:469–76.

Wesselius, J. W. 1990. Joab's Death and the Central Theme of the Succession Narrative (2 Samuel IX–1 Kings II). *VT* 40:336–51.

Wharton, James A. 1981. A Plausible Tale: Story and Theology in II Samuel 9–20, I Kings 1–2. *Int* 35:341–54.

Whitelam, Keith W. 1979. *The Just King. Monarchical Judicial Authority in Ancient Israel*. JSOT Sup 12. Sheffield: JSOT.

———. 1984. The Defense of David. *JSOT* 29:61–87.

Whybray, R. N. 1968. *The Succession Narrative. A Study of II Samuel 9–20; I Kings 1 and 2*. SBT 2,9. London: SCM.

Willis, John T. 1973. The Function of Comprehensive Anticipatory Redactional Joints in I Samuel 16–18. *ZAW* 85:294–314.

———. 1995. The Newly Discovered Fragmentary Aramaic Inscription from Tel Dan. *RQ* 37:219–26.

Wolf, Herbert M. 1967. The Apology of Hattusilis Compared with Other Ancient Near Eastern Political Self-Justifications. Unpublished Ph.D. diss., Brandeis University.

Würthwein, Ernst. [1974] 1994. *Die Erzählung von der Thronnachfolge Davids— theologische oder politische Geschichtsschreibung*. Theologische Studien (B) 115. Zürich: Theologischer Verlag. Reprinted in *Studien zum Deuteronomistischen Geschichtswerk*. BZAW 227. Berlin: W. de Gruyter.

Wyk, W. C. van, ed. 1986. *Studies in the Succession Narrative*. OTWSA Proceedings 1984–85.

Yadin, Yigael. 1963. *The Art of Warfare in Biblical Lands*. London: Weidenfeld and Nicolson.

Zakovitch, Yair. 1995. *From Shepherd to Messiah*. Y. ben–Zvi. (Hebrew)

Zehnder, Marcus. 1998. Exegetische Beobachtungen zu den David-Jonathan-Geschichten. *Bib* 79:153–79.

Zwickel, Wolfgang. 1995. David als Vorbild für den Glauben: Die Veränderung des Davidbildes im Verlauf der alttestamentlichen Geschichte, dargestellt an 2 Sam 6. *BN* 79:88–101.

Index